THE
STORY OF THE BIBLE

By
EDGAR J. GOODSPEED

UNIVERSITY OF CHICAGO PRESS
CHICAGO · ILLINOIS

UNIVERSITY OF CHICAGO PRESS · CHICAGO 37

Agent: THE CAMBRIDGE UNIVERSITY PRESS · LONDON

COPYRIGHT 1936 BY THE UNIVERSITY OF CHICAGO. ALL RIGHTS
RESERVED. PUBLISHED SEPTEMBER 1936. NINTH IMPRESSION
APRIL 1946. COMPOSED AND PRINTED BY THE UNIVERSITY OF
CHICAGO PRESS, CHICAGO, ILLINOIS, U.S.A.

INTRODUCTION

There are two ways to use the Bible. One is the old childhood way of using a text from here or there, regardless of the time and circumstances of its origin. The other is the grown person's way, of reading it a book at a time, as it was written to be read, and with some understanding of the time and circumstances in which each book was written. It is obvious that only in this latter way can the major values of the Bible be realized. The Bible is far from being a child's book. No book in the world is more definitely addressed to the mature mind. And yet many people never get beyond their childhood approach to it, or seek to understand its books in the light of the historical situations that called them forth.

The Old Testament is full of dramatic situations and great religious truths, but these are dimly perceived by most people nowadays. Grotesque elements in its art sometimes completely overshadow its most tremendous religious values—as in the story of Jonah. Superficial reading of its books often leaves us with no idea at all of the situations in which they were written and without which they cannot be understood.

For the Old Testament is a very difficult book. It

is not easy to recover the occasions on which its great utterances were first formulated or the needs to meet which its books were written. Read solely in the order in which we possess it, the order of its subject matter rather than of its literary origin, it is often very obscure. That orderly corpus of twelve books from Genesis to II Kings is indeed a masterpiece of literary organization, and embodies obvious and indispensable values. But there are in the literature other values less obvious but just as indispensable, which demand another order of treatment to bring them out. For the Hebrew religion did not, after all, begin with the priests but with the prophets, and this fact is reflected in its literature. To follow the emergence of its great ideas as the great literary prophets advanced them one after another gives us a truer and even more dramatic picture of that amazing religious development. Great mountains may be looked at from conventional points of view, as the Jungfrau is from Interlaken, or Mont Blanc from Chamonix, but there are other views of them just as true and just as stupendous.

So it is with the Old Testament. We shall know it better if we study it not simply in the familiar order of its subject matter, but in the order of its origins, of its composition, and of its authors. Great progress has in recent years been made in these directions, and while it is of course impossible to claim unanimity on all points, some things about the writings of the Old Testament have gradually become tolerably clear. The progress of archaeology; the decipherment of Assyrian, Babylonian, and Egyptian remains; and the study of ancient religions have helped immensely to the understanding of the Old Testament.

The task is complicated by the fact that many books of the Old Testament have sustained accretions and undergone revision by later hands. It is as though they had been revised and amplified again and again, and come to us in the last form that they assumed—a sort of final revision. One must choose between dividing their material, taking it up part here and part there, or placing them at a point in history which their major interest, their literary or historical center of gravity, suggests. The former method has often been followed, but seems more likely to confuse than to help the reader.

I have therefore arranged the books in the general order of their composition, realizing that it is difficult to be wholly consistent in any arrangement that refuses to break the books in pieces. It is true, for example, that Jeremiah began to preach before Nahum, but the mass of Jeremiah's work falls after the mass of Nahum's, and Jeremiah can be better understood after Nahum than Nahum after Jeremiah.

It is true that the story of the Old Testament cannot be written with the same definiteness with which the story of the New can be told. And yet there is room for such a book, as a guide to the reading and the study of the Old Testament, the great religious values of which are so little appreciated even by intelligent people today. Many problems supposedly quite modern are tellingly dealt with in the Old Testament; indeed, our social reformers are simply saying over again just what the Hebrew prophets said twenty-five hundred years ago. We still need the voice of the prophets. And after all it was they rather than the priests who were the real makers of Israel's religion.

It must always be remembered that Christianity did not spring from the New Testament but the New Testament from Christianity. Christianity did not begin as a religion of books but as a religion of spirit. There was neither time nor need to write books when the Lord Jesus was at the very doors. Still less was there need of authoritative books to guide men whose dominant conviction was that they had the Mind of Christ, the very Spirit of God, guiding them constantly from within.

But the ancient Christians did write. Situations arose that drew letters from them—letters of acknowledgment, thanks, criticism, recommendation, instruction, or advice. These letters, like our modern letters, were written to serve an immediate and pressing need. Situations arose which even drew forth books from these early Christians—books to save people from perplexities or mistakes, or to comfort them in anxiety or peril; but always books to serve some fairly definite circle, in a particular condition of stress or doubt. This practical and occasional character of the books of the New Testament can hardly be overemphasized, for it is only in the light of the situations that called them forth that these books can be fully understood. Only when we put ourselves into the situation of those for whom a given book of the New Testament was written do we begin to feel our oneness with them and to find the living worth in the book.

It may be helpful to conceive the writings of the New Testament as grouped about four notable events or movements: the Greek mission, that is, the evangelization of the gentile world; the fall of Jerusalem; the persecution of Domitian; and the rise of the early sects. The New Testament shows us the church first deep in its missionary enterprise, then seeking a religious explanation of contemporary history, then bracing itself in the midst of persecution, then plunged into controversy over its own beliefs.

The New Testament contains the bulk of that extraordinary literature precipitated by the Christian movement in the most interesting period of its development. Christianity began its world-career as a hope of Jesus' messianic return; it very soon became a permanent and organized church. The books of the New Testament show us those first eschatologi-

cal expectations gradually accommodating themselves to conditions of permanent existence.

The historical study of the New Testament seeks
to trace this movement of life and thought that lies
back of the several books, and to relate the books to
this development. It has yielded certain very definite positive results which are both interesting and
helpful. Through it these old books recover something of the power of speech, and begin to come to
us with the accent and intonation which they had
for the readers for whom they were originally meant.

The short chapters of this book are designed to
present vividly and unconventionally the situations
which called forth the several books of the Bible,
and the way in which each book or letter sought to
meet the special situation to which it was addressed.
It is hoped that a brief constructive presentation of
the background of each book without technicality
or elaboration may bring back particularly to intelligent laymen and young people the individuality
and vital interest of the writings of the Bible.

The purpose of this work is threefold: (1) It may
be read as a continuous narrative, without regard to
the Suggestions for Study at the close of each chapter. It will then afford exactly what its name im-
plies, the story of the Bible. The references to which
the occasional superior numerals relate will be found
at the beginning of the Suggestions for Study which

follow each chapter. (2) After each chapter the corresponding book of the Bible may be read, preferably at one sitting, and thus each piece of literature may make its own appeal on the basis of the introductory interpretation. (3) The book may be used as a basis for definite study of the Bible individually or in classes. The Suggestions for Study are prepared for this purpose. General and special bibliographies for further reading will be found at the end of the book. The student is advised not to attempt a detailed investigation of specific parts of the various books, but to seek to get the large general aim which controlled each individual writer.

EDGAR J. GOODSPEED

CHICAGO
March 24, 1936

THE OLD TESTAMENT

CONTENTS

CHAPTER I

THE BOOK OF AMOS

Jewish literature begins with a plea for justice for the poor. It was made by a poor Hebrew working-man of the eighth century before Christ. His name was Amos. He lived in Tekoa, a village a few miles south of Jerusalem, where he worked as a shepherd and a dresser of sycamore trees.[1]

Long before the time of Amos, the kingdom of David and Solomon had broken into two kingdoms, Israel and Judah, and Amos sometimes found his way up to Bethel, a great sanctuary of the Northern Kingdom, to sell his produce. There, as at Jerusalem itself, he was stirred by the misery of the poor and their oppression by the rich. Even then it was urban life that enhanced these differences and embittered them.

The prophets had fallen into disrepute. They were mercenary and insincere. So when Amos at Bethel burst forth with denunciations of the rich for their selfish cruelty to the poor, and foretold the destruction that such courses would bring upon Israel, the priest Amaziah ordered him off, contemptuously advising him to tell his story in Jerusalem, where reflections on the rival Northern Kingdom would be better received and rewarded. Amos indignantly replied that he was not a prophet nor a member of any prophetic order, but a simple workingman, whom the Lord had taken from following his flock, to send to prophesy to his people Israel. Amos predicts ruin and death for Amaziah, and destruction and exile for the Northern Kingdom.[2]

Amos uttered his prophecies about the middle of the eighth century before Christ, 765–750 B.C., and within a generation the Northern Kingdom fell before the Assyrians under Sargon, who in 721 B.C. carried the inhabitants of Samaria into captivity.[3]

The activity of Amos fell in the reign of Jeroboam II of Israel, 781–740 B.C., for Amaziah reported his seditious utterances to that king.[4] It was a time of political success, for Jeroboam had won back all that the Syrians had taken from the kingdom before his time.[5] With this came material prosperity and its attendant luxury and indulgence. It is against this background of wealth and splendor— ivory houses, palaces of hewn stone, with ivory couches, wine and revelry, lyre and song[6]—that Amos sees in sharp contrast the condition of the poor, set aside and trampled upon by corrupt judges, priests, and nobles, who make the measure small and the price great, and use false scales, so as to sell the innocent for silver and the needy for a pair of sandals;[7] men who are so absorbed in business that they can hardly wait for feast days and Sabbaths to pass, so that they can resume their trade in wheat, though it is only the poorest of it that they will sell to the common people of the land.[8]

Upon all this luxury and exploitation Amos proclaims the judgment of God. Israel has sinned like the nations around, and God will not spare her. Destruction and captivity are to overtake her. The palace songs will become dirges, the shout of the revelers will pass away, the pampered ladies of Samaria, the "cows of Bashan," who oppress the weak and crush the needy, will be dragged forth dead from the city, and thrown unburied on the rubbish heaps.[9] They have treasured up the fruits of violence and robbery in their palaces.[10] But the Assyrians will gather about Samaria and carry her into exile beyond Damascus.[11]

The centers of Israel's hypocritical worship will not be spared.

"The high places of Isaac shall be laid waste;
And the sanctuaries of Israel shall be ruined;
And I will rise against the house of Jeroboam
   with the sword."[12]

Most of Amos' prophecies were directed against Israel. But he looked abroad upon the nations around and saw in each some great sin to condemn, and for every one—Syria, Philistia, Ammon, Moab, Israel—he predicted punishment and overthrow.[13] Amos saw that peace and prosperity have their outrages no less than war, and he denounces the eco-

nomic vices of Israel just as strongly as the more
violent crimes of her neighbors. In this recognition
of God as no mere national deity but as supreme
over the nations and impartial in his judgment upon
them we see for the first time what has been called
the ethical monotheism of the prophets.

Amos saw no hope for the Northern Kingdom.
Its fate was sealed. Such passages in the Book of
Amos as promise restoration are the work of later
hands, through which his writing has passed.[14]

Many things mark this earliest of the literary
prophets with distinction. His lofty idea of God, supreme over the nations and absolutely just; his own
deep moral earnestness, fearlessly assailing the sins
of the rich and privileged of his own nation; his religious insight and his splendid rhetoric mark this
herdsman of Tekoa out in the annals of literature
and of religion.

"The Lord roars from Zion,
  And from Jerusalem he utters his voice"; . . . .
When the lion roars, who does not fear?
When the Lord God speaks, who will not
    prophesy?[15]
He who made the Pleiades and Orion,
Who turns dense darkness to dawn,
And darkens day into night.[16]

"Prepare to meet your God, O Israel!"[17] . . . .
Let justice roll down like waters,
And righteousness like a perennial stream."[18]

The literature of Western Asia was usually anonymous, growing up as a social product out of many minds, and connected with no individual's name. The great exception is the literary prophets of Judaism. Their utterances were so individual, and so definitely related to specific occasions and situations, that their names were attached to them, and they became the first "authors" of the Bible. Their messages and oracles were usually cast in poetic form so that these early prophets were also poets.

But above all they were the fearless and unsparing critics of the national life and morals. Their poetic and literary gifts were steadily directed to the reformation of their people. Their condemnation was directed not so much at neglect of law or cultus, or what might be called specifically religious duties, but at moral wrong—cruelty, dishonesty, and social injustice. In these they saw the most serious disobedience to the will of God, and against these they waged unceasing war, at no matter what cost to themselves. This is the greatest glory of the Hebrew prophets.

SUGGESTIONS FOR STUDY

1. *References:* [1]Amos 1:1; 7:14; [2]Amos 7:10–17; [3]II Kings 17:4–6; [4]Amos 7:10; [5]II Kings 14:23–25; [6]Amos 3:15; 5:11; 6:4,5; [7]Amos 2:6; [8]Amos 8:5,6; [9]Amos 4:1–3; [10]Amos 3:10; [11]Amos 3:9; 5:27; [12]Amos 7:9; [13]Amos, chap. 1; [14]Amos 9:9–15; [15]Amos 1:2; 3:8; [16]Amos 5:8; [17]Amos 4:12; [18]Amos 5:24.

2. Where did Amos live and what was his occupation?

3. In what literary form did he cast his prophecies?

4. Where did he do most of his prophetic work?

5. What was the political condition of the Kingdom of Israel in his day?

6. What are the sins which Amos especially condemns?

7. What punishment does he threaten Israel with?

8. Relate Amos' interview with Amaziah.

9. What was the current estimate of prophets in his time?

10. What is meant by the ethical monotheism of the prophets?

11. Locate the nations of chapters 1 and 2 on the map.

12. On the oracle against Edom, 2:11, 12, compare Obadiah and its parallels.

13. What became of the Northern Kingdom?

14. What picture of Israelitish civilization appears in Amos?

15. What was the character of the Assyrians?

16. What was the prevailing view of the origin of books in Western Asia?

17. Is there any modern application of the ideas of Amos, or are they obsolete and out of date?

CHAPTER II

THE BOOK OF HOSEA

The prophets taught by deeds as well as words. They dramatized and acted their messages. By their strange and arresting conduct they would attract popular attention to what they wished to convey, and thus impress it deeply upon the public. They did not hesitate to do very sensational things to this end. The most sensational of these prophetic acts was the marriage of Hosea.

Hosea was a prophet of the Northern Kingdom of Israel. He was profoundly convinced that his nation had been unfaithful to God. Israel was strongly infected with the fertility cult that was current in Palestine, with its deification and worship of the forces of nature. The people were abandoning the simpler worship of God to follow this form of nature worship. But Hosea thought of God and the nation as husband and wife, and this adoption of another religion appeared to him an act of conjugal infidelity.

To bring this home to his people he felt it his religious duty to make his own marriage a parable of the nation's sin, and married a notoriously immoral woman, named Gomer, buying her like a slave for a few pieces of silver and a few quarts of barley. In

her unfaithfulness he saw the symbol of Israel's unfaithfulness to God. Israel was no better than an
adulteress, who abandoned an honorable marriage
for base intrigues with faithless lovers.

Gomer's children were given names suggestive of
Israel's disloyalty and disobedience. The boy Jez-
reel[1] recalled Jehu's massacre of Ahab's family in
that city, a crime that was yet to be avenged upon
Jehu's house.[2] The names of the other children,
Lo-ruhamah ("Unpitied") and Lo-ammi ("Not-my-
people")[3] mark them as disowned and repudiated, as
Israel will be disowned and repudiated by God.

This extraordinary story of Hosea's marriage is
told twice: first in the third person, in chapter 1,
and again in the first person, in chapter 3. It is evident from it that the rescue of his nation from its
religious lapse was the one absorbing passion of his
life, compared with which all other ties and hopes—
home and wife and family—were as nothing.

Hosea sometimes includes Judah in his denunciations of Israel, but his appeal is principally addressed to the people of the Northern Kingdom.
The Lord has a quarrel with the inhabitants of the
land, because there is no fidelity, no kindness, and
no knowledge of God in the land:

"Cursing, lying, murder, theft and adultery—
   They break out and one crime follows hard upon
      another."[4]

Their immoral practices are intertwined with their idolatry. Their sons "go apart with harlots and sacrifice with temple-prostitutes."[5] Their daughters, too, are immoral, and their sons' wives are adulterous, but God will not punish them, since their brothers and husbands are no better. This single standard for men and women is a startling thing to find in this ancient oriental prophet.

The indications of Israel's idolatry and its adoption of the fertility cult are numerous in Hosea. Their altars, their sacred pillars, their high places, their Anath and Asherah, their Baals, their idols:

"In Gilgal they sacrifice to demons . . . .
   A maker of images is Ephraim;
   He has set up for himself a fat bull! . . . .
   I loathe your bull, O Samaria! . . . .
   A mechanic made it,
   And it is not God."[6]

For all this betrayal of the love and care of God, the nation must suffer. They sowed the wind, and they shall reap the whirlwind.[7] They shall say to the mountains "Cover us!" and to the hills "Fall upon us!"[8] Because of their wicked deeds God will drive them out of his house.[9] Ephraim shall return to Egypt, and Assyria shall be his king.[10] They shall go to Assyria. Egypt shall gather them, Memphis shall bury them.[11] The calf of Beth Aven shall be carried to Assyria, as tribute to the Great King.[12]

"My God will reject them,
  Because they have not listened to him,
  And they shall become wanderers among the
    nations."[13]

While nothing can avert this penalty of exile, Hosea is not without hope of the ultimate restoration of his people. He is supremely the prophet of the unalterable love of God.

"When Israel was a child, I came to love him,
  And from Egypt I called him. . . . .
  It was I who taught Ephraim to walk,
  I took them up in my arms; . . . .
  How can I give you up, O Ephraim?
  How surrender you, O Israel?"[14]

In the figure of the temporary separation of Hosea and Gomer, the prophet sets forth his expectation of a period of exile, to be followed by the return of Israel to his own land.

"They shall come fluttering like a bird from
    Egypt,
  And like a dove from the land of Assyria,
  And I will bring them back to their homes."
             It is the oracle of the Lord.[15]

"I will betroth you to myself forever;
  I will betroth you to myself in righteousness
    and in justice,
  And in kindness and mercy."[16]

"Whereas it was said to them, 'You are not my
  people,'
It shall be said to them, 'Sons of the living
  God!' "[17]

Hosea's preaching fell a few years later than that
of Amos. Both worked in the days of Jeroboam II,
of Israel, but the work of Amos was over by the
middle of the century, while that of Hosea fell between 745 and 735 B.C. In those years the Assyrian
armies under Tiglath-pileser III were coming nearer
and nearer. In 738, Menahem, king of Israel, sent
tribute to that monarch. In 730, Israel under King
Hoshea became a vassal of Assyria. When he rebelled, about 725, Assyria, now at the zenith of its
power, set out to crush Israel altogether, and in 721
Samaria fell before the Assyrians under Sargon.

Hosea remains the prophet of the unalterable love
of God, as Amos is that of his impartial justice.

SUGGESTIONS FOR STUDY

1. *References:* [1]Hos. 1:4; [2]II Kings, chaps. 9, 10; [3]Hos.
1:6, 9; [4]Hos. 4:2; [5]Hos. 4:14; [6]Hos. 12:11; 4:17; 8:5, 6;
[7]Hos. 8:7; [8]Hos. 10:8; [9]Hos. 9:15; [10]Hos. 11:5; [11]Hos. 9:6;
[12]Hos. 10:5, 6; [13]Hos. 9:17; [14]Hos. 11:1, 3, 8; [15]Hos. 11:11;
[16]Hos. 2:19; [17]Hos. 1:10.

2. How did Hosea's domestic life embody his religious
message?

3. What was the religious condition of Israel in his day?

4. How did the names of Hosea's children bear upon his
work?

5. What penalty does Hosea declare the nation must pay for its sins?

6. When did he prophesy?

7. What was the subsequent fate of Israel?

8. What were the sins he most strongly denounced?

9. Had he any hope for the future of his nation?

10. What is the great religious idea of Hosea?

11. Compare him with Amos.

CHAPTER III

THE BOOK OF MICAH

The crimes and dangers of Israel must have made a very deep impression upon the thoughtful men of the eighth century, for they stirred Micah as well as Amos and Hosea. With him we are brought still nearer to the catastrophe, for he prophesied between 730 and 721 B.C. and in the latter year Samaria fell before the Assyrians under Sargon, and the Northern Kingdom became extinct.

Micah, like Amos, was a peasant. He spoke for the oppressed peasantry, crushed under the tyranny and greed of the rich. His home was the little town of Moresheth Gath, near the Philistine border of Judah. His point of view was rural and provincial rather than urban and metropolitan, and the chief cities of his time seem to him so full of violence and wrong that they are positive crimes:

> What is Jacob's transgression?
> Is it not Samaria?
> And what is Judah's sin?
> Is it not Jerusalem?[1]

These cities seem to the prophet to be built of sin and wrong:

> Who build Zion with blood,
> And Jerusalem with guilt.[2]

Prophets, priests, and judges alike fall under Micah's savage invective:

Her chiefs pronounce judgment for a bribe,
And her priests declare oracles for hire,
And her prophets divine for cash.[3]

You are my people's foe.
You rise against those who are at peace.[4]

For the sake of a mere trifle,
You take a heavy mortgage.[5]

They covet fields, and seize them,
And houses, and carry them off.[6]

If a man, walking in a false spirit, should lie,
"I will prophesy to you of wine and strong drink,"
He would be this people's prophet![7]

"Is it not your place to know justice,
You who hate the good and love wickedness,
Snatching their skin from upon them,
And their flesh from upon their bones?"[8]

The iron has entered into the soul of Micah, and he champions the cause of his class in no uncertain terms. The ruling classes have betrayed their trust. Israel as well as Judah is guilty, and both alike shall be punished:

I will turn Samaria into a ruin of the field,
Into a planted vineyard. . . . .
All her images shall be burned with fire,

And all her idols I will lay waste.
For from the harlot's hire they were gathered,
And unto the harlot's hire they shall return.[9]

The leaders of Judah still hope that they will escape. They rely upon the sanctity of the temple, which they believe God will not permit their enemies to profane:

They lean upon the Lord, saying,
"Is not the Lord in the midst of us?
No misfortune can befall us."[10]

But the punishment that is to fall upon Israel will involve Judah also:

For her stroke is incurable;
For it has come even to Judah.
It reaches the gate of my people,
Even to Jerusalem.[11]

Therefore, because of you,
Zion shall be plowed like a field,
And Jerusalem shall become a ruin,
And the temple hill a high place in
a forest.[12]

This bold rustic prophet was in fact the first to predict the destruction of Jerusalem. It would be difficult to imagine anything more repugnant and shocking to Micah's fellow-countrymen. It contradicted their fundamental convictions, both political and religious, and must have made a profound im-

pression. It was quoted in Jerusalem a hundred
years later, when Jeremiah's predictions of the desolation of the city so infuriated the priests and the
prophets that they called for his execution.[13] Some
of the elders of the land saved him, however, by appealing to the case of Micah, who had said just such
things about Jerusalem and thus caused the people
to repent and reform. For Jerusalem did not fall until 597 B.C., when the Babylonians took it. They destroyed it after their second seizure of it, in 586.

Of the seven chapters of Micah only the first
three can with confidence be called the work of Micah himself. It was probably in about this extent
that the book was known to Jeremiah and his times.
As so often happens, this little collection of dirges in
time gathered to itself kindred poems from later
hands, some of which seemed to supply elements
wanting in Micah's own work.

The second part of our book, chapters 4 and 5,
consists of seven short poems or fragments, none of
them probably earlier than the period of the Exile,
597–538, dealing with the Remnant, the restoration, and the Messianic Age and King. The splendid picture of the Golden Age of peace, 4:1–5, and
of the prince from Bethlehem, 5:1–3, are among the
noblest things in Jewish prophecy:

They will beat their swords into plow-shares,
And their spears into pruning-hooks.

Nation shall not lift up sword against nation,
Nor shall they learn war any more.[14]

And you, O Bethlehem Ephrathah,
Too little to be among the clans of Judah,
From you, one shall come forth for me,
Who shall be ruler over Israel.[15]

That this is really a collection of prophetic poems from different hands is shown by the fact that 4:1-3 is found also in Isa. 2:1-4.

The third part of the book, chapters 6 and 7, is almost equally varied, yet part of these chapters may be as old as the time of Micah, if he lived until the reign of Manasseh. The closing verses, 7:14-20, are clearly as late as the Exile. Denunciations of the city for its sin mingle with visions of the ultimate restoration of Jerusalem. Here is found that perfect description of true religion which is on every account one of the gems of religious literature:

Yet what does the Lord require of you,
But to do justice, and to love kindness,
And to walk humbly with your God?[16]

Small in quantity as what we possess of Micah's own work really is, in fire and vigor he is second to none of the Jewish prophets, but is, as he himself expressed it, full of power

To declare to Jacob his crimes,
And to Israel his sins.[17]

ad-
to be
-prophet,
of his day,
of his faith in

done in the reigns of
Hezekiah,[2] but he may
es of Manasseh, 693-639
is said by tradition to have
, by being sawn asunder.
ve chapters of the book consist of
saiah denouncing the sins of Judah—
justice, bribery, superstition, idolatry, in-
ce, and want of faith—and declaring that
will destroy the nation because of them. Isa-
ah's call is described and there is an account of his interview with Ahaz when Syria and Israel were threatening Judah. Isaiah foresees the desolation of the land. He comes to see that the Assyrian is to be the rod of God's anger and the staff of his fury;[3] he will sweep through Judah like an overwhelming flood.[4] A terrible day of judgment is coming, when the pride of man will be brought low.[5]

Isaiah's children, like Hosea's, were given names

SUGGESTIONS FOR STUDY

1. *References:* [1]Mic. 1:5; [2]Mic. 3:10; [3]Mi
2:8; [5]Mic. 2:10; [6]Mic. 2:2; [7]Mic. 2:11; [8]Mic.
1:6, 7; [10]Mic. 3:11; [11]Mic. 1:9; [12]Mic. 3:12;
[14]Mic. 4:3; [15]Mic. 5:1; [16]Mic. 6:8; [17]Mic. 3:8.

2. When did Micah prophesy?
3. Where did he live?
4. What was his station in life?
5. What great wrongs moved him to preac
6. What was the burden of his message?
7. What did he think of the cities of Israel
8. Why are his prophecies, chaps. 1–3, s
dirges?
9. What did he teach as to the future of S
Jerusalem?
10. How does he compare with Amos and H
11. What is the character of chaps. 4 and 5?
12. What subjects are dealt with in chaps. 6
13. When was Jerusalem captured and whe
stroyed?

taken by them in 711, and in 701, under Sennacherib, they invaded Judah itself.

All this Isaiah witnessed, with intense anxiety,
from the vantage-point of the capital of Judah
Again and again he sought to shape events by
dressing the king with counsels which he fel
divinely guided. He was thus a statesma
participating actively in the political lif
and interpreting its events in the lig
God.

Isaiah's prophetic work was
Uzziah, Jotham, Ahaz, and
have lived until the ti
B.C., under whom h
suffered martyrd

The first tw
sermons of
luxury, i
dulge
Go

history. In 735–734 Syria and Israel made war upon
Judah in the effort to force her to join them in re-
sisting Assyria. Every year the Assyrians were coming nearer. They took Damascus in 732, Samaria in
721, and Carchemish in 717. In 715 they defeated
Hanno of Gaza in the battle of Raphia. Ashdod was

related to his prophecies. One born in the midst of
the apprehension of the Syro-Ephraimitic War was
given a name to indicate how soon the wealth of
Damascus and the spoil of Samaria would be carried
away by the king of Assyria.[6] Another was named
in honor of the remnant which, Isaiah taught, was all
that would return to the service of God.[7] Isaiah's
hopelessness as to the mass of the people, reflected
in his call,[8] is echoed here, as well as in his purpose
to seal up his disregarded testimony, and to seal his
teaching in the hearts of the disciples whom he
gathered around him,[9] and in whom he saw the beginnings of that remnant which would some day return to the mighty God.[10] Indeed, there is little
hope in the preaching of Isaiah. The beautiful
prophecies of the Prince of Peace[11] and the Age of
Gold[12] reflect the hopes that sprang up long after in
the dark years of the Babylonian Exile.

Of the eight parts into which Isaiah may be divided, the second, chapters 13–23, consists of oracles dealing with various crises between the Syro-
Ephraimitic War, 735–734 B.C., and the invasion of
Sennacherib, 701 B.C. But with these are combined
passages like 13:1—14:23 and 21:1-10, which
clearly belong to the time of the Exile.

The third part, chapters 24–27, which is probably
as late as the time of Alexander the Great, 332 B.C.,
forms a preface to the fourth part, chapters 28–33,
which has mostly to do with the deliverance of Jeru-

salem; while the fifth part, chapters 34 and 35, forms an eschatological appendix to the preceding section, describing God's judgment upon Edom and the Golden Age to come:

> The wilderness and the parched land shall be
>   glad,
> And the desert shall rejoice and blossom; . . . .
>
> Then shall the eyes of the blind be opened,
> And the ears of the deaf shall be unstopped; . . . .
>
> They shall come to Zion with singing,
> And with everlasting joy upon their heads.[13]

Part VI, chapters 36–39, made up of extracts from II Kings, relates experiences of Isaiah in the time of the invasion by Sennacherib, and forms the conclusion of this main collection of prophecies anciently ascribed to Isaiah, chapters 1–39. Sennacherib's sudden and mysterious raising of the siege of Jerusalem and withdrawal from Judah may have been occasioned by some reverse suffered by his main army which was threatening Egypt.[14] The result was that the doctrine of the inviolability of Jerusalem as the Holy City of God himself became established in Jewish religious thought.[15]

The seventh and eighth parts of the book, chapters 40–55 and 56–66, reflect very different situations and periods from what has gone before. In chapters 40–55 Babylon has replaced Assyria as Judah's

overshadowing foe, which has carried the people
into exile. The captive nation is the suffering servant of God, and looks to Cyrus, the Persian conqueror, chapter 45, for deliverance from its bondage.
Babylon fell before the Persians in 538, and Cyrus
began to return the exiles to their homes. These
chapters beautifully reflect the joy of the return:

"Comfort, O comfort my people,"
    Says your God;
"Speak to the heart of Jerusalem,
    And call to her—
That her time of service is ended,
    That her guilt is paid in full." . . . .

On a high mountain get you up,
    O heralds of good news to Zion!
Lift up your voice with strength,
    O heralds of good news to Jerusalem . . . .
Say to the cities of Judah,
    "Behold your God!"[16]

The final chapters of the book, Part VIII, chapters 56–66, again present a change of scene. They
deal with the situation of the returned exiles, who
found it difficult to induce the population of Jerusalem to conform to the legal developments the Hebrew religion had undergone during the Exile, and
were probably written about the middle of the fifth
century before Christ, not long before the times of
Nehemiah and Ezra.

It will be seen that about the great name of Isaiah there has gathered a wide range of prophetic messages, some of them Exilic or post-Exilic; indeed, it is probable that our Book of Isaiah is the combination of several collections of this kind, so that it has become a veritable anthology, or rather a treasury, of the most brilliant and varied Hebrew prophecy.

The work of Isaiah himself is found, with some other material, in the first, second, fourth, and sixth parts of the book, chapters 1–12, 13–23, 28–33, 36–39. His prophecies passed through many editions and sustained many accretions before they reached the form in which they have come down to us, and it cannot have been far from 300 B.C. that the Book of Isaiah received the last of those varied additions that together with the work of Isaiah himself make it the most brilliant and splendid book in all Jewish literature. He was supremely the prophet of the holiness of God.

SUGGESTIONS FOR STUDY

1. *References:* [1]Isa. 6:1–13; [2]Isa. 1:1; [3]Isa. 10:5; [4]Isa. 8:5–8; [5]Isa. 2:17; [6]Isa. 8:4; [7]Isa. 7:3; [8]Isa. 6:9, 10; [9]Isa. 8:16–18; [10]Isa. 10:20, 21; [11]Isa. 9:1–7; [12]Isa. 11:1–9; [13]Isa. 35:1, 5, 10; [14]Isa. 37:36, 37; [15]cf. Isa. 37:35; [16]Isa. 40:1, 2, 9.

2. What part of the Book of Isaiah relates to Isaiah and his work?

3. Where did he live?

4. What was his social station?

5. Describe his call to the prophetic office.
6. What attribute of God most impressed Isaiah?
7. What political events form the background of his work?
8. What hopes of success had Isaiah for his work?
9. What use did he see in it?
10. What measures did he take for its perpetuation?
11. What future for Judah does he foresee?
12. How did other prophecies come to be added to Isaiah's?
13. Who was Cyrus and why was he so glorified by the prophets of the Exile?
14. What parts of the Book of Isaiah deal with the Return?
15. To what period do the closing chapters of the book belong?

CHAPTER V

THE BOOK OF ZEPHANIAH

The prophets felt themselves to be the preachers of a true and lofty religion, which their people for the most part refused and disobeyed. This led them to a mood of deep pessimism. The end, they felt, could be nothing but destruction, utter and hopeless, as Amos had described it, in his fearful vision of the Day of the Lord.[1]

The teaching of the herdsman Amos was echoed more than a century after his time, by a young aristocrat of Jerusalem named Zephaniah, a descendant of King Hezekiah. The Scythians spoken of in Herodotus[2] had made their appearance in Palestine (627 B.C.), and this seemed to Zephaniah to mark the beginning of the end. The destructive Day, of which Amos had spoken, was at last to come, and overwhelm Judah and the sinful nations around.

Later Judaism came to suppose that from an earlier condition of general piety and godliness the Jewish people in the prophets' time had fallen into idolatry and wickedness. It would be truer to think of the prophets in religious development as far in advance of their countrymen, who were still very largely polytheistic and idolatrous. The prophets faced the enormous task of raising these backward masses to something approaching their own moral and religious elevation, and it is not strange that sometimes the undertaking seemed hopeless.

The Scythians had swept into Western Asia from the north, and, encountering the rising power of the Medes, had defeated them, and pressed on into Palestine, with the intention of passing through it to Egypt. But Psammetichus of Egypt met them and made terms with them, so that they presently retired.

Their stay in Palestine was probably not long but it made a deep impression, as both Jeremiah and Zephaniah show. To Zephaniah, these half-savage hordes seemed the prelude to the awful Day of the Lord that the wickedness of the world made him expect. The whole earth must suffer the agonies of judgment:

"I will utterly sweep away everything
From upon the face of the ground.
I will sweep away man and beast;
I will sweep away the fowl of the heavens and the
    fish of the sea.
And I will cause the wicked to stumble,
And I will cut off mankind from upon the face of
    the ground."
It is the oracle of the Lord.[3]

The half-idolatrous people of Judah, with their pagan proclivities, will suffer for their sins:

"And I will stretch out my hand against Judah,
   And against all the inhabitants of Jerusalem.
   And from this place I will cut off Baal to the last
      remnant,
   The name of the priestlings with the priests;
   And those who prostrate themselves upon the
      roofs
   To the host of the heavens;
   And those who prostrate themselves before the
      Lord,
   And swear by Milcom;
   And those who have withdrawn from following
      the Lord,
   And those who have not sought the Lord,
   Nor inquired after him."[4]

This terrible prospect of frightful and complete
destruction Zephaniah declares to be close at hand:

   Silence before the Lord God,
   For the day of the Lord is near at hand! . . . .
   Near at hand is the great day of the Lord;
   Near and speeding fast!
   Near at hand is the bitter day of the Lord.
   Then the warrior will cry in terror!
   A day of wrath is that day;
   A day of trouble and distress,
   A day of desolation and waste,
   A day of darkness and gloom,
   A day of cloud and thundercloud;

> A day of trumpet and battle-cry,
> Against the fortified cities,
> And against the lofty battlements.[5]

The principal damage done by the Scythians in Palestine seems to have been at the Philistine city of Ascalon, where, Herodotus says, they destroyed the temple of Venus (Astarte). Zephaniah has much to say of Philistia's doom:

> Gaza shall be deserted,
> And Askelon a waste.
> Ashdod—at noon they shall expel her,
> And Ekron shall be uprooted. . . . .
> The word of the Lord is against you,
> O Canaan, land of the Philistines,
> And I will destroy you so that there
> shall be no inhabitant.[6]

The rising power of the Medes in the farther east had borne the first brunt of the Scythians' attack, as their hordes, so like the Mongols in the thirteenth century, burst into Western Asia. Even Assyria had been threatened, and the purpose of the invaders in entering Palestine had been to reach Egypt. Zephaniah sees in their coming the doom of Assyria and Egypt:

> You, too, O Ethiopians,
> Shall be slain by my sword!

And he will stretch out his hand against the
    north,
    And destroy Assyria.
And he will make Nineveh a desolation,
    A drought like the desert.
And herds shall lie down in the midst of her,
    Every beast of the field.
Both screech owl and porcupine
    Shall lodge in her capitals.
The owl shall hoot in the window,
    The bustard on the threshold.
For I will destroy her city.
This is the exultant city,
    That dwelt in security!
That said to itself,
    "I am, and there is none else."
How has she become a ruin,
    A lair for wild beasts.
Everyone that passes by her hisses,
    And shakes his fist![7]

This picture of the desolation of Nineveh recalls
Xenophon's visit to its site more than two hundred
years later, in 401 B.C. He found only "a great wall
lying deserted, belonging to a city called Mespila,
which had once been inhabited by the Medes."[8]

The doom the prophet has foretold for Philistia,
Ethiopia, and Assyria is to overtake Judah also.
Jerusalem is an oppressing city, which has not ac-

cepted correction or drawn near to her God. Idolatry, injustice, and corruption are rampant in Judah:

> Her princes within her are roaring lions;
> Her judges are wolves of the night,
> Who long not for the morning.
> Her prophets are reckless, treacherous men;
> Her priests profane holy things;
> They do violence to the law.[9]

The punishments of the surrounding nations which should have been a lesson to Judah she has disregarded. Instead of reforming, her people

> ". . . . have zealously made
> All their doings corrupt."[10]

The announcement of the doom of Moab and Ammon, 2:8-11, and the closing lyrics of the book, which deal with the deliverance of Jerusalem and the future renown of Israel, 3:8-20, are later additions to the work of Zephaniah, and probably belong to the time of the Exile.

The destruction of Assyria and Judah was not, however, to be the work of the Scythians, but was reserved for other hands. Yet it was not long delayed. Fifteen years later Assyria fell before the Medes and Babylonians; Nineveh, the capital, was captured in 612 B.C., and fifteen years after, in 597, Jerusalem was taken by the Babylonians. Zephaniah's terrible picture of the Day of the Lord was

revived in the Middle Ages in the great hymn of
Thomas of Celano, A.D. 1250, the first line of which,
"Dies irae, dies illa," is quoted from the Vulgate
Latin translation of Zeph. 1:15: "A day of wrath is
that day!"

SUGGESTIONS FOR STUDY

1. *References:* [1]Amos 5:18–20; 8:7–10; [2]Herodotus, 1.
103–5: "A numerous horde of Scyths, under their king
Madyes, son of Protothyes, burst into Asia in pursuit of the
Cimmerians whom they had driven out of Europe, and
entered the Median territory. . . . . The Scythians, having
invaded Media, were opposed by the Medes, who gave them
battle, but, being defeated, lost their empire. The Scythians
became masters of Asia. After this they marched forward
with the design of invading Egypt. When they reached Palestine, however, Psammetichus the Egyptian king met them
with gifts and prayers, and prevailed on them to advance no
farther. On their return, passing through Ascalon, a city of
Syria, the greater part of them went their way without doing
any damage; but some few who lagged behind pillaged the
temple of Celestial Venus. . . . . The dominion of the Scythians over Asia lasted eight and twenty years, during which
time their insolence and oppression spread ruin on every
side. . . . . They scoured the country and plundered every
one of whatever they could" (Rawlinson's translation);
[3]Zeph. 1:2, 3; [4]Zeph. 1:4–6; [5]Zeph. 1:7, 14–16; [6]Zeph. 2:4, 5;
[7]Zeph. 2:12–15; [8]Anabasis, iii:4. 10; [9]Zeph. 3:3, 4; [10]Zeph.
3:7.

2. What menacing situation led Zephaniah to prophesy?
3. From what earlier prophet did he take his text?
4. What is the subject of his prophecy?
5. What fate does he anticipate for the nations around
Judah?

6. What is Judah herself going to experience?

7. What does Zephaniah think of Judah and Jerusalem?

8. What does he describe as their chief failings?

9. When did Nineveh fall?

10. What remains of Nineveh did Xenophon find when he passed that way with the Ten Thousand two centuries later?

11. What do you think of Zephaniah's moral ideals?

12. What do you think of his literary skill?

CHAPTER VI

THE BOOK OF NAHUM

The Jew has always had a strong race-consciousness, a keen sense of his Jewish blood and heritage. The most conspicuous example of this attitude among the prophets is Nahum, who is also probably the greatest poet among them.

Nahum is stirred to write by the impending fall of Nineveh, which seems to be immediately in prospect, if it has not just actually taken place. Nineveh had long overshadowed and threatened the little kingdom of Judah, but now that cruel, devastating empire is facing its own doom. Half a century before, about 661 B.C., the Assyrians under Ashurbanipal had captured and plundered Thebes, the ancient capital of Egypt, but now their time has come and their own capital is to be taken and sacked. This allusion to the fall of Thebes helps us to date the prophecy of Nahum. He evidently writes after that event, and when the fall of Nineveh before the Babylonians and Medes is a certainty of the near future. Nineveh fell in 612 B.C. and Nahum probably uttered this prophecy about that time.

The Assyrians had for centuries been the terror of the smaller kingdoms of Western Asia. One by one they had fallen before her, Israel among the rest. Once Sennacherib had invaded Judah itself and laid siege to Jerusalem. This event of ninety years before is probably what is referred to in 1:11:

> Did not one go forth from you plotting evil
>   against the Lord,
> Counselling rascality?

For the Assyrians were not, like some conquerors, benefactors of the peoples they conquered. And while the nations of the ancient East were all cruel, the Assyrians, if not actually the most cruel of them all, certainly took the most satisfaction in recording their atrocities in their inscriptions.

All this and much more besides lies back of the prophecy of Nahum. If we could assemble in our minds all that we nowadays most hate and abhor in the modern world, it would be pale and insignificant compared with the mass of memories and pictures that filled the mind of Nahum as he thought of Nineveh and the doings of the Assyrians through three centuries of invasion, deportation, and barbarity. Only thus can we fairly understand the bitterness of his hatred. And in the destruction of Assyria he sees God's punishment of her for her crimes.

The Assyrians had built up by sheer force of arms the greatest empire the world had yet seen. They had developed the provincial system of organization, and to keep their conquests in subjection had devised the policy of deporting conquered peoples to other distant parts of their empire, where they would be less likely to rebel. Thus Sargon had carried more than twenty-seven thousand people away from Samaria, in 721, and the long grief of exile was added to the humiliation of defeat. Judah and Jerusalem had narrowly escaped a similar fate twenty years later.

But now a power had arisen in the East that could actually try conclusions with Assyria herself and push her from her place. Centuries before, the Babylonians had been the masters of the Eastern world, and now after a long period of quiescence, under a new dynasty they resumed their old position. They were enabled to do this by the appearance of the Medes in the farther east, and their combined forces enabled them to capture Nineveh, conquer the Assyrian Empire, and divide it between them.

Nahum's eyes are fixed upon the dramatic point in this great upheaval—the capture of Nineveh. He greets her downfall with unrestrained delight. The confusion of the siege and sack of the city give his unequaled descriptive powers ample scope:

Oh city, bloody throughout,
Full of lies and booty!
Prey ceases not.

The crack of the whip, and the noise of the rum-
bling wheel,
And the galloping horse, and the jolting chariot,
The charging horseman, and the flashing sword,
And the glittering spear, and a multitude of slain,
And a mass of bodies, and no end to the corpses!
They stumble over the corpses![1]

The earlier prophets had been greatly impressed
with the military organization of Assyria. Isaiah described it in one of his most brilliant passages:

No loin-girdle of his is loosed,
No sandal-thong is snapped;
His arrows are sharpened,
His bows are all bent;
His horses' hoofs are counted like flint,
His wheels like the whirlwind.[2]

Nahum exultingly describes it as now driven to
self-defense:

The shatterer is come up against you;
Keep the rampart;
Watch the road; brace your loins.
Strengthen your forces to the utmost. . . . .

The chariots will rage in the streets,
Dashing to and fro in the open spaces.
Their appearance will be like that of torches,
Darting about like lightning.
He summons his nobles; they stumble as they
go;

They hasten to the wall,
And the battering ram is set up.

The gates of the rivers are opened
And the palace melts away.
Its mistress is brought forth; she goes into
    captivity,
While her maidens mourn,
Moaning like the sound of doves,
Beating upon their breasts.
And Nineveh is like a pool of water,
Whose water escapes.

There is emptiness, and desolation, and
    waste,
And a melting heart and trembling knees;
And anguish is in all loins,
And the faces of all of them become livid.
Where is the den of the lions,
And the cave of the young lions,
Whither the lion went bringing in spoil,
The lion's cub, with none to disturb?[3]

Nineveh is now to suffer what she had so often
made others suffer. Half a century before she had
destroyed Thebes:

"Are you any better than Thebes,
    That sat by the great Nile,
    (Water was around her)
    Whose rampart was the sea,

Whose wall was water? . . . .
Yet even she became an exile;
She went into captivity. . . . .
You too shall reel and swoon,
You too shall seek refuge from the foe. . . . .

"Draw yourself waters for the siege;
    strengthen your forts. . . . .
But there fire shall devour you,
The sword shall cut you off.

"Your shepherds slumber, O king of Assyria,
    Your nobles sleep! . . . .
There is no healing for your wound,
    Your hurt is incurable.
Everyone who shall hear the news about you
    Will clap his hands over you.
For against whom has your malice not con-
    tinually gone forth?"[4]

To Nahum's fiery oracles a later hand has prefixed an acrostic poem on the avenging Wrath of
God, 1:2–10, probably in the time of the Exile,
when such alphabetic poems began to become common. It has the effect of making Nahum's song of
triumph over Nineveh an illustration of God's dealings with the wicked.

SUGGESTIONS FOR STUDY

1. *References:* [1]Nah. 3:1–3; [2]Isa. 5:27, 28; [3]Nah. 2:1,
4–8, 10, 11; [4]Nah. 3:8, 10, 11, 14, 15, 18, 19.

2. What political situation led Nahum to utter his
prophecy?

3. What was the substance of his message?

4. What had Assyria done to stir him so deeply?

5. What combination of forces led to the fall of Nineveh?

6. What use does Nahum make of the fate of Thebes?

7. What was the policy of the Assyrians in dealing with conquered peoples?

8. What scenes does Nahum most realistically describe?

9. What do you think of his poetry?

10. What relation does 1:1-10 bear to the rest of the book?

11. Does Nahum take up the question of forgiving one's enemies?

CHAPTER VII

THE BOOK OF DEUTERONOMY

It was the eighteenth year of the reign of Josiah.
The half-heathen reigns of Manasseh and Amon
were over, and under King Josiah efforts were being
made to undo the evil effects of their times. Among
other reforms the temple was repaired, and in the
course of this work somewhere in its recesses an old
book of law was discovered. A dramatic account of
the incident is found in II Kings, chapters 22 and
23. The book was taken to the young king and read
to him, and it led him to further reforms in the religious life of the nation. He put a stop to the idolatrous practices of the people, sought to confine sacrifice to the temple in Jerusalem alone, and had the
Passover celebrated in Jerusalem by all the people.

Just these things are prescribed in the Book of
Deuteronomy, and it was that book, in substance,
that was found and put into effect by Josiah in
621 B.C.

Deuteronomy is the embodiment of the long
struggle of the prophets with the old idolatry of the
land and with the foreign forms of worship that kept
creeping in. In it the great prophetic ideals of religion, as something that should pervade and purify
the whole life of the nation, are powerfully present-

ed. The reforms undertaken by Hezekiah (721–693)[1] had been more than undone under Manasseh (693–639),[2] but now Josiah made the most vigorous attempt in the whole history of the kingdom to carry out the prophetic ideals. Isaiah had taught that the Temple in Jerusalem was the dwelling-place of God, but now it was conceived to be the only sanctuary where he could be acceptably worshiped.

The prophets had always emphasized morals rather than ritual, and had laid little stress upon sacrifice as a way of pleasing God. But now they laid hold of it as a concession to the practical religious needs of the people, purifying and interpreting it, so as to make it a real religious symbol of obedience and devotion to God. Prophetic and priestly interests thus combine in what we know as Deuteronomy. The ceremonial worship of God was to carry with it high ideals of personal morality and social justice.

These ideals were embodied in a series of laws, which were felt to represent the aims and purposes of Moses himself, their great liberator, to whom they looked back as the founder of their religion, six hundred years before. These laws are an expansion and revision of an earlier code which had long existed, and which is preserved in Exod. 20:20—23:33, the so-called "Book of the Covenant." Some things contained in that code were entirely out of date when Deuteronomy was written, like the com-

mand to exterminate the Canaanites; but in general
Deuteronomy reformulates and reinterprets existing
laws, seeking to adjust them to contemporary conditions and fill them with a nobler spirit and with
loftier sanctions. Obedience is to rise not from fear
or self-interest but from the people's love of God:

"Listen, O Israel; the Lord is our God, the Lord
alone; so you must love the Lord your God with all
your mind and all your heart and all your
strength."[3]

How had the mysterious book of law which Hil-
kiah found come into existence? It was probably
written in the dark days of Manasseh, when the
prophets who had guided the reformation under
Hezekiah had been put to death or silenced. Isaiah
is supposed to have suffered martyrdom at that
time and Micah too may have perished. Heathen-
ism once more pervaded the land. The prophets
could not speak; their fair hopes for a righteous and
God-fearing nation were cruelly disappointed. Some
survivor of their group, however, solaced himself in
secret, about 675–650 B.C., by rewriting the old law in
the new prophetic spirit, and casting it into a great
prophetic appeal, in the form of an oration by Moses
himself. And years after, when Manasseh was dead,
this masterpiece of prophetic religion came to light
and became the first Bible of the Jewish people. In
it, rather than in the prophets, we have the actual

nucleus of the Jewish scriptures. From this time on Judaism rallies about a book, and that book is Deuteronomy.

The unknown prophet who wrote Deuteronomy was one of the chief masters of Hebrew prose. He put his work in the form of an oration addressed by Moses to the Israelites as the people approached the promised land, toward the end of the forty years' wandering, when Moses was about to leave them. It is his great valedictory.

It comprises Deuteronomy, chapters 5–26 and 28, and seeks to revise and refine the old law in the spirit of the prophets. Chapters 5–11 form the introduction and chapter 28 the conclusion. The main legal section, chapters 12–26, represents a reorganization of current laws, including the Book of the Covenant, Exod. 20:22—23:33, on a higher plane, with more regard to social and human values. There is more justice, and more recognition and protection for women, slaves, employes, aliens, and the poor.

The Book of the Covenant was itself the fruit of a long development, and reflects a much more primitive time than that of Deuteronomy. It may date from the reform under Asa, king of Judah, about 900 B.C.[4] It in turn grew out of the still more primitive law-code of Exodus, chapter 34—the Little Book of the Covenant, which is probably the germ of the whole Hebrew legislation.

The religious laws of Deuteronomy are particularly interesting. The old local sanctuaries are to be done away; only in Jerusalem can sacrifices be offered to God. The multiplicity of places of sacrifice had made return to idolatry too easy, and against every form of idolatry and paganism Deuteronomy is very severe. The Passover, too, must be celebrated in Jerusalem and nowhere else. This unification of religion in Jerusalem made its control in the interests of monotheism much easier and more effective.[5]

The reforms of Judaism contemplated in Deuteronomy had definite and significant results; Josiah did his utmost to carry them out. But even greater was the influence of the Book of Deuteronomy itself upon contemporary and subsequent Jewish writers. The ideas it embodied powerfully and usefully affected later religious thought, and its appearance marked a new epoch in Jewish religion. It is especially significant as an effort to blend priestly with prophetic ideals of religion, and to fill the sacrificial forms of worship with spiritual meaning.

To this masterpiece of the prophetic spirit were later added chapters 1-4, 27, and 29-34, probably when about 350 B.C. it was wrought into the great encyclopedia of Jewish history, religion, and law which we know as the Hexateuch. Its Greek name, Deuteronomy, the "Second Giving of the Law," was applied to it when in the third century before Christ it was translated, along with Genesis, Exodus, Leviticus, and Numbers, into Greek. And beyond any other single book in the Old Testament it is the germ of what we know as the Bible.

SUGGESTIONS FOR STUDY

1. *References:* [1]II Kings 18:4, 5; [2]II Kings 21:3–16; [3]Deut. 6:4, 5; [4]I Kings 15:9–15; [5]Deut. 16:5, 6, 11, 15, 16.

2. Read Deut., chaps. 5–11, which has been said to embody the noblest religious and social thought ever expressed.

3. Compare Deut., chaps. 12–26, with Exod. 20:20—23:33, the "Book of the Covenant."

4. Compare Exod. 20:20—23:33 with Exod., chap. 34, the "Little Book of the Covenant." Which seems to be derived from the other?

5. When was the Book of Deuteronomy written?

6. When was it adopted as law?

7. What did its writer intend to accomplish by it?

8. What are its leading religious ideas?

9. What reforms in worship was it meant to effect?

10. In what literary form is it cast?

11. What were some of its results?

12. What priestly interests did it serve?

13. What prophetic ideals did it embody?

CHAPTER VIII

THE BOOK OF HABAKKUK

The Hebrew prophets believed firmly in a righteous God, but they saw the world falling a prey to one cruel and brutal tyranny after another, with no apparent reference to right or wrong. Judah herself was wicked enough; her sins roused the prophet Habakkuk to cry to God for punishment upon her. He uttered his prophecies in the last years of the Kingdom of Judah, in the reign of Jehoiakim, 608–597 B.C., a few years after the fall of Assyria before the Medes and Babylonians. The prophets rejoiced in the downfall of Assyria, but it soon became evident that in the Babylonians a new power just as ruthless had taken its place.

Habakkuk is distressed at the violence, injustice, and wrongdoing that prevail in Judah:

> How long, O Lord, must I cry for help,
> > And thou not hear?
> And call out to thee "Violence,"
> > And thou not save?[1]

The solution of the matter presently comes to him. The Babylonians are to be God's instrument of punishment. They will come down upon Judah and destroy it. This must have been in the days of

Babylonia's rise to power, after the fall of Assyria and before the fall of Jerusalem. God answers the prophet's appeal:

"Look out upon the nations and see,
And be utterly amazed.
For a deed is being done in your days
That you would not believe, were it told you.
For behold I am raising up the Chaldeans,
That savage and impetuous nation,
That marches through the breadth of the earth,
To seize habitations that are not his own.

"Terrible and dreadful is he; . . . .
Swifter than leopards are his horses,
And keener than wolves of the desert. . . . .
Terror marches before him;
And he gathers up captives like sand.
He makes scorn of kings;
And rulers are a joke to him!
He laughs at all fortresses,
And heaps up dirt and captures them."[2]

The fall of Nineveh in 612 B.C. before the Babylonians and Medes must have astonished the ancient world, so long accustomed to Assyrian supremacy. And now this new power is turning westward, toward Palestine, and it begins to look as though Judah's time had come and the sins the prophet had denounced were to be punished. The Babylonians had met the Egyptians at Carchemish

in 605 B.C. and decisively defeated them, driving
them out of Palestine, which they had long controlled, and leaving Judah at the mercy of the vic-
tors. In so short a time had the new power of Babylon overcome both the great powers of the day—
Assyria and Egypt. It was indeed an incredible
achievement, "a deed that you would not believe
were it told you."

The dialogue continues. The prophet sees that
the sinfulness of Judah is to be punished, but only
by a power more sinful still, the cruel and brutal
Babylonians. Must this series of violent oppressors
go on forever? Will God keep silent when the wicked swallows up him that is more righteous than
himself? To the conqueror men are no more than so
many fish that he gathers in his net:

> Shall he keep on emptying his net forever,
> And never cease slaying the nations?[3]

Like a watchman upon his lookout the prophet
looks expectantly to God for light upon this question:

> I will take my stand upon my watch-tower,
> And station myself upon the rampart;
> And watch to see what he will say to me,
> And what answer he will make to my complaint.[4]

The answer comes to him:

> "Write the vision clearly upon the tablets,
> That one may read it on the run. . . . .

Verily, the wicked man—I take no pleasure in
    him;
But the righteous lives by reason of his faithful-
    ness.
How much less shall the faithless man live, ...
Shall not all these take up a taunt song against
    him,
And a sharp satire against him, saying,
'Woe to him who enriches himself with what is not
    his own'? . . . .
You will become spoil for them!
Because you have spoiled many nations,
All the rest of the peoples shall spoil you."[5]

God takes no pleasure in the triumphs of the
wicked, but the upright shall live because of his
faithfulness; that is, his devotion will be in some
sense rewarded. Habakkuk has raised the problem
of evil, and the solution he offers for it seems no
better than the old, timeworn Hebrew solution that
piety will bring prosperity. Yet later minds found
in it a deeper meaning, and long after it became a
war-cry for Paul and Luther.

To God's woe pronounced against the rapacious
invaders the prophet adds four more, for their ag-
gression, violence, and idolatry.[6] We seem now to
be in the times of the invasion and conquest of Judah, the fall of Jerusalem, and the carrying of the
Jews into captivity, 597 B.C. The Babylonian who

had at first appeared as the instrument of God's
wrath is now seen to be the archenemy of his people,
cruel and hateful. Plunder, bloodshed, violence, and
wrong are everywhere. But the tyrant's time will
come, and he in his turn will go down to destruction
before some new invader. The heathen nations do
indeed wear themselves out for naught:

> But the earth shall be filled with the knowledge of
>   the glory of the Lord,
> As the waters cover the sea![7]

To be conquered and humiliated by idolaters was
particularly distressing to the prophets. It seemed
as though their religion had suffered defeat, for to
the oriental mind a nation's gods stood or fell with
the nation. But it came to be clear to the prophets
that the deepest things in their faith were not at the
mercy of Assyrian, Egyptian, or Babylonian armies,
and that the triumph of the idols was not real:

> Woe to him who says to wood, "Wake up,"
> To a dumb stone, "Arise."
> Can it give oracles? . . . .
> But the Lord is in his holy temple;
> Be silent before him, all the earth![8]

Yet this reference to the temple as standing seems
to put this woe against idolatry into a later time
than the fall of Jerusalem before Nebuchadnezzar in
597, and the destruction of the Temple by the
Babylonians in 586, and it probably belongs, like

the following chapter, to the period of the rebuilt Temple, after the Exile.

The last chapter of the Book of Habakkuk is a psalm, written long after, probably even after the Exile, for it contains many reminiscences of Hebrew literature, especially Ps. 77:17-20. It describes God in stormy majesty as the judge of the nations, and in one of the noblest pieces of Hebrew poetry expresses that indomitable trust in God—whatever happens—which had been the underlying conviction of Habakkuk:

> Though the fig tree do not flourish,
> And there be no fruit on the vines;
> Though the product of the olive fail,
> And the fields yield no food;
> Though the flock be cut off from the fold,
> And there be no cattle in the stalls;
> Yet I will exult in the Lord;
> I will rejoice in my victorious God!
> God, the Lord, is my strength;
> And he makes my feet like the feet of hinds,
> And makes me walk upon my heights.[9]

SUGGESTIONS FOR STUDY

1. *References:* [1]Hab. 1:2; [2]Hab. 1:5-10; [3]Hab. 1:17; [4]Hab. 2:1; [5]Hab. 2:2, 4-8; [6]Hab. 2:9-20; [7]Hab. 2:14; [8]Hab. 2:19, 20; [9]Hab. 3:17-19.

2. With Hab. 2:14 compare Isa. 11:9. Which seems to you a quotation of the other?

3. With Hab. 3:3 compare Deut. 33:2. Which seems to you to have been influenced by the other?

4. With Hab. 3:10–12, 15 compare Ps. 77:17–20. Which seems to you a quotation of the other?

5. With Hab. 3:18 compare Mic. 7:7. Which seems to you to have quoted the other?

6. With Hab. 3:19 compare II Sam. 22:33, 34 and Ps. 18:34. Is there literary dependence here?

7. What aroused Habakkuk to prophesy?

8. What view did he come to take of the rise of Babylon?

9. What did he think would be her fate?

10. What great problem did Habakkuk raise? Did he solve it?

11. What is the message of the psalm that now concludes the book?

CHAPTER IX

THE BOOK OF JEREMIAH

The Scythian hordes whose appearance in Palestine had seemed to Zephaniah to herald the dreadful Day of the Lord awoke the spirit of prophecy in another young Jew, named Jeremiah. He lived in the village of Anathoth, four miles northeast of Jerusalem. But his sermons, unlike Zephaniah's, are not confined to the time of the Scythian invasion but reflect the history of his people through a period of forty years, 627–586 B.C. These years witnessed great changes in the empires of the East and in the fortunes of Judah: the Scythian advance (627), the fall of Assyria (612), the death of Josiah at Megiddo (609), the rise of Babylon, her defeat of Egypt at Carchemish (605) and consequent control of Judah, the capture of Jerusalem and first deportation (597), and the destruction of the city and final deportation (586). And early in this period occurred the religious reforms of Josiah and the introduction of the Deuteronomic law, discovered in 621. Through these momentous years the great voice of Jeremiah makes itself heard now and again, in crises of political or religious life.

Jeremiah felt himself called to be a prophet to the nations, with authority

To root up and to pull down, to wreck and to
ruin, to build and to plant.[1]

Like a boiling pot out of the north all the kingdoms
of the earth seemed to come against Judah; as Israel, Syria, and Assyria had in the years before come
down against her, now the Scythians were coming,
and later the Babylonians were to come.[2] In all this
Jeremiah sees the just punishment of his people's
idolatry and wickedness.

Jeremiah felt quite unequal to the task set for
him:

"Ah, Lord God! I cannot speak;
For I am only a boy."
But the Lord said to me,
"Do not say, 'I am only a boy';
For to all to whom I send you shall you go,
And all that I command you shall you speak."[3]

Jeremiah was by nature a shrinking, sensitive
man, but he developed a heroic tenacity in his difficult and thankless work. He did not hesitate to denounce the priests and prophets as well as the kings
and princes of Judah for their shortcomings: "On
your hands is found the blood of the innocent poor."[4]

It is not only the character of Jeremiah that is
appealing and affecting; his literary art is equally
striking and has enriched the diction of the world.

The sermons of chapters 1–6 belong to the years
627–621 B.C., before the Deuteronomic reformation.

The changes demanded by Deuteronomy must have been welcome to Jeremiah, as far as their discouragement of idolatry was concerned, but the emphasis they laid upon the Temple, sacrifice, and the formal exercises of religion was extremely distasteful to him, for he put the emphasis in religion upon moral uprightness and the inner life (chaps. 7, 8, 11).

The sin and failure of his people stir Jeremiah to the bitterest outcries; no wonder he has been called the "Weeping Prophet":

> Is there no balm in Gilead?
> Is there no physician there? . . . .
> Oh that my head were waters,
> And mine eyes a fountain of tears,
> That I might weep day and night
> For the slain of the daughter of my people!
> Oh that I had in the desert
>   A traveller's inn,
> That I might leave my people,
>   and be quit of them.
> For they are all adulterers,
>   a company of traitors. . . . .
> They cheat each one his neighbor,
> And no one speaks the truth.[5]

It is in kindness, justice, and uprightness that God delights, and he will punish the nation with destruction:

"I will make Jerusalem a heap of ruins,
    a lair of jackals."[6]

After the death of King Josiah in 609, Jeremiah caused his sermons and memoirs to be written down, and a roll containing them was laid before King Jehoiakim, in the fourth year of his reign, 604 B.C.[7] The king scornfully cut the roll to pieces with his knife and burned it up. This led Jeremiah to have a second, more comprehensive collection made by his secretary Baruch, and this, together with biographical material by his disciples, formed the basis of our Book of Jeremiah, which may be described as at least the third edition of Jeremiah. The first edition, sent to Jehoiakim, probably contained little more than chapters 1–17.

The final overthrow of Judah came at the end of a long series of disasters. Josiah had been killed at Megiddo (609) by Necho of Egypt, who thus became master of Judah. But Necho was defeated at Carchemish in 605 by the Babylonian crown-prince Nebuchadnezzar, and so Judah became a vassal of Babylon. But the Jewish king Jehoiakim withheld his tribute, and Nebuchadnezzar in 597 besieged and captured Jerusalem and carried into captivity ten thousand men of the better class. Zedekiah, the puppet king he appointed, being encouraged by Egypt, rebelled, and in 586 the city was again taken, a great body of captives was transported to Babylonia, and the Temple, the pride of all Jewish hearts, was destroyed.

Most of these tragic happenings are reflected in the pages of Jeremiah. He had been the friend of Josiah, and the unsparing critic of Jehoiakim. Zedekiah consulted him but would not take his advice to offer no resistance to the Babylonian army.[8] Jeremiah's bold prediction of the destruction of Jerusalem and the Temple had offended the religious and political feelings of both court and priesthood and involved him in the gravest danger.[9] For a hundred years the inviolability of the Temple had been a cherished Jewish conviction. Jeremiah was imprisoned and put in the stocks. He was lowered into a cistern and left to die, but the intercession of an Ethiopian eunuch saved his life.[10] When the city was taken for the second time and the Temple was destroyed,[11] he found himself left behind in a desolated and hopeless Judah, from which the glory had utterly departed.[12] Even then his troubles were not over. The turbulent remnant rose against their new rulers and killed them, and to escape the consequences, most of the Jewish community fled to Egypt for safety, taking Jeremiah with them.[13] There he disappears from our view, still protesting against idolatry and striving to keep his miserable companions faithful to their religion.[14]

No Hebrew prophet reveals himself to us so completely as Jeremiah. His anguish over his hopeless task, his resentment against God himself for his situation, his extreme sensitiveness of spirit, combined with his courage and tenacity of purpose, make him a unique figure, at once pathetic and heroic. It was his hard task to distinguish Jewish religion from Jewish national fortunes, and show that they did not stand or fall together; that the Jewish faith did not perish with the Temple, and above all that religion is an individual and inner, not a national and outward, possession and experience.[15] This perception is the great contribution of Jeremiah to Israel's religion.

SUGGESTIONS FOR STUDY

1. *References:* [1]Jer. 1:10; [2]Jer. 1:13–16; [3]Jer. 1:6, 7; [4]Jer. 2:34 (cf. 5:31); [5]Jer. 8:22; 9:1, 2, 5; [6]Jer. 9:11; [7]Jer., chap. 36; [8]Jer. 38:14–28; [9]Jer., chap. 26; [10]Jer. 37:11—38:13; [11]Jer. 39:1, 2, 4–10; [12]Jer. 39:14; [13]Jer. 41:1–3; 43:4–6; [14]Jer., chap. 44; [15]Jer. 31:27–34.

2. In what period of Jewish history did Jeremiah live?

3. Name some important events of that period.

4. Where was his early home?

5. What great movement is reflected in his early preaching?

6. Read Jer. 4:5—6:26 in the light of that movement.

7. What other prophet dealt with it?

8. What steps did Jeremiah take for the preservation of his memoirs and sermons? Read chap. 36.

9. What was his attitude to the Deuteronomic reformation of Josiah? Read chaps. 7, 8, 11.

10. What was his relation to Josiah? To Jehoiakim? To Zedekiah?

11. What prophecies of Jeremiah made him unpopular with the court and the priesthood?

12. What was the character of Jeremiah?

13. What were the leading traits in his message?

14. What is the story of Jeremiah's Temple address and what came of it? Read chap. 26.

15. In connection with the defeat of the Egyptians at Carchemish read chap. 46.

16. For Jeremiah's inner life read Jer. 15:10–21; 20:7–18.

17. For his characteristic message read Jer. 31:27–34.

CHAPTER X

THE BOOK OF EZEKIEL

The most creative period in Hebrew literature was the Exile. It was only when it was uprooted from its own land and social habits that the Hebrew genius fully expressed itself and the Hebrew faith rose to its true stature.

The first of the exiles to lift up his voice was Ezekiel. He was a priest who had been carried into captivity in the first deportation of 597 B.C., when the better class of the population of Jerusalem was taken. Ezekiel dates his visions from that sad event,[1] which is also described as the exile of King Jehoiachin.[2] Jehoiachin was the unfortunate son of Jehoiakim who became king at eighteen and after a reign of three months was taken captive by Nebuchadnezzar and carried to Babylon, where he remained in prison until the death of his conqueror, thirty-seven years later. Nebuchadnezzar's successor, Evil-merodach, released him, and for the rest of his life he was treated with consideration.[3] Even in his exile and captivity Ezekiel evidently regarded him as the rightful king of Judah, as did the authors of the closing paragraph of Jeremiah and of II Kings.

Ezekiel was called to prophesy in the fifth year of

Jehoiachin's exile, 592 B.C. Ezekiel was then living with other exiles at Tel Abib, on the banks of the Chebar, the Grand Canal in Babylonia. Much of his prophecy is cast in the form of visions. His first vision was of four living creatures drawing a topaz chariot supporting a sapphire throne, with the shining figure of God, who commissioned him to speak in his name to the rebellious household of Israel. His task is to be as hopeless as Isaiah's was:

"They will not listen to you, for they will not listen to me. . . . . But I will make you as hard-faced and stubborn as they; I will make you like adamant, harder than flint."[4]

Ezekiel's call laid on him a great responsibility. He was appointed watchman to the household of Israel. If he failed to warn them, their blood would be upon his head. The prophet felt a terrible responsibility for the moral life of his people, now in their exile in the midst of a triumphant idolatry more likely than ever to wander from their faith.

From distant Babylonia, Ezekiel watched the progress of events at home in Judah. He felt the unrepentant wickedness of the Bloody City.[5] He foresaw the final destruction of city and Temple. He saw the Glory of the Lord depart in awful splendor from the Temple.[6] In this vision, as in the account of his call (chap. 1), his symbolism is colored by what he had seen of Babylonian art, with its giant winged bulls, or cherubs, with human faces. Ezekiel shows the influence of earlier Jewish prophets too—Hosea, Isaiah, Jeremiah—but he is no mere imitator, but a creative and original mind.

His writings are full of vision, allegory, and symbol. His great vision of the Glory of God is thought of as pre-eminently the Vision of Ezekiel,[7] but hardly less significant is the Vision of the Valley of the Dry Bones,[8] in which he foretells the return of the exiles to Judah. Of his allegories, those of the Faithless Wife,[9] the Eagles and the Vine,[10] and the Two Sisters, Samaria and Jerusalem,[11] are the most impressive. And by striking symbolic actions he pictured and interpreted the second fall of Jerusalem of 586 B.C., and the second deportation.[12] His refusal to mourn over the death of his wife was also a symbolic prophecy.[13]

Ezekiel gives a dramatic account of the arrival of a messenger with the news that what he had so long foretold had happened; Jerusalem had again fallen.[14] This confirmation of his earlier unwelcome preaching must have greatly strengthened his position as a prophet, yet the people were too much absorbed in their business pursuits to give much heed to him:

"You are to them like a singer of love-songs, with a beautiful voice, and able to play well on the instrument: they listen to your words, but they will not obey them. Only when the hour comes—and it is coming—they shall know that a prophet has been in the midst of them."[15]

Ezekiel is the great representative of the religious worth of the individual and of personal responsibility in religion. Jeremiah had declared religion to be an individual matter, and Ezekiel carries that teaching out to important conclusions.[16] The exiled Jews were inclined to think they were paying for their fathers' sins. But Ezekiel declares that iniquity and uprightness are not hereditary; they are the fruit of the individual's own choices. No man, no matter how good he is, can save another.[17] Even within the life of the individual, if an upright man does wrong, he will be held accountable for it, and if an unrighteous man repents and reforms, he will live and not die.

"Repent, then, ... get you a new heart and a new spirit. Why should you die, O household of Israel? For I have no pleasure in the death of anyone who dies," is the oracle of the Lord God.[18]

Ezekiel declares almost everything he says to be the oracle of God, going farther in this than any of his prophetic predecessors. Most of his prophecies that can be dated were uttered between 592 and 584 B.C., but they were probably committed to writing about 570 B.C. or soon after. They are not arranged in chronological order, but the dates Ezekiel connects with them cover a period of about twenty-five years, from 592 to 567 B.C.

In general, chapters 1–24 gather up the prophecies of judgment uttered before the final destruction of Jerusalem in 586 B.C. Chapters 25–32 pronounce judgment upon the nations surrounding Judah, and probably belong to the time after the complete collapse of Judah, when these heathen peoples seemed to have triumphed over her and to be glorying in her downfall. Chapters 33–48 look forward to the restoration of the nation and the national worship.

Ezekiel foresaw a gigantic attack, a kind of grand offensive against the future nation, when the heathen powers of the world should unite under the leadership of Gog of the land of Magog, to destroy God's people Israel, so happily settled again in Palestine, at the center of the earth.[19] But when that happened, God himself, with all the forces of nature, would rise in their defense and destroy the impious Gog and all his host.

Ezekiel explained the destruction of the Temple by the fact that God had abandoned it. This is the meaning of his vision of the Departure of the Glory of God from it.[20] After the second capture of the city and the demolishing of the Temple, his thoughts turned to a future day when the purified exiles should be brought back to their land and when the Glory should return to the Temple hill. The old sanctuary had been profaned by the admission to it of idolatrous worship; it was such things that had driven God's presence from it. But Ezekiel now looked forward to a new sanctuary, carefully guarded and walled about, and protected from any possible profanation, with an inner court for the priests and an outer court for the people. The service was to be in the hands of the old Jerusalem priesthood, the sons of Zadok, while the menial duties should be performed by the Levites, who had been the priests of the old local sanctuaries. The cultus itself was also to be reformed and new sin-offerings instituted to insure the holiness of the people. To such a temple God would return.

This new law of the Temple is developed in chapters 40–46, and reminds us that Ezekiel is not only a prophet but a priest, who looked forward to the restoration of the worship of God in the Temple on a nobler plane and on behalf of a reformed people. Prophet though he was, as a priest he sought to mold the religious life of his people into stricter ecclesiastical terms. For this reason he has been called the Father of Judaism.

SUGGESTIONS FOR STUDY

1. *References:* [1]Ezek. 33:21; [2]Ezek. 1:2; [3]II Kings 25:27, 28; [4]Ezek. 3:7–9; [5]Ezek., chap. 22; [6]Ezek., chap. 10; [7]Ezek., chap. 1; [8]Ezek., chap. 37; [9]Ezek., chap. 16; [10]Ezek., chap 17; [11]Ezek., chap. 23; [12]Ezek., chaps. 4, 12; [13]Ezek. 24:15–27; [14]Ezek. 33:21–33; [15]Ezek. 33:32, 33; [16]Ezek., chap. 18;

[17]Ezek. 14:13–20; [18]Ezek. 18:30–32; [19]Ezek., chaps. 38, 39; [20]Ezek. 10:1–22; 11:22–25.

2. When did Ezekiel begin to prophesy?

3. What new situation did he face?

4. In what form is his message cast?

5. What hope of success had he?

6. What was the "Vision of Ezekiel"?

7. What were some of his other great visions?

8. Into what three parts does the book fall?

9. How long did Ezekiel continue to prophesy?

10. What was the purpose of the new law in the closing chapters?

11. What important contribution did Ezekiel make to the Hebrew religion?

12. Why has he been called the Father of Judaism?

CHAPTER XI

THE BOOKS OF SAMUEL AND KINGS

It was about 1000 B.C. that David had been made king. In his reign of almost half a century Hebrew literature really began. There had long been songs and stories, sung or told from memory. But now men began to write them down, in the new script adapted from that of the Phoenicians, and before 900 the oft-told stories of tribal heroes like Saul and David were committed to writing.

It is of such materials, among others, that the work known to us as Samuel and Kings was made. It has come down to us as four books, but it forms a unit, and was finally shaped and organized by a single writer. But in his work he used, sometimes almost unaltered, sources so old that they must have been contemporary with the times they dealt with.

The most notable of these is the narrative that forms the core of the books of Samuel. So vivid, well informed, and objective is this story that it has been conjectured that it may actually be the work of David's lifelong friend Abiathar the priest, who was forced into retirement after the accession of Solomon, about 955 B.C.[1] One is tempted to imagine him in his old age beguiling his banishment at Anathoth by writing with unsparing candor the story of

the two kings, from the times of his forefather Eli to
the death of David. His father Ahimelech had lost
his life for giving David shelter, and Abiathar had
fled to David when he was in the Cave of Adullam,
and shared his fortunes thenceforth.[2] Certainly no
one was in a better position to tell the story than he.

This is only a conjecture, of course, but it is certain that these narratives are masterpieces of the
oriental story-teller's art, and historical materials of
the utmost value and interest. David was the national hero of the Hebrews, and what we know of
him is gained altogether from this absorbing narrative.

Hardly less important is the Northern Israel narrative of the deeds of the great northern prophets
Elijah and Elisha, which was committed to writing
about 800 B.C. or soon after.[3] Elijah possesses great
importance for the history of Israel's religion because he advanced the doctrine that only the Lord
God should be worshiped in Israel; all other deities
should be rigidly excluded. This was an extreme position, for it was customary in the Orient for a new
king to marry and take into his harem the daughters
of friendly monarchs, and these women, like Solomon's Egyptian wife, or Ahab's wife Jezebel, naturally expected to continue to worship the gods of
their fathers.

The book is a history, in something much better
than the ancient manner, of the Hebrew monarchy,

from its very beginnings to the bitter end. The narrative opens with the birth of Samuel, the king-maker, and relates the hero stories about Saul and David, the glory of Solomon, the division of the kingdom, and the successive reigns that followed, until the Assyrians destroyed the Northern Kingdom in 721, and the Babylonians the Southern in 597 and 586. The last paragraph of all contains the pathetic account of how poor Jehoiachin, the boy of eighteen who had reigned three months and then been taken captive to Babylon, had in the thirty-seventh year of his captivity (561 B.C.) been released from prison and at last shown some consideration by his Babylonian masters.

This makes it very plain that this Book of Reigns was completed in the course of the Babylonian Exile, 597–538 B.C. It was based upon a variety of written sources which had grown up from David's time onward. The writer occasionally refers to such earlier works: the Book of the Records of Solomon;[4] the Book of the Chronicles of the Kings of Judah;[5] the Book of the Chronicles of the Kings of Israel.[6]

After the fall of the Northern Kingdom, its books were preserved and read in the Southern Kingdom of Judah. And there, out of such sources as these, some Jew of the seventh century before Christ, after the appearance of Deuteronomy, began to weave the old Judean and Ephraimitic narratives into an organized whole, approving or condemning the various kings as they appeared from his prophetic point of view. He was in deep sympathy with the Deuteronomic Law, which had come into force under Josiah in 621,[7] and traces of his attachment to it color his telling of the ancient story at many points. He shared the conviction, which Isaiah had expressed and Deuteronomy had encouraged, that God would never give Jerusalem up to its enemies.[8]

But these hopes were disappointed in the Babylonian conquest and the destruction of Jerusalem. And long after these events, some later Jewish exile solaced himself in his captivity, and in the midst of the national depression, by completing the story of the reigns, or kingdoms, with the overthrow of the Jewish monarchy and the two deportations, even down to the thirty-seventh year of the captivity of the ill-fated Jehoiachin, 561 B.C. It must therefore have been late in the Exile, and not long after that very date, that the book was completed.

In it we possess the framework of the main period of Jewish history, from the last days of the Judges to the midst of the Exile. This is enriched with many admirable narratives of the heroic times of Saul and David, and stirring scenes from the lives of Elijah and Elisha, the great prophets of the North. The whole is reviewed from the strongly prophetic point of view.

The man who gave final form to this great sketch of the Jewish state belonged to Judah and found

more to approve in the history of the Southern
Kingdom than in that of the Northern. Yet he felt
that Judah, too, had sinned and deserved the misfortunes that had overtaken her. The history of the
Northern Kingdom was indeed a terrible series of
bloody usurpations. But in the south the Davidic
line continued unbroken for four hundred years,
and its restoration and perpetuation were the dream
of the prophets of the Exile.

While the books of Samuel and Kings form one
continuous narrative and received their present
form from one writer, the Jews treated them as two
books, Samuel and Kings. The Greek translators of
the Hebrew Bible, in the third century before
Christ, divided each of them into two parts, to ac-
commodate them to the ordinary size of a convenient
papyrus roll, calling them First, Second, Third, and
Fourth Reigns or Kingdoms. Our names for them
are a combination of the Greek and Hebrew sys-
tems.

Sixty years ago little more was known of the history of Western Asia than was afforded by the books
of Samuel and Kings, supplemented by a few pages
of Herodotus. But now the discoveries of the cunei-
form records of Assyria and Babylonia have revealed
the histories of those empires to us with a fulness
even yet hardly realized. And these tablets and inscriptions also enable us to fill in the political and
religious backgrounds of this history of the Hebrew

kings and give us a new understanding of the conditions under which for a little more than four centuries the Jewish state endured.

1. *References:* [1]I Kings 2:22–27; [2]I Sam., chap. 22; [3]I Kings 17:1—II Kings 13:21; [4]I Kings 11:41; [5]II Kings 21:25; [6]II Kings 10:34; [7]II Kings, chap. 22; [8]II Sam. 7:16; I Kings 9:3; 11:36; II Kings 8:19.

2. What is the scope of the books of Samuel and Kings?

3. Were they originally one, two, or four books?

4. From what point of view were they written?

5. What sources were used by the writer?

6. Through what stages has the work passed?

7. What is its relation to Deuteronomy?

8. When and where was it completed?

9. How did its author regard the Northern Kingdom?

10. How does he explain the overthrow of the Jewish state?

11. Who are the chief figures in the history of the united kingdom? Of the Northern Kingdom? Of the Southern Kingdom?

12. When did Hebrew literature begin?

13. What additional sources for the history are now available?

14. What military power destroyed the Northern Kingdom and when?

15. What military power destroyed the Southern Kingdom and when?

16. How does the writer contrive to tell the story of the two kingdoms simultaneously?

CHAPTER XII

THE BOOK OF JUDGES

The Exile made the full observance of the Deuteronomic Law impossible; the Temple was destroyed and the people were deported to Babylon. But much of that law was moral and personal in character, and thoughtful exiles were thrown back upon those sides of it which could still be obeyed. So strong was its influence upon them that they began to review their past history in the light of it and to recognize illustrations of its truth in the earlier experiences of the nation.

Among their books was one relating the exploits of their various tribal heroes in the confused and obscure period in the twelfth and eleventh centuries before Christ, when the Hebrews were struggling with the Canaanites and Philistines for the possession of the land. It was the story of one champion after another who arose in response to some pressing situation and for a while succeeded in leading and controlling his own tribe and its neighbors, for these tribal leaders did not command the support of all the tribes, which were only beginning to grope their way toward national consciousness.

Some of these stories were very ancient, and among them was included the oldest considerable piece of literature in the Old Testament, the War-Song of Deborah, which has been called the most important source in existence for the history of Israel, and probably comes from the twelfth century before Christ.[1] It begins with the Lord riding upon the storm from his home on Mount Sinai to aid his people in their battle, and exultingly describes the victory of the valiant tribes who rallied around Deborah and Barak to fight the Canaanite kings in the Plain of Esdraelon.[2] The book takes its name from these temporary leaders, who were called "judges" because the administration of some rude sort of justice was one of their duties. But those were times of violence and tumult, and it was the bold and shrewd soldier who usually made himself chief. Some of them were only names even to the ancient chronicler —Tola, Jair, Ibzan, Elon, Abdon. But about others clustered whole groups of legends like those connected with the name of Gideon, Jephthah, and Samson. Sometimes brutal, sometimes humorous, and always very primitive, these stories faithfully reflect the rough, wild, half-savage period with which they deal.

The Philistines, who were possessed of a somewhat developed civilization, had come over the sea perhaps from Crete, having been driven from their homes by barbarous Greek invaders, and had taken up their residence in Palestine. They had failed in an attempt to enter Egypt, but established them-

selves in the twelfth century before Christ along the
seacoast of Palestine, which takes its name from
them. The tribe of Dan came into collision with
them, both claiming the desirable rolling country
between the coast plain and the hills. Samson was
the Danite champion and alternately fraternized
with the Philistines and harried them.[3]

The Midianites, who belonged east of the Red
Sea, came up through Moab and crossed the Jordan,
into the Plain of Esdraelon. But Gideon mobilized
the tribe of Manasseh against them and drove them
back.[4] The Gileadites were harassed by the Am-
monites, but taught them a severe lesson, under the
leadership of Jephthah.[5] Their next quarrel was
with their brothers the Ephraimites, against whom
Jephthah again led them to victory.[6]

So one tribe fought another or its outside enemies
generation after generation, through the days of the
judges, and the tales of their warlike exploits, told
over and over, were at length committed to writing
and united into one book, probably in the seventh
century before Christ. Then later, when the appearance of the Book of Deuteronomy had put such
new spirit into Jewish religion, it was revised, probably in the course of the Exile, in accordance with
the ideas of that book. It was at this time that the
characteristic Deuteronomic framework was introduced: The Israelites did evil in the sight of the
Lord, and he delivered them into the power of their

enemies. Then they cried to the Lord and he sent them a deliverer. This was the Deuteronomic interpretation of the ceaseless ebb and flow of the period of the judges. This second form of the book contained substantially Judg. 2:6—16:31.

This prophetic edition was later enlarged by a writer of priestly sympathies, who prefaced it with an ancient summary of the conquest, 1:1—2:5, and added chapters 17–21. This took place after the writing of the priestly history, in the fifth century before Christ, which was to form the latest element in the Hexateuch. The Book of Judges was probably finished toward the end of the fifth century before Christ, seven hundred years after the composition of the Song of Deborah, which is the oldest part of it.

SUGGESTIONS FOR STUDY

1. *References:* [1]Judg., chap. 5; [2]Judg., chap. 4; [3]Judg., chaps. 13–16; [4]Judg. 6:1—8:28; [5]Judg. 10:6—11:40; [6]Judg. 12:1–7.

2. What period of history is dealt with in the Book of Judges?

3. What was the condition of the Hebrew people at that time?

4. Who were the leading figures of that period?

5. What was the character of their work?

6. Against what foes did Samson distinguish himself?

7. Against whom did Gideon lead the people?

8. Whom did Jephthah fight?

9. What is the theme of the Song of Deborah?

10. When were these stories first assembled in writing?

11. What influence did the Book of Deuteronomy exert upon them?

12. What final touches were put upon the book, and when was it finished?

13. What historical value has it?

14. What is its literary value?

CHAPTER XIII

THE BOOKS OF HAGGAI AND ZECHARIAH

One year in the life of the returned exiles is especially rich in prophecy and hence peculiarly well known to us. It is 520–519 B.C., when Haggai and Zechariah preached in Jerusalem. Darius had sent back more of the Jews to Palestine in 520, under the youthful Zerubbabel, the grandson of the unfortunate Jehoiachin, whom the exiles regarded as the last rightful king of Judah. It was eighteen years since Cyrus had sent the first party of returning exiles to Jerusalem, and now this second party had arrived. Yet no steps had been taken to rebuild the Temple; everybody was engrossed in his own affairs.

The wickedness of any longer putting off the rebuilding of the Temple stirred Haggai deeply, and very soon after the arrival of Zerubbabel and his company, he preached a sermon, calling upon Zerubbabel to undertake the work immediately. With Zerubbabel was associated Joshua, son of the last head of the old Jerusalem priesthood, and Haggai appealed to them both:

"Is it a time for you yourselves to live in your panelled houses, while this house lies waste?"[1]

We do not know who Haggai was, or whether he had come with Zerubbabel and had just arrived in Jerusalem. It is probable that he had. It was the twenty-eighth of September when he made this appeal, and Zerubbabel and Joshua led the people at once to the work of rebuilding.

But it was discouraging to see how little they could accomplish in comparison with the old Temple that the Babylonians had destroyed sixty-six years before. Not quite two months later Haggai once more addressed them.

"Who is there left among you that saw this house in its ancient splendor? And how it looks to you now! Does it not seem to you like nothing at all? . . . . Be strong . . . . and work; for I am with you, ... and I will fill this house with splendor; . . . . the future splendor of this house shall be greater than the past, and upon this place I will bestow prosperity."[2]

Two months more passed and early in 519 B.C. Haggai preached again. It was the twenty-fourth day of the ninth month. If they have not prospered, said the prophet, it is because they have been unclean in the sight of God. But now, with the Temple rebuilding, and the sacrifice worthily offered, if they will hold aloof from defiling contacts with their unclean neighbors, a new era of well-being will dawn for them, beginning from that very day.[3]

On the same day Haggai preached another sermon, his fourth and last, so far as we know. The kingdoms of the nations are to be shaken, but God has chosen Zerubbabel, and he shall be a "seal-ring" —a symbol of the highest significance and distinction.[4] These four messages of Haggai all deal with the rebuilding of the Temple in Jerusalem, and they fall within four months.

Two months after Haggai's first sermon, and so toward the close of 520, Zechariah began his preaching. He reminded the returned exiles that God had warned their forefathers, and all that the prophets had threatened them with had come to pass. They, in their turn, must heed his warnings, if they wish to avoid his anger.[5]

Two months after Haggai's last sermon Zechariah preached again to the exiles, assuring them that the Temple should be rebuilt and God would again favor them:

"I will return to Jerusalem in mercy;
My house shall be rebuilt therein; . . . .
The Lord will again have pity upon Zion,
And again choose Jerusalem."[6]

Zechariah's prophecy was of the apocalyptic type, of which we have seen the beginnings in Ezekiel. The vision of the horseman among the myrtle trees, the four horns, the measuring line, the lamp and the olive trees, the flying roll, the woman in the measure, and the four chariots teach the purification and protection of the land and the future glory of the city. Who has despised a day of small things? Jerusalem is to be so great and populous that it will be impossible to inclose it with a wall. Aged men and women shall again be seen in Jerusalem:

"And the streets of the city shall be filled
   With boys and girls, playing in its streets."[7]

Zechariah sought to cheer his struggling companions with the hope of Israel's messianic destiny: "In those days, ten men, from nations of every language, shall lay hold of him who is a Jew, saying, 'Let us go with you; for we have heard that God is with you!' "[8]

So the new Temple was completed, and the old worship was at last resumed.

To the ancient collection that contained the preaching of Zechariah, chapters 1-8, other kindred prophecies from later times have been added. A mention of Greece,[9] combined with allusions to the captivity and the Dispersion and frequent use of the writings of earlier prophets, shows that these are the work of later hands. They echo and enlarge upon Zechariah's bright hopes for the future. Jerusalem is at last to be a truly holy city; the very bells of the horses will be marked "Holy to the Lord."[10] And, best of all, the Messiah is to come and bring in his peaceful reign:

Exult greatly, O daughter of Zion,
Shout with joy, O daughter of Jerusalem.
Lo, your king comes to you;
Vindicated and victorious is he;
Humble, and riding upon an ass,
Even upon a colt, the foal of an ass. . . . .
He shall command peace upon the nations.
His dominion shall be from sea to sea,
And from the river to the ends of the earth.[11]

SUGGESTIONS FOR STUDY

1. *References:* [1]Hag. 1:4; [2]Hag. 2:3-9; [3]Hag. 2:15-19; [4]Hag. 2:23; [5]Zech. 1:2-6; [6]Zech. 1:16, 17; [7]Zech. 8:4, 5; [8]Zech. 8:23; [9]Zech. 9:13; [10]Zech. 14:20; [11]Zech. 9:9, 10.

2. What situation stirred Haggai and Zechariah to preach?

3. When did they prophesy?

4. How much time does the preaching of Haggai, as we know it, cover?

5. What was its effect?

6. What form did the preaching of Zechariah take?

7. What were his hopes for the city and nation?

8. What hopes color the later oracles of chaps. 9 ff.?

CHAPTER XIV

THE BOOK OF MALACHI

Half a century after the rebuilding of the Temple in 516 B.C. religious conditions at Jerusalem were very distressing. The ritual was carried on in a slovenly and mechanical fashion. The priests were as lax in teaching the Law as they were in obeying it. The people offered their poorest instead of their best animals in sacrifice, and withheld the tithes they were supposed to pay for the support of the worship. They were divorcing their Jewish wives and marrying women not of Jewish blood. All sorts of vulgar vices prevailed.

All this roused a prophet of the fifth century to try to stir his people out of their lethargy and baseness. His name is forgotten, but his prophecy, once an appendix to Zechariah, has come down to us under the name of Malachi, from the occurrence of that word, meaning "My Messenger," in chapter 3:

"Behold, I will send forth my messenger,
    And he shall prepare the way before me!"[1]

Malachi—for we have no other name for him—rebukes the priests and the people for their perfunctory and half-hearted service and their miserable offerings.[2] They seem to think very lightly of their God. And he, for his part, would prefer to have the

Temple closed and the service cease than to have it carried on in this careless, uninterested fashion. For he is not dependent upon them:

"For from the rising of the sun, even to its setting,
My name is great among the nations;
And in every place an offering is made, is brought
near to my name,
And a pure offering.
For my name is great among the nations."[3]

This acceptance on the part of God of heathen worship, when it is sincerely offered, no matter whether under Jewish forms or not, shows us once more how the prophets were constantly breaking through even in the most unpromising times to the great realities of ethical religion.

The denunciation of divorce[4] may be quite as much intended as a warning against giving up the old religion and accepting a new one. Like every oracle in Malachi, it has some lines that are unforgettable:

Have we not all one father?
Did not one God create us? . . . .
So take heed to your spiritual life,
And let nobody be faithless to the wife of his
youth.[5]

The people in their wickedness have forgotten the justice of God. But his Judgment Day is surely coming:[6]

"Behold, I will send forth my messenger,
And he shall prepare the way before me! . . . .
And who can endure the day of his coming?
And who can stand when he appears?
For he shall be like a refiner's fire,
And like fullers' soap . . . .
And shall cleanse the sons of Levi."[7]

It was this prophecy of the coming of the Angel of the Covenant to usher in the Great Repentance that was afterward understood of John the Baptist.

In most vigorous terms Malachi calls upon the people to pay their tithes:[8]

"Bring the whole tithe into the storehouse . . . .
And see if I will not open for you the windows of the heavens
And pour out for you a blessing until there is no more need."[9]

Malachi's little book closes with mingled warning and encouragement:[10]

"You say, 'It is useless to serve God;
And what profit is it that we have kept his charge,
And that we have walked in mourning before the Lord of Hosts?
And now we are deeming the arrogant fortunate;
The doers of wickedness, indeed, are built up;
They test God, also, and they escape!' "[11]

The prophet assures them that God has not forgotten them; a book of remembrance has been written concerning them and they will be God's special treasure. His judgment against the wicked is sure to come:

"But for you who revere my name, there will arise
The sun of righteousness, with healing in its
wings."[12]

Malachi gives us an authentic glimpse of Jewish life in a half-ruinous and utterly discouraged Jerusalem, and helped to prepare the way for Nehemiah, who came in 444 B.C., to rebuild its walls.

SUGGESTIONS FOR STUDY

1. *References:* [1]Mal. 3:1; [2]Mal. 1:6—2:9; [3]Mal. 1:11; [4]Mal. 2:10-16; [5]Mal. 2:10, 15; [6]Mal. 2:17—3:5; [7]Mal. 3:1-3; [8]Mal. 3:6-12; [9]Mal. 3:10; [10]Mal. 3:13—4:5; [11]Mal. 3:14, 15; [12]Mal. 4:2.

2. What is the origin of the name Malachi?

3. When and where was the book written?

4. What was the condition of the Temple at that time?

5. What was the state of Jewish religion?

6. What abuses are especially attacked by Malachi?

7. What great religious truth did he utter?

8. What other Old Testament prophets show hostility to Edom? (1:2-5).

9. What was the ground of this bitterness?

10. What is the relation of Malachi to Zechariah? Compare Mal. 1:1 with Zech. 12:1.

11. What has the Book of Malachi to offer for modern religious life?

CHAPTER XV

THE BOOK OF OBADIAH

The kingdom of Judah was ringed about by hereditary enemies, and when it was conquered and Jerusalem fell, they rejoiced in its downfall. Especially Edom, to the southeast, showed indecent haste in co-operating with Judah's conquerors and harassing her fugitives. They joined in the pillage of the city and afterward appropriated what they could get of the Judean territory.

This graceless inhumanity stirred the indignation of the prophet Obadiah. He speaks almost like a participant in some of the scenes he describes, but he can hardly have witnessed them as he reflects the condition of Edom a century later, when the Arabs were already dispossessing the Edomites:

"The men who were at peace with you have overpowered you.

Your associates have put a foreign people in your place."[1]

The Edomites had gloated over the Jews in their adversity; they had laughed at their trouble. They had cut off the fugitives and betrayed the refugees. They had shared in the plunder of the stricken city when it could no longer protect itself. Obadiah

draws a striking picture of the vulture-like behavior
of Edom, glad to devour the prey that bolder peoples had brought down. When Esau should have
come to the support of his brother Jacob, he had
basely sided against him instead.[2]

All this reflects the atmosphere of the destruction
of Jerusalem by Nebuchadnezzar in 586 B.C. and the
subsequent aggressions of the Edomites. Ezekiel
says of them in the days of the Exile: "In the fire of
my indignation I speak against the rest of the nations, and especially against Edom—the whole of
it—who with malicious glee and bitter contempt
took over my land as a possession for themselves, to
hold it as a prey."[3]

Edom had seized the opportunity to take possession of a good part of Judah's former territory. But
she herself was soon to feel like pressure from the
south. She trusted in her mountainous situation
and her rocky retreats—

"You who dwell in the clefts of the cliff,
    And set your dwelling on high,
    And say to yourself,
    'Who can bring me down to the earth?' "[4]

But against her in the sixth century were already
moving the Arabs of the southern desert, who even-
tually, in 312 B.C., actually captured her capital
Petra, with its rock-hewn palaces. Something of this
dawning peril was known to Obadiah, and he sees in

it the inevitable judgment of God for Edom's crimes against Judah:

"Though you build your nest high like the eagle,
And set your nest even among the stars,
From there I will bring you down."[5]

Edom is to be pillaged in its turn:

"How Esau is ransacked,
And his treasures plundered!
They have cast you forth to the boundary,
All those who were in league with you have betrayed you."
"In that day,"—it is the oracle of the Lord,—
"I will certainly destroy the wise men from Edom,
And intelligence from Mount Esau. . . . .
For the violence done to your brother Jacob,
Shame shall cover you and you shall be cut off forever."[6]

This will be but a part of the dreadful Day of the Lord, when judgment shall overtake the nations, Edom with the rest:

"As you have done, it shall be done to you,
Your deed shall return upon your own head."[7]

A considerable displacement of Edomites by Arabs from the south took place in the fifth century before Christ, and this is probably the time when Obadiah wrote his bitter reproach of Edom. With his wrath against it and the other nations is coupled hope for the future supremacy of Judah and the utter destruction of Edom:

"The house of Jacob shall be a fire,
And the house of Joseph a flame;
And the house of Esau shall be stubble,
And they shall lick them up and devour them;
And there shall be no survivor to the house of Esau."
For the Lord has spoken.[8]

Like Jeremiah before him, Obadiah used as the text[9] for his invective against Edom the words of some older prophet, which appear also in Jer. 49:14-16, 9 f. and 7. We might suppose Obadiah was here quoting Jeremiah, if it were not that the verses stand in a more natural and original order in Obadiah than in Jeremiah. His bitter outcry against Edom has a number of parallels in Old Testament prophecy. There was the unknown prophet from whom Jeremiah was quoting, in 49:7-22. There was Jeremiah himself; there was the oracle against Edom that has found a place in Amos 1:11, 12; and there was the prophecy of the hideous day of vengeance upon Edom that forms the thirty-fourth chapter of Isaiah. So hatred of Edom forms a dark thread in the pattern of Hebrew religious thought in the sixth and fifth centuries before Christ.

SUGGESTIONS FOR STUDY

1. *References:* [1]Obad. 1:7; [2]Obad. 1:10–14; [3]Ezek. 36:5; [4]Obad. 1:3; [5]Obad. 1:4; [6]Obad. 1:6–10; [7]Obad. 1:15; [8]Obad. 1:18; [9]Obad. 1:1–9.

2. What is the subject of the prophecies of Obadiah?

3. When did he prophesy?

4. What other prophets dealt with the same subject?

5. What had so stirred their indignation?

6. What is the explanation of the resemblance of 1:1–9 to Jer. 49:7–22?

7. What force was at this time pressing upon Edom and what later resulted from it?

CHAPTER XVI

THE BOOK OF JOEL

The mysterious Book of Joel reveals a desperate condition of things among the Jews. They are a little religious community—the "congregation"—gathered about the rebuilt Temple, headed by priests and elders instead of kings, and subject to the Persian Empire. Now the locusts have settled upon the land and eaten up the crops, until there is neither food nor fodder. To their ravages are added the horrors of drought. Famine confronts man and beast. So great is the scarcity that even the daily offering at the Temple that united the congregation with its God has had to be given up. The people are so impoverished that some of them have actually sold their children to the Philistine slave-dealers, to be carried off to the Greek west.[1] Even today such things happen in desperate times in Asia.

It was this situation that roused Joel, about 400 B.C., to utter the brief prophecies by which we know him. He was steeped in the prophetic literature of his people; the works of a dozen earlier Jewish writers are reflected in his few pages. He draws a powerful picture of the plague and the drought. There has never been anything like it:

What the shearer left, the locust ate;
And what the locust left, the hopper ate;
And what the hopper left, the destroyer ate.[2]

Joel summons the people to fasting and prayer:

Return to the Lord your God;
For he is gracious and merciful, ...
Assemble the people; order a holy congregation.

Let the priests, the ministers of the Lord, weep,
And let them say, "Spare thy people, O Lord!"[3]

The longed-for relief came:

The Lord became solicitous for his land,
And had pity upon his people.[4]

Hope revived, and the peril passed. The early and the later rains came down as of old.

Joel saw in the plague of locusts a portent of the awful Day of the Lord of which the prophets so often spoke. They had come over the land like an invading army:

They look like horses,
And they run like war-horses . . . .
Like a mighty people
Arrayed for battle.[5]

The Day was to be a day of darkness and gloom, a day of clouds and deep darkness. But after the people's repentance and God's forgiveness, it takes on a brighter aspect:

"It shall come to pass afterward,
   That I will pour out my spirit upon all flesh;
   Your sons and your daughters shall prophesy;
   Your old men shall dream dreams,
   And your young men shall see visions."[6]

But Joel still, like the prophets of old, denounces vengeance upon the heathen. God will gather the nations into the neighboring valley of Jehoshaphat ("Jehovah Judges") for judgment.

> There will I sit to judge
> All the nations from every side.
> For the harvest is ripe! . . . .
> For the wine-press is full! . . . .
> For their wickedness is great.[7]

A golden age to come still beckons the prophet's hope. God is again to dwell in Zion, his holy mountain. Jerusalem shall be holy, and inviolable once more:

"Egypt shall become a waste,
   And Edom shall be a barren steppe; . . . .
   But Judah shall abide forever,
   And Jerusalem for generation after generation."[8]

With such dreams of a great future for his people and his religion Joel reanimated the little Jewish community in one of the darkest hours of its later history. He was a striking embodiment of that indomitable spiritual hope that was the soul of Judaism.

SUGGESTIONS FOR STUDY

1. *References:* [1]Joel 3:3, 6; [2]Joel 1:4; [3]Joel 2:13, 16, 17; [4]Joel 2:18; [5]Joel 2:4, 5; [6]Joel 2:28; [7]Joel 3:12, 13; [8]Joel 3:19, 20.

2. What situation is reflected in the Book of Joel?

3. What great idea of Amos and Zephaniah did this recall to his mind?

4. What did Joel call upon the priests and people to do?

5. What followed?

6. What further picture of the future came to his mind?

7. What is Joel's view of the heathen and their destiny?

8. What are his hopes for Judah and Jerusalem?

CHAPTER XVII

THE BOOK OF RUTH

The return of the exiles created new and serious problems. Some of the Jews had married women not of Jewish descent. These mixed marriages were sternly condemned by Ezra the Scribe, about 397 B.C., who obliged such men to divorce these wives and put away the children they had had by them.[1] He felt that the nation had suffered terribly for its former laxity in religious matters, and long residence in heathen and hence "unclean" lands had intensified in him the traditional Jewish aversion to foreigners.

This harsh action naturally caused great unhappiness and injustice. Over against Ezra and his strict and rigorous policy many people held that in religion there were other things that counted quite as much as pure Jewish descent. Loyalty, piety, and goodness were acceptable to God in other people besides Jews.

In this spirit of protest the Book of Ruth was written. It is an idyllic story. The scene is laid in the time of the Judges. Driven by famine, a man of Bethlehem with his wife and his sons moved eastward into Moab, where he died. There his sons married women of Moab, and there they afterward died.

Their mother Naomi prepared to return to Bethlehem, and her daughters-in-law set out with her.[2] But she bade them remain in their own country, and one of them did so. The other, Ruth, would not leave her and insisted upon going with her to Bethlehem:

"Do not press me to leave you," she said, "to turn back from following you; for wherever you go, I will go; and wherever you lodge, I will lodge; your people shall be my people, and your god my god; wherever you die, I will die, and there will I be buried. May the Lord requite me and worse, if even death separate me from you."[3]

Arrived in Bethlehem, Ruth was allowed to gather what barley the reapers left in the field of Boaz, a rich relative of Naomi's husband. Under the Jewish law, a man's widow should be married by his brother or his next of kin. In view of this, Naomi instructed Ruth to approach Boaz as he slept in the field after the threshing and claim her right to become his wife. Boaz acknowledged her claim, and after the proper formalities before the elders of the city he married her. Their son became the grandfather of David.[4]

So out of the memory of a Moabite strain in the ancestry of David came this story of the devotion and piety of a Moabite girl to her Jewish mother-in-law. If the children of such marriages were unclean in the sight of Ezra, what of David himself, whose grandfather was the child of just such a mixed marriage? And were not women like Ruth worthy to stand with the women of Israel?

The breadth and understanding of the Book of Ruth make it stand out against the narrow exclusiveness of its times, and the naturalness of its simple yet vivid style marks it as one of the gems of Hebrew literature. Even in the midst of the legalism that was already beginning to stifle Judaism, there were some who could see, as Paul did long after, that the real Jew is not one who is so outwardly; the real Jew is the one who is so inwardly, whose praise is not from men but from God.

SUGGESTIONS FOR STUDY

1. *References:* ¹Ezra 9:1—10:17; ²Ruth 1:1–7; ³Ruth 1:16, 17; ⁴Ruth, chaps. 2–4.

2. What is the story of Ruth?

3. In what time is the scene laid?

4. What situation called it forth?

5. How did it apply to the situation?

6. What is its literary quality?

7. How did Paul afterward express its fundamental idea?

8. What serious and lasting consequences did the harsh policy as to mixed marriages have? See Neh. 13:28; Josephus, *Antiquities* xi.8.2.

9. Why does the book stand next after Judges in the Bible?

CHAPTER XVIII

THE BOOK OF JOB

Hebrew literature is rich in varied forms of expression, but it developed no great drama. The nearest approach to it is the Book of Job, which may be described as a drama without action. It is in substance a discussion of the old problem of suffering in human life. What is its cause? What is its meaning? Why do upright people suffer? But the book makes so little real contribution to that subject that it is perhaps truer to say that its purpose is to correct the current notion that disaster and misfortune are tokens of God's disapproval of one's sins, while prosperity and good fortune are signs of his approbation and favor.

Ezekiel speaks of Job as a conspicuously righteous man, along with Noah and Daniel,[1] and his vague figure has been made the hero of this parable of human experience.

The germ of the book, which is probably older than the rest, is formed by the prologue, chapters 1 and 2, and the epilogue, 42:7–16, which tell the story of Job, a patriarch of Edom, perfectly upright and yet pursued by misfortune until he is almost driven to despair. Into this older narrative a Hebrew philosopher early in the fourth century before

Christ introduced the speeches by Job and his three
friends which form the main part of the book.

It is a terrible thing to endure misfortune which
you have done nothing to incur, and doubly so when
all the world interprets it as a just punishment for
some sin you have committed. This was the ancient
attitude to calamity, and must have greatly embittered the lot of many godly and upright people who
were overtaken by misfortune. It is against this
cheap view of suffering that the Book of Job is directed.

The poet-philosopher who first expanded this
sought to describe the thoughts of Job and of his
three friends who had come to comfort him in his
misery. Perhaps their long seven-day silence led
Job to think that they were in their hearts taking
the conventional view of his condition. At any rate
it is Job who at length breaks the silence. He la-
ments that he was ever born, and from the first sentence you know that you are in the presence of one
of the world's greatest poets.

Job is answered by his first friend, Eliphaz, who
voices the common view of adversity: "Who that
was innocent ever perished? . . . . Those who plow
guilt and sow sorrow, reap it. . . . . Can a mortal
man be righteous before God? . . . . Man is born
for trouble, even as sparks fly upward!"[2] But there
is more than pessimism or mere resignation in the
speech of Eliphaz:

"I, however, would seek for God,
And to God I would state my case."[3]

And there is a meaning and a discipline in suffering, for the man who accepts it in the right spirit:

"Happy . . . . is the man whom God reproves,
So do not reject the instruction of the Almighty."[4]

Job answers bitterly, hurt by his friend's easy assumption of his guilt.[5]

His second friend, Bildad, then speaks, urging Job to seek God in his distress:

"If you yourself would seek God, ...
If you were but pure and straight,
Then, indeed, he would bestir himself in your behalf."[6]

Bildad, too, is of the conventional school but he holds out some hope to Job:

"God will not reject a perfect man, ...
He will yet fill your mouth with laughter,
And your lips with shouting."[7]

Job answers in a passage of the profoundest pathos.[8] He is conscious of no fault, yet how can he hope to convince God? He has that terrible feeling of abandonment. God has departed from him; he knows not why. His third friend, Zophar, then speaks, rebuking Job,[9] and Job bursts forth in scornful invective against them all:

"No doubt but you are the people,
　And wisdom will die with you! . . . .
　I know that I am innocent" . . . .

"Wherefore dost thou hide thy face,
　And reckon me as thy foe?
　Wilt thou scare a driven leaf,
　And chase the dry stubble?"[10]

This concludes the first cycle of the great debate.
The second is opened by Eliphaz, whom Job answers. Bildad speaks again and Job replies. Zophar
continues the argument and Job answers him, completing the second cycle. The third cycle follows the
same course: Eliphaz, Job; Bildad, Job; Zophar,
Job, for 27:7–23 and perhaps also chapter 28, the
poem in praise of Wisdom, should probably be understood as Zophar's third speech. In his final
speech in his debate with his friends Job eloquently
contrasts his former felicity with his present wretch-
edness:

"Oh that I were as in months of old,
　As in the days when God guarded me . . . .
　When the friendship of God was over my tent,
　When the Almighty was still with me! . . . .
　But now they laugh at me,
　Those who are younger than I,
　Whose fathers I disdained
　To set with the dogs of my flock."[11]

Then in a series of great stanzas Job protests his innocence of one sin after another. He has always abstained from evil and given himself to good; why has God forsaken him?

"Here is my signature! Let the Almighty answer
  me!" . . . .
The words of Job are finished.[12]

Then the Lord answered Job from the whirlwind, saying:

"Who is this that obscures counsel
  By words without knowledge? . . . .
Where were you when I laid the foundations of
  the earth? . . . .
Who fixed its measurements,—for you should
  know? . . . .
Or who laid its corner stone,
When the morning stars sang together,
And all the gods shouted for joy? . . . .
Have you ever in your life commanded the morn-
  ing? . . . .
Have you gone to the sources of the sea? . . . .
Can you bind the chains of the Pleiades,
Or loosen the girdle of Orion?"[13]

Job acknowledges his utter insignificance: "What can I answer thee?"[14] God speaks again, declaring his incomparable might, and Job acknowledges his own ignorance and dulness:

"I had heard of thee by the hearing of the ear,
  But now my eye has seen thee.

Therefore I retract and repent
In dust and ashes."[15]

In the end Job's problem is left unsolved, except
that in the infinite wisdom of God undeserved suffering must have an explanation beyond our com-
prehension. This is, after all, the simple doctrine of
faith, which does not insist upon explaining everything, but trusts the fundamental love and care of
God in prosperity and adversity alike. It is not
stated in Job in terms of Christian warmth and love
but it is nevertheless there. Job's inward experience
of God at last satisfies him that there is a deeper justice and a deeper meaning in life than we can sometimes see. God speaks to him and he is satisfied.
It is not mere misfortune that has staggered him, it
is the agonizing delusion that God has abandoned
him.

To a later Hebrew poet it seemed wrong that Job
should thus triumph in the debate over his conventional friends, and he introduced the four speeches
by Elihu that immediately follow Job's agonized appeal to God.[16] They present over again the old popular Jewish view that misfortune is the punishment
of sin, but with far less power and genius than the
original author possessed. They also destroy the
symmetry of the poem and defeat its dramatic
movement, for they separate God's answer from
Job's impassioned appeal, which logically and emo-
tionally it directly follows. For at the end of chapter 31 Job is clearly waiting for God to answer him,

and God's first words in 38:2—"Who is this that obscures counsel by words without knowledge?"— unmistakably refer to Job. The interpolated chapters add little to what the three friends had already said, and their literary quality must strike every reader as inferior to that of the rest of the book. If Job was written about 400 B.C., they were probably added a century or more later.

SUGGESTIONS FOR STUDY

1. *References:* [1]Ezek. 14:14, 20; [2]Job 4:7, 8, 17; 5:7; [3]Job 5:8; [4]Job 5:17; [5]Job 6:1—7:21; [6]Job 8:5, 6; [7]Job 8:20, 21; [8]Job 9:1—10:22; [9]Job 11:1–20; [10]Job 12:1; 13:18, 24, 25; [11]Job 29:2, 4, 5; 30:1; [12]Job 31:35, 40; [13]Job 38:1, 2, 4–7, 12, 16, 31; [14]Job 40:4; [15]Job 42:5, 6; [16]Job, chaps. 32–37.

2. What was the conventional view of misfortune and suffering among the Jews?

3. What change in this does the Book of Job seek to make?

4. What three stages can be traced in the growth of the book?

5. What is the literary quality of the book?

6. What parts of it contain the noblest poetry?

7. What is the aim of the Elihu speeches?

8. What is chap. 28?

9. What attitude toward the problem is taken in Ps. 22?

10. What light do the suffering and death of Christ throw upon it?

11. What attitude is expressed in Henley's *Invictus?*

12. What is the Christian attitude toward misfortune and suffering?

13. Is it identical with that of Job or of his friends?

14. Did the Book of Job prepare the way for it?

CHAPTER XIX

THE HEXATEUCH

The most commanding work of Hebrew genius sprang not out of the years of national power and prestige but out of the days of obscurity and depression that followed the return from exile. It is that great body of history, tradition, and law that we know as the Hexateuch—the books of Genesis, Exodus, Leviticus, Numbers, Deuteronomy, and Joshua. It was completed not long after 400 B.C., but it arose from sources and forces many centuries older.

The oldest of these elements was a Judean account of the nation's story from the beginning of the world to the conquest of Canaan by the tribes. It was the first sustained history to be written anywhere. The writer of it believed that the march of events was simply the working-out of divine purposes. Babylonian myths and legends and Canaanite popular tales he freely appropriated to his great purpose of enforcing morality and the worship of one God. Sometimes crude old superstitious ideas still cling to some of these.

The writer of this ancient record was a prophet, and told the story from the prophet's point of view. He wrote his book about 850 B.C. in the Southern Kingdom of Judah.

A hundred years later, in the Northern Kingdom of Israel, another prophetic writer gathered up the thrice-told tales of his world into a great historical narrative. It began with the story of Abraham, but its masterpiece was the story of Joseph. It is more tender and scrupulous than its great predecessor of Judah, as we might expect in the times of the prophet Amos. The writer was influenced by the work of Elijah, the great prophet of the North, and was controlled by the idea that Israel must serve God alone.

After the fall of the Northern Kingdom before Assyria in 721 B.C., its literature passed into southern hands, where the great Judean history had so long been current. It was inevitable that the two narratives, so alike in religious interest and so often parallel in material, should be combined, and this was done in Judah, in the course of the seventh century before Christ, the last century of the Judean kingdom. In this work Hebrew prose reached its highest level.

In that same period, as we have seen, when reaction under the half-heathen king Manasseh drove the prophets into hiding, they produced the Book of Deuteronomy.[1] This, with the new history just described, the Jews carried with them into captivity, after the disasters of 597 and 586 B.C. And in the captivity in Babylonia these books were combined into a great composite work of history and law, all conceived from a fundamentally prophetic point of view.

The Exile was a time of great literary activity on the part of the Jews. Faced with the collapse of their national fortunes, they seem to have found their literary heritage all the more precious, and to have sought in every way to preserve and enhance it. They were, moreover, dreaming of a return to their own land and devising means to prevent the recurrence of the catastrophe that had plunged them into exile.

They now felt that their desolation was caused by their failure to please God and serve him faithfully, and to safeguard the nation in the future and insure its holiness, priestly exiles like Ezekiel produced the temple legislation of Ezekiel, chapters 40–48, and the still earlier Holiness Code of Leviticus, chapters 17–26, written probably between 597 and 586, with its undertone: "You must be holy, for I, the Lord your God, am holy."[2] Their ideal was theocratic; God himself was to be the head of the state in the future. The nation was to exclude from itself all unclean heathen elements, and devote itself wholly to the service and the worship of God.

In such a spirit, after the Exile, priestly authors created a new history. It began with a majestic account of the Creation, which was represented as culminating in the institution of the Jewish Sabbath.[3] Its narrative was supplemented with painstaking genealogies—for purity of Jewish blood had assumed religious importance—and accounts of

tribal arrangements, and especial attention was
given to matters of law and religious ceremonial.
There was a covenant relation of the most solemn
kind between Israel and God, and this underlay the
whole religious practice of the nation.

This great expression of the priestly conception of
religion and its institutions was completed toward
the middle of the fifth century before Christ, taking
its place beside the great older prophetic book of
history and law which had taken shape about the
Book of Deuteronomy. The new work was probably
the textbook of Ezra's reforms of 397 B.C. The two
works were so parallel and so supplementary that
they were soon combined into a single whole, pre-
serving and as far as possible adjusting and harmonizing the leading features and materials of both.

So at last, not long after 400 B.C., arose the
Hexateuch. The extraordinary thing about it is its
scope, for it seeks to unify and organize the whole
range of human history, society, institutions, law,
and religion. It was a cosmogony, an outline of
history, an account of human origins and social institutions, a system of worship, and a handbook of
religion and morals—all rolled in one. It would be
difficult to find in the world's literature any parallel
to the sweep of this tremendous work, into which
some great Jew late in the Persian period wrought
the diverse literary inheritance of his nation.

The literary problem presented by the Hexateuch and its sources is one of the most intricate in the whole range of literature. But it may be substantially summarized as follows: The Judean history arose about 850 B.C.; the Ephraimitic history, about 750 B.C.; they were combined in the following century, before the publication of Deuteronomy in 621 B.C., and presumably before its composition, perhaps about 650 B.C.; in the following century, 600–500 B.C., this joint history was in turn united with Deuteronomy; late in the fifth century the priestly book of history and law was written, and early in the fourth century, or soon after 400 B.C., this too was united by priestly hands with the great corpus of ancient history and law that had thus grown up, to form substantially what we know as Genesis to Joshua. The Hexateuch was therefore almost five hundred years in the making.

This work, which by itself is almost as long as the whole New Testament, was a single book, but it was soon divided into six parts, which we know by the Greek names given them when they were translated into Greek, in Egypt in the third century before Christ: Genesis (Beginning); Exodus (Going Out); Leviticus (the Levitical Book); Numbers (from the Numbering of the People, chaps. 1–4, 26); Deuteronomy (the Second Giving of the Law), and Joshua (the hero of the sixth book).

The reverence with which Deuteronomy had been regarded from the time of its discovery gradually extended to all the books that preceded it in the Hexateuch, and these five, Genesis–Deuteronomy, came to be called the Law and formed the core about which the rest of the Hebrew scriptures, the Prophets and the Writings, later gathered.

SUGGESTIONS FOR STUDY

1. *References:* [1]Chap. vii; [2]Lev. 19:2; [3]Gen., chap. 1.
2. What is the Hexateuch?
3. Compare the priestly account of creation (Gen. 1:1—2:3) with the prophetic account (Gen. 2:4–25).
4. What are the four main sources of the Hexateuch?
5. When did each of them arise?
6. Through what stages of combination did they pass?
7. What is the scope of the narrative of the Hexateuch?
8. What part of it reflects the work of Ezekiel?
9. What part of it did Ezra urge upon the people?
10. To what part of it do we owe the story of Joseph?
11. What social institutions does it explain?
12. What has it to say about the beginnings of arts and crafts?
13. What explanation does it offer for the unity and harmony of nature? What other explanations occur to you?
14. What are some of its characteristic religious and social attitudes? (Cf. Lev., 11; 19:18; 20:27; 24:20.)
15. How did the makers of our present six books divide the materials of the Hexateuch?
16. What do you consider the most important and significant portions of each book?

CHAPTER XX

THE BOOK OF JONAH

The Jewish prophets thought of their nation as peculiarly chosen and favored by God, and yet they saw the world controlled generation after generation by cruel heathen powers. The chosen people, as they considered themselves, were conquered and scattered, and the prophets denounced and condemned their conquerors in strong and bitter terms. Yet the nation did not recover, but fell into a state of settled insignificance and impotence. Assyria, Egypt, Babylon, and Persia dominated it one after the other, and the proud claims and high hopes of Judaism seemed farther from fulfilment than ever. For the few who still cherished those claims and hopes, the religious adjustment to all this disappointment and humiliation was indescribably hard.

At length it dawned upon the Jewish mind that there was a nobler solution of the great enigma than the old familiar one of meeting hatred with hatred and bitterness with bitterness. That had risen out of the old narrow way of conceiving God as peculiarly their own, and supremely concerned with their welfare. But suppose he really cared for other nations and peoples just as much as he cared for the Jews? That would put the whole matter in a different perspective.

Of course the way had been prepared for this by the sublime ethical monotheism of the earliest literary prophets, and by Jeremiah's doctrine of religion as an individual matter and Ezekiel's teaching of personal responsibility. Ezekiel had seen that God took no pleasure in the death of the wicked: "I have no pleasure in the death of the wicked, but rather in this, that the wicked man turn from his way and live."[1]

But Ezekiel had said this of the Jews: "Why should you die, O household of Israel?"[2] It remained for a later prophet, about the middle of the fourth century before Christ, to rise to the splendid thought that this was as true of the heathen as of the Jews, and that God as creator had the same concern, the same forbearance and compassion, for all his creatures, whether Jew or Gentile.

Such a teaching was particularly timely after the days of Ezra, when Jewish life became so permeated with narrowness and arrogance. It was to correct that harsh and unlovely attitude in late Judaism that the Book of Jonah was written. The followers of Ezra had gone to one extreme, but the position in which it left them was religiously intolerable. It filled the heart with bitterness instead of peace. The true remedy must lie in the very opposite direction; in the direction of breadth, sympathy, and love, even for one's enemies. This is the most difficult of all lessons, and the most indispensable.

This is the message of the Book of Jonah. Jonah

the son of Amittai, was a Galilean prophet of the eighth century before Christ; he is mentioned in II Kings.[3] Four hundred years later he was made the hero of a story or parable to teach the great new lesson that, as Paul afterward said, God does not belong to the Jews alone; he belongs to the heathen also.[4]

Jonah is called by God to go to Nineveh, the Assyrian capital, and preach against it, but instead of obeying he flees in the opposite direction, and takes passage in a ship for Tarshish, to get away from the presence of the Lord. His amazing adventures on the voyage make up the best-known story in the Bible and perhaps in the world. Escaped from the storm and from the fish, Jonah is once more called to warn the Ninevites. This time he obeys, and preaches to them with such success that they all repent and are forgiven. God is pleased, but Jonah is not; he is bitterly disappointed. He did not wish the Ninevites to be saved; he wished them to be lost. He supposed he had the congenial task of pronouncing doom upon the enemies of his people, and now it seemed that he had simply been opening the way for their repentance and God's forgiveness. He felt that he had been deceived and betrayed into giving his heathen enemies his own choicest and exclusive possession—the favor of God. No wonder Jonah is angry enough to die. But God rebukes him for his anger and bitterness, and declares his pity for the untold thousands of the great heathen city: "You had pity on the gourd, ... and should not I, indeed, have pity on Nineveh, that great city?"[5]

Nineveh had been the archenemy of the Jewish people, and it was asking a great deal to require Jonah to rejoice over its conversion and salvation. It was a hard lesson that the Book of Jonah sought to teach. But religion is something to be not hoarded but shared. Jonah is the first missionary book in the world. There's a wideness in God's mercy like the wideness of the sea, and the love of God is broader than the measure of man's mind. This is the imperishable truth of the Book of Jonah, and its unknown author cast it in such inimitable forms that his three-page story is among the masterpieces of the world.

The psalm in chapter 2 is a subsequent addition, in the latest Hebrew lyric style. It is manifestly in origin not a prayer for deliverance but a thanksgiving for a deliverance already accomplished.

SUGGESTIONS FOR STUDY

1. *References:* [1]Ezek. 33:11 (cf. 18:23); [2]Ezek. 18:31 (cf. 33:11); [3]II Kings 14:25; [4]Rom. 3:29; [5]Jonah 4:10, 11.

2. In what period is the scene of the story of Jonah laid?

3. Tell the story.

4. What did Nineveh stand for in Jewish experience?

5. How did the Jew feel about his relation to God?

6. How does the teaching of Jonah affect this?

7. What is its great religious lesson?

8. To what form of literature does the Book of Jonah belong?

CHAPTER XXI

THE SONG OF SONGS

Hebrew poetry was not all religious. The Hebrews were orientals and fully alive to the passionate appeals of existence. Their first literary expressions were war-songs and dirges.[1] The imprecatory psalms and the taunt-songs of the prophets show how they could hate, and their amorous impulses found full expression in one great love poem, the Song of Songs.

This form of title, like the King of Kings, or the Book of Books, means the greatest of songs. It was also called Solomon's Song, because Solomon was regarded as the greatest of the Hebrew song-writers; and so the greatest song would naturally be ascribed to him. He was said to have written five thousand songs.[2]

But the Song of Songs was not a product of court life, nor is it as ancient as the time of the undivided kingdom. It is in fact not a single song but a group of songs. Now it is the girl who sings, now it is her lover. They are village lovers, from some place not far from Jerusalem, as the references to scenes and places show. Each in turn gives utterance to the frankest and most passionate terms of affection.

It is still the custom in Syria for a bridal pair to

be treated as king and queen in their village during the week of the celebration of their marriage. The bridegroom is brought in state to the threshing floor where he is enthroned upon the threshing sledge with his bride, and hailed as king. The beauty of the bride is dwelt upon in great detail in the "wasf" or "description," and the passionate attachment of each for the other is described in the first person.

The significance of this for the Song is very clear. The bridegroom is called Solomon because Solomon was such a famous king, and he is "Solomon" for his week, in his village. And if he is Solomon, she is Shulammith,[3] which is clearly just a feminine form of the same name, as though he were called, as in Latin, Salomo, and she, Salome.

In chapters 4–7 at least we have such a series of songs, celebrating the beauty of the bride and the attractions of her lover, and hailing them as king and queen of the village:

Ah, it is the litter of Solomon.
Sixty warriors are around it,
    of the warriors of Israel. . . . .
O maidens of Jerusalem, go forth,
    and gaze upon King Solomon.[4]

In fact, the whole Song is most naturally understood in this way. The bride and the bridegroom are represented as singing the solos and the villagers form the chorus. The bride exults in the affection of her lover, 1:2–4. The bride and bridegroom lavish compliments upon each other, 1:7—2:2. The bride declares to the villagers her devotion to him, 2:3—3:5. The chorus hails the bridegroom, enthroned on the threshing sledge, 3:6–11. The bridegroom rejoices in the beauty of the bride, 4:1–15. The bride declares the physical perfections of her lover, 5:10–16. The bridegroom returns the compliment, 6:4–10. As the bride dances the sword-dance the villagers dilate with the utmost frankness upon her charms, 6:13—7:6. The bridegroom and the bride, encouraged by the chorus, acknowledge the overwhelming power of love and their devotion to each other, 7:7—8:14.

We cannot be sure that the songs are in the order followed in such country weddings, but there is no serious reason for thinking they are not. The whole may at any rate be regarded as a little anthology of Hebrew wedding songs, rejoicing in the strong mutual attraction of the sexes culminating in happy and honorable marriage.

Efforts have been made to understand the Song as a little drama in six acts and twelve scenes, telling the story of a Shulamite girl brought to Solomon's court, but longing for her shepherd lover, with whom she is finally reunited. It would be gratifying to have even so small a fragment of Hebrew drama, but the explanation breaks down at too many points.

Others see in it a survival of the old nature-wor-
ship of Palestine, so denounced by the prophets. In
the succession of the seasons this worship saw in the
autumn the death of Tammuz and explained the
spring as caused by his resurrection and marriage to
the goddess Ishtar. In the Song, such interpreters
say, Solomon was presently brought in and the goddess became the bride. This, too, is confused and
difficult; the Song does not read in that way at all,
though such old religious hymns may have influenced these songs.

The religious interpretations of the Song are also
full of difficulty. Jewish thought has endeavored to
see in it the union of God and his people, and Christian interpreters have understood it of Christ and
the Church, or of Christ and the soul. When the
bold oriental figures of which the Song is full are
really understood, however, these fanciful religious
interpretations are seen to be far-fetched and incon-
gruous. Yet the Song is still publicly read among the
Jews in celebration of the Passover.

The songs are, in fact, in their present form altogether wanting in religious feeling and interest.
But it is a satisfaction to the student of Hebrew life
and literature to have some of the purely secular
poetry of the Hebrews, and the Song of Songs, with
its rich oriental feeling and imagery, is all that we
possess of that. It belongs late in Jewish history,
probably in the fourth or the third century before

Christ, in the period of the Persian or the Greek domination.

SUGGESTIONS FOR STUDY

1. *References:* [1]Judg., chap. 5; II Sam. 1:19–27; [2]I Kings 4:32; [3]Song of Songs 6:13; [4]Song of Songs 3:7, 11.

2. Name some varieties of Hebrew poetry.

3. To which of these does the Song of Songs belong?

4. What is the meaning of its name?

5. Why is it sometimes called Solomon's Song?

6. What are some modern interpretations of the Song?

7. What is the probable explanation of it?

8. How does this explain the use of the names Solomon and Shulammith?

9. Was Judaism an ascetic religion?

10. What is the literary value of the Song?

11. What place has the Song in modern Jewish practice?

CHAPTER XXII

THE BOOKS OF CHRONICLES, NEHEMIAH, AND EZRA

The conquests of Alexander left the Jewish community after his death subject to the Greek masters of Egypt, and no nearer than before to the independence and influence of which they dreamed. It was not strange that they found solace in these times of insignificance and humiliation in recalling the glories of the nation's past, and in repainting in glowing colors its departed splendors. The priesthood and the ritual had become more and more central and dominant in Jewish life. The priestly book of history and law had been written and its influence was at its height. It was natural that the nation's story, from the death of Saul to the reformation under Ezra, should be retold from the point of view of priestly standards and ideals.

It is this that is done in the books known to us as Chronicles, Ezra, and Nehemiah. They were originally a single continuous work, for the most part paralleling the narratives of II Samuel and I and II Kings. But here the colors are much deeper. Good kings are depicted as better, bad kings as worse, than in Samuel and Kings. Armies are larger, tribute is heavier—in general, figures and statistics are exaggerated. The priestly system and atmosphere are read back into the distant past. The Temple organization is credited to David in great detail, and all its appointments when it was erected under Solomon are dwelt upon at length, but the work of the prophets Elijah and Elisha is passed over in silence. The writer's interest is clearly in Temple and priesthood, and in the response of the kings to duties specifically religious.

II Kings stopped in the midst of the Exile, at the thirty-seventh year of the captivity of King Jehoiachin, or 561 B.C. But the Chronicler did not stop there. He went on with the decrees of Cyrus authorizing the Jews to return to their own land, and the work of Nehemiah and Ezra in reorganizing the emancipated Jews. For this part of his work he seems to have had further written sources, among them a very moving account by Nehemiah himself of his work,[1] and one Aramaic narrative from which he takes over short passages without translating them into Hebrew;[2] as though both languages would be equally intelligible to his readers.

He makes the work of Ezra precede that of Nehemiah, but careful modern study has established that Nehemiah's work began in 444 B.C. and Ezra's in 397 B.C., or perhaps even later. It is probable also that the humbler people who had never been carried into captivity played a larger part in rebuilding the city and Temple than the Chronicler indicates. In

Nehemiah,[3] the succession of high priests is brought down to Jaddua, whom Josephus mentions as high priest in the time of Alexander the Great.[4] The Chronicler's work must have been written soon after that time.

The vigorous stand of Ezra against intermarriage with foreigners is reflected in the Chronicler's great concern for unbroken Jewish genealogies, such as occupy chapters 1–8 of I Chronicles, and frequently intersperse the narrative, making the whole work a sort of Golden Book of Jewish ancestries. The scope of these genealogies—Adam, Seth, Enosh—shows that the writer knew not simply the books of Samuel and Kings but the great record of history and law known to us as Genesis to Joshua, indeed the whole historical literature of his people. His pious and priestly interest leads him to drop out of sight the recreant Northern Kingdom; he makes no effort to retell its story, and his interest in the Levites and his knowledge of Temple music make it clear that he himself is a Levite and a Temple musician.[5]

He re-writes the story of the kingdom of Judah not as Samuel and Kings had related it but on the understanding that the developed religious law of his own day had been in force through its whole history. His book is an imaginative priestly recast of Jewish history. It has been described as an ecclesiastical chronicle of Jerusalem.

To the historian the most convincing part of the

Chronicler's record is his picture of Nehemiah, and his coming to Jerusalem, surveying the ruined walls by night, and setting about their restoration. The first exiles to return had come back in 538 B.C., and began by building houses to live in. In 520, at the instance of Haggai and Zechariah, steps were taken to rebuild the Temple.[6] With Nehemiah, in 444, the walls are rebuilt.

But the condition of the people was still far from satisfactory from the new priestly point of view, and when Ezra the priest came in 397 B.C., or soon after, he called upon those who had married foreign wives to divorce them and cast off their children, for he looked upon such unions as pernicious and unclean.[7] This harsh position was sustained by the heads of families whom he called into conference on the matter, but it did not go unchallenged, as the Book of Ruth shows. Ezra represents the unflinching application of the priestly law to the people of Jerusalem, and the Chronicler reads back this law into all the previous history of the kingdom of Judah.

Sincere and high-minded as Ezra's purpose doubtless was in his reforms, they nevertheless tended to foster and establish in the Jewish mind those narrow ideals of legalism and exclusiveness that so blighted the subsequent course of Judaism, and have driven many of its best spirits, in ancient and modern times, out of its fellowship.

SUGGESTIONS FOR STUDY

1. *References:* [1]Neh. 2:11-20; [2]Ezra 4:7-23; 5:3—6:15; [3]Neh. 12:10 f.; [4]*Antiquities* xi. 7. 2; 8. 4; [5]I Chron., chaps. 24-26; II Chron. 5:12, 13; 35:15, etc.; [6]chap. xiii; [7]Ezra, chaps. 9, 10.

2. What period of Jewish history is covered by the books of Chronicles, Nehemiah, and Ezra?

3. What is the writer's distinctive point of view in writing?

4. What do we know of his position and interests?

5. How does he alter the picture given in Samuel and Kings? (Cf. I Kings 22:43 with II Chron. 17:6.)

6. What has he to say about the work of the prophets?

7. Why does he neglect the history of the Northern Kingdom?

8. What sources had he for the later period of Nehemiah and Ezra?

9. What was the work of Nehemiah?

10. What reforms did Ezra undertake?

11. What is the historical value of the books of Chronicles as compared with Samuel and Kings?

12. What was the writer's view of religion?

CHAPTER XXIII

THE BOOK OF LAMENTATIONS

Some of the earliest Hebrew poems that have come down to us are dirges. David composed one over Abner,[1] and a greater one over Saul and Jonathan:[2]

> "How have the heroes fallen! . . . .
> Swifter than eagles were they,
> They were stronger than lions. . . . .
> How have the mighty fallen,
> And the weapons of war perished!"

Amos sings a dirge over Israel:

> "Fallen, not to rise again,
>   is the virgin Israel;
> Prostrate on her own soil,
>   with none to raise her up."[3]

Amos wrote a generation before the fall of the Northern Kingdom, and a century and a half before the Babylonians took Jerusalem. The grief the Jews felt when the city was actually taken and the national life extinguished was far keener. It found expression in the dirges that form the main part of the Book of Lamentations.

Lamentations, or Dirges, consists of five poems, each forming a separate chapter in our modern ver-

sions. They deal with the misery of the conquered
city and people. The first, second, and fourth of
them are dirges lamenting the overthrow of Jerusalem as that of an individual, the daughter of Zion.
The third is a lament over the writer's own sufferings, of course representing those of his people. The
fifth is a prayer describing the misery and shame of
the exiles.

The first four chapters are not only in the Hebrew
elegiac meter, but are acrostic poems, the lines of
each stanza beginning with the successive letters of
the Hebrew alphabet. In chapters 1–3 these stanzas
consist of three lines, but in chapter 4 of two.
Strangely enough, in chapters 2, 3, and 4 the fifteenth and sixteenth letters of the Hebrew alphabet
are transposed, but in chapter 1 they are in the conventional modern order. This suggests that these
three poems are older than chapter 1, but the acrostic form of poetry was a late development of Hebrew
literature and the whole book was written long after
the events it so touchingly describes, probably some
time in the third century before Christ.

The misery of the captured and pillaged city is
movingly depicted in the first dirge:

How lonely the city sits,
    once so crowded with people! . . . .
Judah . . . . has to live among the nations,
    she can find no home; . . . .

> Her people are all moaning,
>   in their search for bread;
> They give of their treasures for food,
>   to keep themselves alive. . . . .
> Ho, all you who pass along the road,
>   look and see,
> If there is any pain like my pain,
>   which has been dealt to me.[4]

The poet acknowledges the sinfulness of his people as the just cause of their misery, and only asks that God will punish his oppressors in their turn, for their misdeeds.

The second dirge brings out more plainly the divine judgment on Jerusalem; it was God himself, in his fierce anger, who brought all this misery upon them. It is he that has destroyed not only their palaces and fortresses, but his own pavilion, meeting-place, and altar. The picture is clearly that of the final destruction of the city in 586 B.C. Children are starving in the streets, women devour their own offspring, and priest and prophet are slain in the very Temple itself.

> Lift up your hands to him
>   for the life of your children,
> Who faint for hunger
>   at the head of every street.[5]

In the third poem the poet sees in God the author of all his affliction. He speaks as a prisoner, living in the dark, loaded with chains and walled in with stones. He might be speaking for Jehoiachin, who became king at eighteen, reigned for three months, and was imprisoned for thirty-six years. But he is not hopeless:

"It is good that one should wait quietly
    for help from the Lord;
It is good for a man,
    that he should bear the yoke in his youth.
Let him sit alone in silence,
    since it has been laid upon him. . . . .
To crush under foot
    all prisoners in the world.
To deprive a man of his rights,
    in the face of the Almighty,
To subvert man in his cause,
    the Lord does not countenance."[6]

The poet still clings to his faith in God's eternal justice:

O Lord, thou didst plead my cause,
    thou didst redeem my life.
O Lord, thou hast seen the wrong done me;
    give me justice.[7]

In the third dirge, the fourth chapter, the wretched condition of the sacked and ruined city is powerfully described:

The children are begging bread
    with none to offer it to them. . . . .
Better off are those stricken by the sword
    than those stricken by hunger. . . . .
No kings of the earth believed,
    nor any of the inhabitants of the world,
That the oppressor and enemy could enter
    the gates of Jerusalem.
It was for the sins of her prophets,
    the iniquities of her priests,
Who shed in her midst
    the blood of the righteous.[8]

When Jerusalem fell the Edomites who lived southeast of Judah had joined in plundering them, and this memory long rankled in the Jewish heart and colors the closing stanzas of this dirge.[9]

The final chapter of Lamentations is a prayer for God's mercy, and describes the sorrows of the exiles and their longing for home:

But thou, O Lord, art enthroned forever;
Thy throne endures from age to age. . . . .
Restore us, O Lord, to thyself, so that we may return;
Renew our days as of old.[10]

These poems of lamentation bear witness to the lasting impression made on the Jewish mind by the Babylonian conquest and Exile. They show the Hebrew dirge in its most developed form, and constitute the largest single group of acrostic poems in Hebrew literature. Their especial concern for the sufferings of children reflects a highly developed sensibility. They were anciently ascribed to Jeremiah, but they present more contrasts than resemblances to his characteristic ideas and ways of expression.

SUGGESTIONS FOR STUDY

1. *References:* [1]II Sam. 3:33, 34; [2]II Sam. 1:19–27; [3]Amos 5:1, 2; [4]Lam. 1:1, 3, 11, 12; [5]Lam. 2:19; [6]Lam. 3:26–28, 34–36; [7]Lam. 3:58, 59; [8]Lam. 4:4, 9, 12, 13; [9]Lam. 4:21, 22; [10]Lam. 5:19, 21.

2. To what type of Jewish literature do the Lamentations belong?

3. What parts of the book do you find particularly moving?

4. Read David's dirge over Abner (II Sam. 3:33).

5. Read David's dirge over Saul and Jonathan (II Sam. 1:19–27).

6. With what national experience do the Lamentations chiefly deal?

7. What is the central topic of Lamentations, chaps. 1, 2?

8. Who seems to be impersonated in the third poem?

9. Why are the Edomites so bitterly spoken of in chap. 4?

10. How many of these poems are in the acrostic style?

11. What other such poems does the Old Testament contain? (Cf. Nah., chap. 1; Prov., chap 31; Pss. 9–10, 25, 34, 37, 111, 112, 119, 145.)

12. What peculiarity in the order of the alphabet distinguishes chap. 1 from chaps. 2, 3, and 4?

13. Why were the Lamentations ascribed to Jeremiah? Why was he called the Weeping Prophet?

CHAPTER XXIV

THE BOOK OF PROVERBS

Every people has its proverbs. They spring out of the wit and insight of the common people and can hardly be described as literary expressions. Their beauty lies in their brevity and detachment. Their life is not in books but on the lips of living men and women.

The Hebrews had such proverbs. But with them such detached aphorisms developed into a regular form of moral and even religious instruction. The proverb became a conscious, didactic method. Most proverbs are naïve instinctive expressions of homely, practical wisdom. But among the Hebrews the composing of proverbs was cultivated as an art.

The men who studied the writing of proverbs were the Wise Men, the Sages of Israel and in later times, under the Persian and Greek rule, they became the professional teachers of the Jewish youth. They would produce a whole series of proverbs, more or less connected, and embodying not simply worldly wisdom but religious ideas as well.

Sometimes they abandoned the brief proverb form and developed their thought into an extended poem usually in praise of Wisdom: the Appeal of

Wisdom, the Worth of Wisdom, the Blessings of Wisdom, the Invitation of Wisdom, Wisdom and Folly, and the like.[1] They also made it a practice to collect and edit proverbs, so that little books of them came into existence.

Studious and traveled men brought home from other lands foreign proverbs and put them into Hebrew, adapting them to Jewish ideas of God and religion. We have seen that after the Exile some Jews took refuge in Egypt, where they established a colony at Elephantine, near the First Cataract. Such refugees translated into Hebrew an old Egyptian work, the Wisdom of Amen-em-ope, which we know as Prov. 22:17—24:22. This ancient fragment of Egyptian Wisdom was probably composed some centuries before the Exile, long before the Jews had taken up the writing of proverbial literature, or Wisdom, and is the oldest part of the Proverbs.

The next oldest part of the book is the immediately preceding portion, 10:1—22:16, which probably comes from the Persian period, the fifth and fourth centuries before Christ. Chapters 1–9 are later, perhaps from the Ptolemaic times, especially the third century before Christ—which were more favorable to Jewish life.

The two main collections of independent proverbs in the book are 10:1—22:16, already mentioned, and chapters 25–29. The first of these, which is the oldest collection of native Hebrew proverbs, consists chiefly of simple two-line proverbs:

> Hope deferred makes the heart sick,
> But desire fulfilled is a tree of life.[2]

> A gentle answer turns away wrath,
> But harsh words stir up anger.[3]

In the second collection, chapters 25–29, the proverbs are often much longer, extending to four or even eight lines.

It is evident that the book is a collection of collections. Eight of these can be distinguished: 1–9; 10:1—22:16; 22:17—24:22 (the Words of the Wise); 24:23–34 (an appendix: further Words of the Wise); chapters 25–29 (the Proverbs of Solomon); chapter 30 (the Words of Agur); 31:1–9 (the Words of Lemuel); and 31:10–31 (the alphabetic poem on the Ideal Wife).

Nothing is known of Agur and Lemuel, but their connection with Massa points to Arabia as the reputed source of their wisdom. It is Agur who says "Give me neither poverty nor riches."[4] The final poem, on the Ideal Wife, reflects a higher position for Hebrew womanhood than was conceded her until long after the Exile. She is the symbol of thrift, industry, and foresight. "Her children rise up and bless her."[5]

The Sages have been called the humanists of Israel, and, like the greatest humanists, they were deeply religious. "The beginning of wisdom is reverence for the Lord" was the cornerstone of their work.[6] Our collection of Proverbs was probably completed in the third century before Christ, but it was followed in the second century by Ecclesiastes and the Wisdom of Jesus ben Sirach, and by the Book of the Wisdom of Solomon, who became the symbol of Wisdom not only to the Jews but to the Arabs. The authors of the Book of Kings said that his wisdom surpassed the wisdom of all the eastern Arabs and all the wisdom of Egypt, for he was wiser than all men, and uttered three thousand proverbs.[7] They came in this way to ascribe to him their proverbs just as they ascribed to David their psalms.[8]

The proverb is so portable a form of truth that it has always remained popular down to modern times, as the *Adages* of Erasmus and *Poor Richard's Almanac* show. And the division of the Bible into verse paragraphs in the sixteenth century has led most people to treat all its books as though they were made up of proverbs, each verse being considered an independent statement of truth. So the proverb style has dominated the use of the Bible, although properly it is confined to the Book of Proverbs.

SUGGESTIONS FOR STUDY

1. *References:* [1]Job, chap. 28; [2]Prov. 13:12; [3]Prov. 15:1; [4]Prov. 30:8; [5]Prov. 31:10–31; [6]Ps. 111:10; Prov. 9:10; [7]I Kings 4:30–32; [8]Prov. 1:1.

2. Repeat a few current proverbs.

3. What is the difference between such proverbs and those in the Book of Proverbs?

4. Who produced the proverbs?

5. What other books did they write?

6. Were all the proverbs of native Hebrew origin?

7. Through what stages of collection have they passed?

8. What are some of the most familiar ones?

9. Show how the proverb form grew among the Hebrews, from the simplest to the most developed kind.

10. When was our Book of Proverbs formed?

11. What kind of wife is described in the closing acrostic poem?

12. Is its form a mark of early or late date?

13. Does the ideal of womanhood it presents belong early or late in Hebrew development?

CHAPTER XXV

THE BOOK OF DANIEL

The efforts of the kings of Syria to impose Greek ideals of life upon their subjects were strongly resisted by the more pious Jewish groups, and when in 168 B.C. Antiochus Epiphanes, wishing his people to have one civilization, proposed to obliterate everything that made the Jews different from the rest of his subjects, the situation became desperate. The observance of the Sabbath was forbidden, the Temple was plundered and desecrated, and Judaism was outlawed.

Some Jews gave way before this systematic persecution and abandoned their religion. But the Pious, as they were called—the Saints or Chasidhim—would not give way. They refused to give up the copies of their scriptures and endured martyrdom rather than apostatize. At the little Judean town of Modein where the Jews were commanded to attend a heathen sacrifice, an old priest named Mattathias and his sons killed the Syrian officer and broke up the ceremony. This was the beginning of the Maccabean uprising, which was to emancipate Judea from Syrian rule and make it once more for a time a free and independent state.

The struggle was a hard one and must often have

seemed hopeless. But the Jews encouraged themselves with memories of the heroes of other days and the difficulties they had surmounted. The chief of these heroes was Daniel. He stood in Jewish legend and tradition for the ideal exile, unflinchingly resolved to maintain the faith of his fathers at all costs. In the intense heat of the Maccabean persecution these memories and traditions were cast into the Book of Daniel.

The book consists of two parts. The first describes the experiences of Daniel and his three companions at the court of Nebuchadnezzar, chapters 1–6. These noble young captives refuse to eat the unclean food of Babylon or to worship the idol set up by the king. Daniel continues to pray to his God in spite of the king's interdict. In short, the exiles do just the things the Jews were forbidden by Antiochus to do, and God delivers them from the fearful penalties thus incurred, the fiery furnace and the lions' den. Daniel's wisdom stands out above that of the heathen and Belshazzar's feast and Nebuchadnezzar's madness show in masterly dramatic style what happens to kings who set themselves against God.

The second part of Daniel, chapters 7–12, is a series of four visions. They are in that apocalyptic style which we have seen already in Zechariah and Ezekiel. They set forth under the characteristic apocalyptic symbolism the series of empires, Baby-

lonian, Persian, Greek, and Syrian, down to the
Maccabean time, when they are to end in destruction. The three and a half years[1] are the years between the termination of the Temple worship by
Antiochus and the resumption of Jewish worship
there under the Maccabees in 165.

The same meaning is conveyed by Nebuchadnezzar's dream, in chapter 2, where the different
parts of the statue represent the successive empires
that between Daniel's time and their own had ruled
the world. The last, the feet of iron and clay, is to
be broken into dust by the stone hewn without
hands from a mountain, which itself becomes a great
mountain that fills the earth.[2] This is the Kingdom
of God.

It was the habit of the later apocalyptists to describe the conditions of their own day under the
name of some great figure of antiquity, such as
Enoch, Seth, Noah, Adam, or Daniel, who is dramatically conceived as writing not for his own time
but solely for the far-off time to come: "Not for
this generation, but for a remote one which is for to
come," as the Book of Enoch puts it.[3] In the words
of the Book of Daniel, "It relates to the distant future."[4]

Daniel was evidently written in the midst of the
Maccabean struggle, between 168 and 165 B.C. The
"little horn" of chapter 8 is the persecuting Antiochus himself,[5] while chapter 11 reflects the contem-

porary history of the Syrian kingdom in its relations with Egypt and Rome in increasing detail until the "contemptible person" (Antiochus Epiphanes) makes his assault upon Judaism and the Temple worship.[6]

Daniel, like Ezra, is written partly in Hebrew and partly in Aramaic. When the Chaldean magicians are introduced in 2:4 they use the Aramaic language, which they might be expected to speak. But the book goes on in Aramaic to the end of the seventh chapter. After that it is Hebrew again. It is evident that when the book was written both Hebrew and Aramaic were familiar to Jewish readers.

The power and vigor of the imagery of Daniel and the strength of its religious faith have given it a high place both in literature and in religion. It served its immediate time by nerving the Maccabean party to resist the attack of their rulers upon the Jewish faith and to throw off the Syrian yoke.

SUGGESTIONS FOR STUDY

1. *References:* [1]Dan. 7:25; [2]Dan. 2:34, 44; [3]En. 1:2; [4]Dan. 8:26; [5]Dan. 8:9, 23–25;[6] Dan. 11:21.

2. What scenes in the Book of Daniel are most familiar to you?

3. To what type of literature does it belong?

4. What are some of the traits of that literature?

5. What situation led to the writing of Daniel?

6. How does it meet the situation?

7. Into what parts does the book fall?

8. What effect did it have upon the situation?

9. What other books of this kind did the Jews produce?

10. Has Daniel a religious lesson for us today, and if so what is it?

11. What literary value has the Book of Daniel?

12. Compare the visions of chaps. 7–12 with the visions of Zechariah.

13. Compare them with the visions of Ezekiel.

CHAPTER XXVI

THE BOOK OF PSALMS

Jewish religion expressed itself not only in laws and sermons but in hymns and prayers, and these were gathered up from time to time into collections, like our hymnbooks. Some of these are very old, going back to the time of the kingdom, and even perhaps to David himself. He was a poet, as his dirges over Abner and Saul show,[1] and Jewish tradition assigned to him almost half of its psalms. The second of the five books of psalms ends with the words, "The prayers of David the son of Jesse are ended,"[2] but eighteen other psalms are ascribed to David in the rest of the Psalter,[3] and the Septuagint or Greek translation of the Book of Psalms adds fifteen more. Thus the Hebrews did honor to their great hero by ascribing to him their choicest songs.

But the Psalter is for the most part the product of the age after the Exile, when the Temple worship became more and more the typical expression of Jewish religion. The older hymns were revised, just as ours have been, to accord with new attitudes and uses, and various collections were formed, some of which may still be distinguished in the Psalter. The psalms of the sons of Korah, 42–49, and those of the sons of Asaph, 73–83, were such collections. The former are spoken of in II Chronicles[4] as Levites who stood up to praise the Lord with an exceedingly loud voice. Asaph, too, was associated by the Chronicler with the ancient psalmody,[5] and was evidently one of the traditional founders of guilds of Temple singers.

Other collections visible within the present Psalter are the Songs of Ascents, 120–34, and the Hallelujah Psalms, 111–13, 146–50. The songs sung at the Passover—the Hallel—Pss. 113–18, also formed a unit in practical use; Pss. 113 and 114 were sung before the Passover supper and Pss. 115–18 after it; they were the "hymn" sung by Jesus and the disciples after the Last Supper.[6]

The presence of independent collections in the Psalter is shown by the duplicate psalms that it contains; Ps. 14 is identical with Ps. 53; Ps. 40:13–17 reappears as Ps. 70; Ps. 57:7–11 and Ps. 60:5–12 make up Ps. 108.

It is clear that our Psalter is a collection of collections—a grand collection that was to embrace them all, and so came to include a few duplicates. The Psalter was thus a growth, and reflects many periods and situations in Jewish religious life, from the kingdom down through the Exile and the second Temple to the times of the Maccabean struggle toward the middle of the second century before Christ. Its somewhat arbitrary division into five books reflects the earlier division of the Law into the five books of

Genesis, Exodus, Leviticus, Numbers, and Deuteronomy. Book I, Pss. 1–41, is probably the oldest collection. A second one was made up of 42–89, including Books II and III, and a third, more liturgical in character, of 90–150, including Books IV and V.

We have noted the appearance of acrostic poetry in the prophets, Nah. 1:2–10; in Proverbs, chapter 31; and in Lamentations, chapters 1–4. It is abundantly represented in the psalms—9–10, 25, 34, 37, 111, 112, 119, 145. Ps. 119, in praise of the Law, the longest of all the psalms, is the most elaborate in structure, each of the first eight lines beginning with the first letter of the alphabet, the next eight with the second, and so on, through all its 176 verses.

In the Psalter, Jewish liturgy found its fullest and finest expression. We can imagine the male choruses of the second Temple, the Korahites, and the "sons of Asaph," singing these great hymns in its service, in the later days of Judaism. In fact, most of the much-discussed superscriptions of the psalms as well as the mysterious "Selah" have to do with directions for their musical and liturgical use. Even after centuries of transmission, we can still easily distinguish solos, antiphonies, refrains, and choruses. The pilgrims as they marched in bands to the regular feasts at Jerusalem sang old songs of Zion:

I was glad when they said to me,
"Let us go to the house of the Lord."[7]

We seem to see them approaching the Temple hill, with a great doubt as to their own fitness to mount it:

> Who can ascend into the hill of the Lord?
> And who can stand in his holy place?[8]

And the answer comes:

> He who has clean hands and a pure heart,
> Who has had no desire for falsehood,
> And has not sworn to a lie.[9]

There are glimpses of religious processions:

> Thy processions are seen, O God,
> The processions of my God, my King, in the sanctuary.
> Singers lead; at the rear, the stringed instruments;
> In the middle, maidens playing timbrels.
> In choirs, they bless God.[10]

Babylonian and Egyptian models influenced some of the psalms. The Babylonians had an extensive literature of penitential psalms, and Ps. 104 closely parallels a solar hymn of Amenhotep IV, about 1370 B.C. But their expressions are thoroughly saturated with the distinctive ideas of Jewish religion.

With surprising clearness the Psalter thus reflects the varied exercises of Jewish religious life: coronations, dedications, processions, pilgrimages.

The greatest of all antiphonies is Ps. 136. The great national experiences are mirrored and celebrated in the Psalter: exile, humiliation, persecution: Ps. 79 describes their distress when Antiochus made his attack upon their religion and worship:

> O God, the nations have come into thy inheritance;
> They have defiled thy holy temple;
> They have laid Jerusalem in ruins.[11]

Bitter memories of the Exile lingered in Ps. 137:

> By the rivers of Babylon,
> There we sat down, and wept, indeed,
> When we remembered Zion.[12]

Edom's malicious encouragement of the destruction of Jerusalem—

> "Raze it, raze it
> To its very foundations!"[13]

must not be forgotten, and the poet hopes in no chastened mood that the children of Babylon will in their turn be dashed to pieces on the rocks.[14] This is vengeful hatred, indeed, and may warn us nowadays not to indulge in hymns of hate.

The advance in Jewish thought toward a nobler and loftier conception of God is reflected in the psalms as is also the dawning consciousness of a great national religious mission, a messianic destiny.

It has been well said that the Psalter was not only the hymnbook but the prayer-book of the second Temple, and the chief modern interest in the psalms is as expressions of personal religious life—remorse, despair, repentance, communion, aspiration, faith, hope, assurance. The psalmist is now lonely in a strange land, now sick and discouraged:

> Out of the depths I cry to thee, O Lord.
> O Lord, hear my voice![15]

And the social value of religion is finely put in the lines:

> Lo, how good and lovely it is
> When brethren dwell together as one.[16]

It is the variety as well as the reality of these inward experiences that makes the psalms an inexhaustible treasure of religion. No one fathoms it all, because no one passes through all the trials it describes. For the psalms are the emotion of many hearts, the thought of many minds, most of them writing under great stress, and it is this deep and varied religious expression that makes the Psalter so universal in its appeal. Sometimes the writer's religion is of the Law and the Temple; he exults in his book of religion, as in Ps. 119, or finds gratification in the exercises of processional and liturgy. Sometimes it is as spiritual and free as anything in the prophets:

Sacrifice and offering thou dost not desire . . . .
Burnt offering and sin-offering thou dost not de-
    mand.[17]

Everyone has his favorite psalms, but the one of
universal appeal is, of course, the Twenty-third,
which stands unsurpassed and perhaps unequaled
among the world's classics of devotion:

The Lord is my Shepherd; I shall not want.[18]

And no book in the Bible speaks more directly
and widely to modern religious life than this wonderful old Hebrew hymnbook, which was so often revised and enlarged, and reached its present size
probably about the middle of the second century
before Christ, or soon after.

SUGGESTIONS FOR STUDY

1. *References:* [1]II Sam. 1:19–27; 3:33, 34; [2]Ps. 72:18;
[3]Pss. 86, 101, 103, 108–10, 122, 124, 131, 133, 138–45; [4]II
Chron. 20:19; [5]II Chron. 29:30; [6]Mark 14:26; [7]Ps. 122:1;
[8]Ps. 24:3; [9]Ps. 24:4; [10]Ps. 68:24–26; [11]Ps. 79:1; [12]Ps. 137:1;
[13]Ps. 137:7; [14]Ps. 137:9; [15]Ps. 130:1, 2; [16]Ps. 133:1; [17]Ps.
40:6; [18]Ps. 23:1.

2. What is the Psalter?

3. What can you say of its history?

4. What historical situations does it reflect?

5. What light does it throw upon Jewish religious practices?

6. What is the lesson of the imprecatory psalms?

7. What do the superscriptions deal with?

8. What light do the psalms throw upon Jewish personal religion?

9. What personal emotions find expression in the book?

10. What is the modern value of the psalms?

11. What are your favorite psalms?

12. When did the Jews sing psalms?

13. What influence have the psalms had upon Christian hymns?

CHAPTER XXVII

THE BOOK OF ESTHER

No story in the Old Testament is more romantic than that of Esther, the beautiful Jewish girl who became a queen and once when her people were in great peril of extinction risked her life to save them.

Esther was the ward of her cousin, Mordecai, who lived in Susa, and when the Persian king, Ahasuerus, or Xerxes, dismissed his wife Vashti for disobeying him, and ordered all the beautiful girls in the provinces of his dominions to be brought to his harem at Susa so that he might select the new queen from them, Mordecai directed Esther to join them. She was chosen by the king out of all the candidates, and became his queen. And later when a plan was formed by Haman, the anti-Jewish vizier, to destroy all the Jews throughout the Empire, Esther's wit and courage defeated it and delivered them, while their enemies were signally punished. The story reflects familiarity with violent anti-Jewish demonstrations, and reports with evident satisfaction that in this case the Jews were able to turn upon their tormentors and kill seventy-five thousand of them in the Persian Empire.

The primitive emotions and lurid colors of this

nationalistic romance have always made it popular
with Jews and Gentiles alike. But its spirit is not at
all religious, and its moral attitude is resentful and
bitter. Yet the story is skilfully told and the action
moves on with well-sustained interest. The book
was really written to explain the origin of Purim, the
latest of the Jewish feasts, which it declares was instituted to celebrate the escape of the Jews from the
danger that threatened them in the days of Esther
and Mordecai. As Xerxes ruled from 486 to 465
B.C., and is described as marrying Esther in the seventh year of his reign, this would push the origin of
Purim back to that time. But its observance is not
reflected elsewhere in Jewish history before the second century, and it is probably about the middle of
that century that Esther was written.

Purim was a joyous festival in the month Adar
(March), the last month of the Jewish year, and is
probably of oriental origin. Mordecai and Esther
sound very much like Marduk and Ishtar, the Babylonian deities, and the scene of the story is laid in
Susa, the ancient capital of Elam. It would seem
that at this season of the year Jews in the east took
up the local practice of keeping this popular festival
and formed the habit of giving dinners and exchang-
ing presents at this time. The Jews of Palestine
were slow to accept the practice, and Esther was
written to justify and popularize it among them. It
is to be noted that no express religious motive or

authority is claimed for its institution. It was a purely secular expression of social Judaism.

That it was written long after the Persian Empire had gone out of existence is also shown by its picture of Persian court and official procedure, which is quite out of accord with what we learn of them from Persian sources. The book thus belongs with Ruth and Jonah as another Hebrew example of the short story, a kind of creative literature of which these three books form almost the beginning. Other Jewish examples are the books of Judith and Tobit in the Apocrypha. Ruth, Jonah, and Esther are all of them short stories with a purpose, though that of Esther is not religious but social. It is more developed in form than the others, and throws new light upon Hebrew literary genius. It belongs to the history of literature rather than of religion, and reminds us that the Old Testament gathers up the literary classics of one of the most gifted peoples of antiquity, which knew the uses not only of law, eloquence, history, and poetry but of fiction as well.

The Book of Esther in Hebrew is very generally given to Jewish boys nowadays, when they reach the age of thirteen, and often in the form of a manuscript roll, so that there are more manuscript copies of Esther in existence today than of any other book of the Old Testament.

SUGGESTIONS FOR STUDY

1. Is it wrong to write fiction?

2. What examples of fiction does Jewish literature contain?

3. What purpose controlled each of these books?

4. How does fiction differ from the work of the oriental story-teller?

5. What types of literature does the Old Testament contain?

6. What types does it lack?

7. Of the three short stories in the Old Testament, which exhibits the most artistic development?

8. What do the names Esther and Mordecai suggest as to the sources of the book?

9. What is the moral weakness of the book?

10. What is its moral strength?

CHAPTER XXVIII

THE BOOK OF ECCLESIASTES

The Greek name Ecclesiastes, meaning "Preacher," was intended as a translation of the mysterious name Koheleth under which the Book of Ecclesiastes was written. Koheleth, the son of David, who was king in Jerusalem,[1] was evidently a way of referring to Solomon, who was considered the wisest of men, and credited in I Kings[2] with an immense number of songs and proverbs.

The writer of Ecclesiastes looked at the facts of life and found no progress or satisfaction in them. They filled him with the most absolute despondency. Nature goes round and round in a purposeless routine (1:1–11):

> "All rivers run to the sea,
>   But the sea is never full. . . . .
>   There is nothing new under the sun."[3]

Learning, too, is a wretched business, and knowing wisdom and folly is simply striving for the wind (1:12–18):

> "For more wisdom is more worry,
>   And increase of knowledge is increase of sorrow."[4]

Indeed, all human effort seemed to him vain. The works of man are so evanescent, his life is so short!

Who can tell what use the future will make of his little accumulations of wisdom or property? "How the wise and the fool alike die! And I hated life, for everything that is done under the sun seemed to me wrong."[5]

Life offers no satisfaction and there is no after-life, declares Koheleth. It is all futility, as he repeatedly says. He is a thoroughgoing pessimist; at least he writes in a mood of utter pessimism. He doubtless lived in a time when religion seemed lifeless and perfunctory, when the pursuit of truth had not revealed its immense attraction for the human mind, and when men had not awakened to the social opportunity afforded by the sheer needs of their fellows. The Greek pursuit of beauty in art and architecture and of truth in philosophy and science had not reached this Jewish philosopher, and the undoubted narrowness, formalism, and complacency of later Jewish thought threw him back upon himself.

It seems quite obvious to us that the real basis of Koheleth's bleak pessimism is his own utter selfishness, and we wonder whether there was no suffering humanity to be helped and comforted in his day. If he had had any disposition to serve God or even his fellow-men, he might have found life full of the deepest satisfactions. And if everybody had approached life as he did, this would today be a much more backward and unlovely world than it is. In

our desperate hours we sometimes cheer ourselves
with thoughts of wise and good women: "Das ewig
Weibliche zieht uns hinan." But even this was denied to Koheleth: "One man out of a thousand have
I found, but not a woman have I found among all
these."[6] He fully shared the Jewish undervaluation
of women.

But his work was afterward embellished by another of the Wise Men of Israel, who sought to light-
en its darkness with some of the shrewd practical
aphorisms of the Sages, and to show that after all
things are not as bad as Koheleth had represented
them. Of course the literary effect of Koheleth's
picture lay in his tremendous overstatement. He
means to paint a very dark picture. But its very
darkness makes every reader protest, and one of
these ancient readers wrought into it the moderat-
ing touches mentioned above. When Koheleth la-
ments that all the labor and all the hard work are
due to men's jealousy of one another, the Sage
pointedly observes, "The fool folds his hands and
devours his own flesh."[7] When Koheleth bitterly
cries, "For whom should I toil and deny myself happiness?"[8] the Sage remarks, "Two are better than
one, for they get a good wage for their toil; and if
they fall, the one can lift up his companion, but if a
solitary person falls there is no partner to lift him
up."[9] This is a keen hint of the social value of life
and work much needed by Koheleth.

But Koheleth needed more than the frigid proverbs of the Wise Men to balance its unreligious bitterness. For while the author acknowledged the existence of God, it seems to have meant almost nothing to him religiously; it did not give him light or hope or courage. This must have been the feeling of the pious Jew who perhaps not many years after its appearance wrought into it those great statements of religion that so enrich and glorify it. When Koheleth told young men to make the most of life's enjoyments while they could, the new voice is heard saying, "But know that for all these things God will bring you into judgment."[10] And a little farther on, in the same poem on the fleeting joys of youth, he sternly interjects, "Remember your Creator in the days of your vigor,"[11] which seriously interrupts and contradicts the flow of Koheleth's words. To fear God and keep his commandments is the thing that most concerns every man, for God will bring every work into judgment.[12] This is the last word of the book, and it is clear that it sounds much more like his religious reviser than like world-weary, disillusioned old Koheleth.

The book was written about the end of the third century before Christ, or not far from 200 B.C. Of its literary power there can be no doubt. The concluding poem, 11:9—12:8, with its inimitable picture of old age and death, is one of the gems of biblical literature. But the book is full of memorable sayings:

"Cast your bread upon the surface of the water,
For after many days you will find it."[13]

It has been finely said that the three hands that
may be distinguished in Koheleth are just those
types of mind mentioned by Paul in I Corinthians[14]
—the scribe, the wise man, and the searcher of this
world. It was the last who wrote the book, and the
wise man and the scribe retouched it. It might be
called "The Three Voices." And when we come to
the last lines of it, we seem to hear each of them
speak in turn:

Furthermore, my son, take warning: of the making of many books there is no end, and much study
is weariness of the flesh.[15]

The words of the wise are like goads; but collections which are given by one teacher are like nails
driven with a sledge.[16]

The conclusion of the matter. Let us hear all:
Fear God and keep his commandments.[17]

It is well that they do all speak. For the modern
man too is faced with the uncompromising material
facts of science, which he must relate to culture and
religion in his turn. And so he can still find a lesson
in this strangest book in the Old Testament.

SUGGESTIONS FOR STUDY

1. *References:* [1]Eccles. 1:1; [2]I Kings 4:32; [3]Eccles. 1:7, 9;
[4]Eccles. 1:18; [5]Eccles. 2:16, 17; [6]Eccles. 7:28; [7]Eccles. 4:5;
[8]Eccles. 4:8; [9]Eccles. 4:9, 10; [10]Eccles. 11:9; [11]Eccles. 12:1;

[12]Eccles. 12:13; [13]Eccles. 11:1; [14]I Cor. 1:20; [15]Eccles. 12:12; [16]Eccles. 12:11; [17]Eccles. 12:13.

2. How are the conflicting statements and attitudes of Ecclesiastes explained?

3. When was it written?

4. What was the writer's general position?

5. What was done to it afterward?

6. To which of the hands that worked upon it would you assign 7:4–6? 7:7–12? 7:19? 10:1–3? 8:14a?

7. Who is meant by Koheleth?

8. Why was the book ascribed to him?

9. Why do we call the book Ecclesiastes?

10. Does anyone today maintain the position taken in the original body of the book?

11. What is the religious answer to that position?

12. How would you distribute the last three verses of the book among the three hands that have worked upon it?

CHAPTER XXIX

THE FORMATION OF THE OLD TESTAMENT

The works of Hebrew literature have come down to us assembled into a collection which we know as the Old Testament. This collection was gradually formed by the Jews for their own religious purposes, but they did not of course call it the Old Testament. They called it the Scriptures, or the Law and the Prophets, or simply the Law. How did it originate, and through what stages did it pass?

The beginning of the Old Testament was the finding of the book of Deuteronomy in the Temple in 621 B.C. That book became the nucleus of the Jewish scriptures. It was gradually expanded through the addition of the prophetic history in the course of the sixth century, only the legal parts of the whole being regarded as authoritative.

When Ezra the priest soon after 400 B.C. stood up before the people and read the Book of the Law aloud to them day after day, it marked not only the introduction of the Synagogue into Palestine, but also a new step in the progress of the Jewish scripture, for the Law he read was probably the new priestly recast of Hebrew history and legislation.[1] This was itself soon combined with the expanded Deuteronomy into our Hexateuch—Genesis, Exodus, Leviticus, Numbers, Deuteronomy, Joshua. But since the Law stopped with Deuteronomy, Joshua naturally fell away, and the Pentateuch, or work of five books remained.

The harsh measures of Nehemiah and Ezra in demanding that marriages with foreign women be annulled met with much opposition. One son of the high priest refused to give up his foreign wife, the daughter of Sanballat the Horonite,[2] and was expelled. Sanballat built him a temple on Mount Gerizim, near Shechem, and the Samaritan church was the result. These Samaritans have always cherished the Law—the five books of Moses, and no more—and they possess to this day a Samaritan manuscript of it for which they claim a great antiquity. This shows that when they broke off from the Jews of Jerusalem the Jewish scripture had reached that stage but no further.

While this Samaritan schism began about 432 B.C., the breach with the Jerusalem community did not at once become complete. Still we may be sure the acceptance by both Jerusalem and Samaria of the completed Genesis to Deuteronomy must have taken place by the middle of the following century. The advocates of the priestly book of law and history would naturally seek to have it combined with the expanded Deuteronomy which contained the nation's law, and this must have happened soon after Ezra's appearance with the priestly book, in

397 B.C. In fact, he may have been active in securing their amalgamation.

With Joshua the books of Judges, Samuel, and Kings were presently grouped, under the title of the Former Prophets. The Jews had begun to collect the works of the literary or writing prophets in the time of the Exile, so that a collection of these Latter Prophets also was already well advanced. The prophetic collection as a whole, including both Former and Latter Prophets, came to be recognized as authoritative between 250 and 175 B.C., for the Chronicler evidently did not regard the Former Prophets as scripture, or he could not have reshaped them so freely into the books of Chronicles. Jesus, son of Sirach, on the other hand, who about 180 B.C. composed his Wisdom, our Ecclesiasticus, in Jerusalem, spoke of the Law, the Prophets, and the rest of the books as making up the sacred writings of his people; at least that expression occurs more than once in the Greek translation of his book made by his grandson at Alexandria about 132 B.C. The collection of the prophets was clearly accepted in their days.

The Latter Prophets included Isaiah, Jeremiah, Ezekiel, and the Book of the Twelve, which we know as the Minor Prophets, Hosea to Malachi. But it was counted as one book by the Jews. This made the number of the Latter Prophets the same as that of the Former, that is, four.

The books of the prophets did not, however, stand on quite the same level of authority as the books of the Law. The prophets were subordinated to the Law, and in many ways discriminated from them in prestige. In these later days of Judaism the priestly had thus prevailed over the prophetic element in final influence.

The Psalms formed the nucleus of the third group of sacred books. They are quoted as scripture in I Maccabees, written probably early in the first century before Christ. With them were associated Job and Proverbs. The Five Rolls also came into this last division of Hebrew scripture: The Song of Songs, Ruth, Lamentations, Ecclesiastes, and Esther, each of which was read at one of the five religious festivals of the Jewish year, from Passover to Purim.

The last group in this part of the scripture was formed by Daniel, Ezra-Nehemiah, and Chronicles, making a total, as the Jews counted, of twenty-four books, corresponding to the number of letters in the Hebrew alphabet, which may be reckoned as either twenty-two or twenty-four.

The Hebrew scripture did not reach these final proportions until the end of the first century after Christ, however, for uncertainty was felt as to the Song of Songs and Ecclesiastes until the synod of Jamnia, about the end of the first century after Christ, and even after that some rabbis did not accept Esther as a book of scripture.

Lessons both from the Law and from the prophets were read in the synagogue every Sabbath in New Testament times, but it must be remembered that in Jewish regard the Law was supreme over both Prophets and Writings.

The theory on which the decision as to the canonicity of doubtful books was reached was that the prophetic period had extended from Moses to Ezra, and that books falling within that period might properly be accepted. Proverbs, Ecclesiastes, and the Song of Songs purported to be the works of Solomon; the Psalms, of David; Esther and Daniel dealt with scenes and persons of the fifth and sixth centuries before Christ. There was, therefore, some color for admitting these books to the Jewish scripture as belonging to the times before Ezra (397 B.C.). This rabbinical conception of a definite prophetic period to which a book must belong if it was to be considered scripture is the key to the last stage in the development of the Old Testament.

SUGGESTIONS FOR STUDY

1. *References:* [1]This is indicated by the fact that the people in response to his efforts kept the Feast of Booths for eight days, as the new priestly law required, not for seven, as the older Deuteronomy provided; Neh. 8:14–18; Lev. 23:36; Deut. 16:13; [2]Neh. 13:28; Josephus, *Antiquities* xi. 7.2; 8.4.

2. What is the source of our Old Testament?

3. What book may be regarded as the nucleus of the collection?

4. Into what did this book develop?

5. What was the book from which Ezra the priest read before the people in 397 B.C.?

6. What became of this book?

7. How did the Samaritan community arise, and what is its scripture?

8. What is meant by the Former Prophets?

9. What constituted the Latter Prophets?

10. When were these collections combined into the Prophets?

11. What religious use was made of the Law and the Prophets?

12. What was the third part of the Hebrew scriptures?

13. What three groups did it contain?

14. What liturgical use was made of some of these?

15. About what books was there most uncertainty?

16. How was it terminated?

17. What is meant by the prophetic period, and how did it affect the problem?

CHAPTER XXX

THE APOCRYPHAL BOOKS

The Hebrews produced many other books besides those preserved in our Bible. Some of these are mentioned in the Old Testament, but have long since disappeared: the Book of Jashar;[1] the Book of the Chronicles of the Kings of Judah;[2] the Book of the Chronicles of the Kings of Israel.[3] In general, the Old Testament (aside from Esther and the Song of Songs) contains only the religious literature of Judaism and by no means all of that.

Of the lost books of Hebrew literature some were fortunately translated into Greek and have survived in that language. The Bible of early Christianity was the Greek translation of the Jewish scriptures, which included some of these books now lost in Hebrew, as well as others that were originally written in Greek. When toward the close of the fourth century after Christ Jerome set about revising the Old Latin Bible, he tried to find the Hebrew originals of all the Old Testament books to help him in his task, and the books he could not find in the Hebrew canon he named the Apocrypha, the Secret Books or Books of Hidden Wisdom. Luther (1534) first grouped them together. As the first English Bible in its Old Testament portion was translated from the German and Latin (1535), the

Apocrypha passed into the English Bible, and they still find a place in all complete printings of the King James Version, of 1611. Though they are in general from a rather late period, they contain much of literary and historical interest, and some passages of real religious value.

The Book of Tobit tells the story of a pious Jew whose steadfast devotion to alms, prayer, tithes, and the observance of the Law was, after a bitter experience of blindness, poverty, and humiliation, finally rewarded. The main episode is the journey of his son Tobias from Nineveh to recover a sum of money previously deposited by Tobit with a friend in Rages. Tobias is accompanied on the journey by the angel Raphael disguised as a guide or dragoman. At Ecbatana, Tobias meets his cousin Sarah and falls in love with her. She had been given to seven husbands in succession, but each of them had been killed on the wedding night by the demon Asmodeus, who loved her. With the aid of Raphael, Tobias routs the demon, the money is brought from Rages, and on their joyful return to Nineveh, Tobit's sight is restored.

The book is a piece of religious fiction, almost a fairy story, written probably in Greek, and in Egypt, where it may have been intended as an answer to a local production, the Tractate of Khons, which was designed to promote the worship of that Egyptian deity, and told how with the aid of Khons a demon was cast out of a princess. The popular Jewish Story of the Wise Ahikar is also reflected. Tobit was written probably between 190 and 175 B.C., and gives a faithful picture of Jewish ideals of piety at that time, in devotion to the Law and the Temple. The appearance of angels and demons—Raphael, one of the seven archangels,[4] and Asmodeus, the evil demon[5]—is a definite development in Jewish ideas, under Persian influence, which was later to play an important part in New Testament times.

The longest of the Apocrypha is the Wisdom of Jesus, the son of Sirach. It is a typical piece of Jewish Wisdom Literature, like Proverbs. It was written by a Jewish scribe of Jerusalem before the outbreak of the Maccabean struggle, and probably about 180 B.C. It was translated into Greek by the author's grandson on a visit to Alexandria about 130 B.C., for the translator states that he had come to Egypt in the thirty-eighth year of King Euergetes, or 132 B.C. The statement of the book that it is a translation has been confirmed in recent years by the discovery of about two-thirds of it in Hebrew manuscripts of the tenth or eleventh century after Christ, which were found in the storeroom of an old synagogue in Cairo, between 1896 and 1900. It is evident that it was in existence in Hebrew in Jerome's day, although he did not succeed in finding it.

The strength and the weakness of the scribal Judaism that began with Ezra are plainly seen in Ecclesiasticus, as the Greeks called the book. His conception of woman is absurdly low; a daughter is to him only an unending source of anxiety.[6] Yet his appreciation of the physician, the scribe, and especially the craftsman[7] is full of understanding. It is of the farmer, the jeweler, the smith, and the potter that he says: "They will maintain the fabric of the world. and in the handiwork of their craft is their prayer."[8]

The closing part of the book is a grand review of the great men of Jewish religious history, ending with Simeon the high priest, who died in 199 B.C. and was evidently a contemporary of the author, who pronounces a splendid eulogy upon him.[9] This review is introduced with the lines in praise of famous men,[10] which is the most quoted passage in all the Apocrypha: "Let us now praise famous men, our fathers before us."

The Greek form of the Book of Daniel contains various additions unknown to the Hebrew, which appear in the Apocrypha of the English Bible. The Prayer of Azariah and the Song of the Three Children are associated with the deliverance of Daniel's three friends from the fiery furnace. Both are pieces of Jewish liturgy—the Prayer from the dark days just before the Maccabean uprising, or about 170 B.C.; the Song a splendid psalm of thanksgiving, from the days of the Maccabean triumph, about 150 B.C.

In Bel and the Dragon, Daniel seeks to convince the king of Babylon of the falsity of his gods. To prove that the image of Bel does not eat the food left in his temple, Daniel has wood-ashes scattered on the floor, to record the footprints of the priests who come in the night to eat the offerings. And the Dragon, or serpent, which the king worships, Daniel kills by feeding him pitch and hair. The story was written to ridicule idolatry, probably in Greek about 100 B.C., when serpents were venerated in oriental and Greek shrines, like that of Aesculapius at Epidaurus.

The Story of Susanna reflects the efforts of the Pharisees in the first century before Christ to reform Jewish legal procedure in the matter of false witness to a capital charge. With many willing to act as informers, two might easily agree and condemn an innocent person to death. If they failed and were themselves convicted, they could not be executed, as no one had actually suffered. The remedy so dramatically urged in the Story of Susanna is twofold: the witnesses must be separately examined; and if their testimony is shown to be false they must be executed, whether the person they have accused has been put to death or not. The Story was probably written in the first quarter of the first century before Christ, in Jerusalem, by some Pharisee, and perhaps in Hebrew, although Julius Africanus, the friend of Origen, offered strong arguments for a Greek original.

The Book of Judith is the romantic account of how a beautiful Jewish woman named Judith, when her town was besieged by an Assyrian army under Holofernes, penetrated into the Assyrian camp, captivated Holofernes, and beheaded him in his sleep, thus delivering her city from its danger. Its purpose is to bring home to its readers the necessity of strict observance of the Jewish Law. In all the exacting situations in which Judith finds herself, she scrupulously observes the fasts, feasts, food laws and ablutions prescribed by the Law, and so earnestly insisted upon by the Pharisees. It is a significant document of Pharisaism.

Judith is extant in a short Hebrew form in a manuscript of the tenth century, and in a much-expanded Greek revision. It was composed probably about 150 B.C., when the Pharisaic movement began to develop actively after the Maccabean struggle, and it assumed its fuller Greek form about a century later.

The book is another example of Jewish religious fiction. The author seems almost to advertise the unhistorical character of his work by his opening statement that Nebuchadnezzar "reigned over the Assyrians in Nineveh." Nebuchadnezzar was the king of the Babylonians and his capital was Babylon, not Nineveh, as every Jew would know, for it was he that had captured and destroyed Jerusalem and carried the Jews to captivity in Babylon. The historical value of Judith lies in its picture of early

Pharisaism, not in any light it might cast upon the reign of Nebuchadnezzar, and its undoubted literary power and interest have given it an enduring place in the world's literature.

The supplementary chapters of Esther appear in the King James Bible as 10:4—16:24, but they appear in the Greek version of Esther scattered through the book. In general they seek to give to the book the religious tone it so manifestly lacks. They were probably introduced into it sometime between 150 and 100 B.C.

I Esdras is in the main an imaginative account, probably of Greek origin, of the rebuilding of the Temple. It tells the story of the three guardsmen of Darius and their answers to the question, "What is strongest?" One said wine, another, the king; and the third, woman, though truth was mightiest of all. He was adjudged the victor, and chose as his reward the rebuilding of the Temple.

The story was written not long after 150 B.C., probably in Alexandria. Its historical value is slight, but its literary interest is considerable. From it comes the famous proverb, "Truth is mighty and will prevail."[12]

II Esdras, in the English Apocrypha, consists chiefly of a series of apocalyptic visions from different hands, composed for the most part late in the first or early in the second century after Christ.

The Prayer of Manasseh is not really a part of the

Greek version of the Old Testament, but stands in a very few manuscripts with other materials at the end of the Psalms. It is a fine prayer of penitence, of Pharisaic color, and was written, probably in Greek, in the first half of the first century before Christ, 100–50 B.C. It was later identified with the prayer said in II Chronicles[13] to have been uttered by the wicked king Manasseh in his distress, and so found its way into some Greek Bibles.

There are four books called Maccabees. I Maccabees is an account of the Maccabean struggle against the persecution of Antiochus Epiphanes, resulting in the rise of the Hasmoneans. It covers the period 175—132 B.C., and was written by a Jew of Palestine perhaps half a century after the latter date. It was written in Hebrew or Aramaic, but was soon translated into Greek, in which form alone it survived. It is an important and generally trustworthy source for the history of its time.

II Maccabees, on the other hand, was written in Greek, and deals in a rhetorical and somewhat fanciful way with the stirring events of 175—160 B.C. It was probably composed in Alexandria, and has no such claims to historical worth as has I Maccabees. But its language influenced the writer of the Epistle to the Hebrews.[14]

III Maccabees is a romantic story of the effort of Ptolemy Philopator to enter the Holy of Holies in Jerusalem. The priests refused to permit this, and he determined to take vengeance upon the Jews of Alexandria. Being providentially prevented, however, he became their protector and patron instead. The book was written in Greek, probably in the first century before Christ.

IV Maccabees is really a discussion of the control of the emotions by reason. The author is a man of Pharisaic and Stoic leanings. Much of his book is occupied by a panegyric upon the Maccabean martyrs. The book was written in Greek, probably early in the first century after Christ.

The Wisdom of Solomon is the work of two authors, the second beginning at 11:2 and continuing to the end. It was written in Greek probably in the latter half of the first century before Christ, for Egyptian Jews, to safeguard them against the perils of skepticism, materialism, idolatry, and persecution. It was well known to more than one New Testament writer—Paul,[15] the authors of Hebrews[16] and Ephesians.[17] It has been called the finest work of Alexandrian Judaism before the time of Christ. It was so congenial to early Christian thought that it was actually included in the earliest list of New Testament books that has come down to us, the Muratorian List, made up probably at Rome, about A.D. 200. To Wisdom we owe the beautiful line, "The souls of the righteous are in the hand of God."[18]

The Book of Baruch represents itself as written

by Jeremiah's friend Baruch in the fifth year after the destruction of Jerusalem by the Babylonians, or 582 B.C., and sent to Jerusalem with a sum of money to help support the cultus there—to buy burnt offerings and sin-offerings and incense,[19] though how this could be done, with the Temple in ruins and the priesthood scattered, is by no means clear. The book is chiefly of a liturgical character, and reflects not only II Maccabees and the ancient Jewish liturgy, but probably the fall of Jerusalem before the Romans in A.D. 70, when Jewish thought would naturally turn back to the similar experience of the Jewish people centuries before. The first section (1:1—3:8) is devoted to the praise of God, the confession of sin, and a prayer for God's mercy. The second (3:9—4:4) revives the counsels of the Sages: Wisdom is what is needed. The third (4:5—5:9) consists of two odes of comfort and cheer, reflecting the later part of Isaiah and the Psalms of Solomon (*ca.* 50 B.C.). The sixth chapter is the so-called Letter of Jeremiah, which seeks to keep the Jews from falling into idolatry. The work as a whole belongs to the end of the first or the beginning of the second century after Christ.

Other Jewish books, like the apocalyptic Book of Enoch (second century B.C.), and the Psalms of Solomon, or Psalms of the Pharisees (first century B.C.), were known and read in Greek by the early Christians. Indeed, it is difficult to set definite limits to the collection of books they admitted to their Old Testament as sacred scripture. But the firm hand of Jerome drew a line between the books extant in Hebrew and accepted by the Jews of Palestine and the books known to him only in Greek, and ruled the former only in the full sense canonical and authoritative, and in this most Protestant churches have followed him.

SUGGESTIONS FOR STUDY

1. *References:* [1]Josh. 10:13; II Sam. 1:18; [2]I Kings 22:45; [3]I Kings 22:39; [4]Tob. 12:15; [5]Tob. 3:8; [6]Ecclus., chap. 42; [7]Ecclus., chap. 38; [8]Ecclus. 38:34; [9]Ecclus., chap. 50; [10]Ecclus., chap. 44; [11]Judith 1:1; [12]I Esd. 4:41; [13]II Chron. 33:12, 13; [14]Heb. 11:35 (cf. II Macc. 6:19, 30); [15]Rom. 9:21–23; [16]Heb. 1:3; [17]Eph. 6:11–20; [18]Wisd. 3:1; [19]Baruch 1:10.

2. What books mentioned in the Old Testament have disappeared?

3. What circumstance has preserved many books now lost in Hebrew?

4. How did these books come to be called the Apocrypha?

5. How did they happen to find a place in the first English Bibles?

6. What is the story of Tobit?

7. When was it written and why?

8. When was Ecclesiasticus written and by whom?

9. What are some of its values?

10. What is the significance of the Story of Susanna?

11. What was the purpose of "Bel and the Dragon"?

12. What is the story of Judith, and what was its purpose?

13. What was the purpose of the Greek additions to Esther?

14. What is the story of the Three Guardsmen?

15. What is the historical value of I Maccabees, and what period does it cover?

16. Characterize the other books of Maccabees.

17. What were the date and purpose of the Wisdom of Solomon?

18. What is the character of the Book of Baruch and when was it written?

19. Do you think these books should be included in the Old Testament, as they are in Greek Bible and the King James Version, or omitted from it, as they were by the Palestinian Jews and the Puritans?

CHRONOLOGICAL SURVEY

B.C.

Ca.	1150	The Song of Deborah
Ca.	850	The Judean History
	765–750	The work of Amos
Ca.	750	The Ephraimitic History
	745–735	The work of Hosea
	730–721	The work of Micah
	740–701	The work of Isaiah
	721	The Fall of Samaria
By	650	The Judean and Ephraimitic Histories combined
Ca.	650	The Book of Deuteronomy
	627	The Scythian Invasion; Zephaniah
	621	The Finding of Deuteronomy
	612	The Fall of Nineveh; Nahum
	608–597	The work of Habakkuk
	627–586	The work of Jeremiah
	597	The Fall of Jerusalem
	597–538	The Exile
	592	The Call of Ezekiel
	586	The Second Capture of Jerusalem
	586–538	The Histories combined with Deuteronomy
	550	The book of Samuel-Kings completed
	538	The Fall of Babylon; the return from Exile; Isa., chaps. 40–55
	520–519	The work of Haggai and Zechariah
Ca.	475–450	The work of Malachi
	444	The work of Nehemiah
Before	400	The Book of Obadiah
		The priestly book of law and history
		The Book of Judges completed

B.C.

Ca.	400	The Book of Joel
Ca.	397	The work of Ezra
Ca.	350	The formation of the Hexateuch
Before	300	The work of the Chronicler
	300–200	The books of Lamentations and Proverbs
Ca.	165	The Book of Daniel
	200–150	The Book of Ecclesiastes
Ca.	150	The completion of the Psalter
Ca.	150	The Book of Esther

BIBLIOGRAPHY

GENERAL

MOORE, G. F. *The Literature of the Old Testament*. New York: Holt, 1913.

BOX, G. H. *A Short Introduction to the Literature of the Old Testament*. London: Rivingtons, 1909.

GRAY, G. B. *A Critical Introduction to the Old Testament*. New York: Scribner, 1913.

FOWLER, H. T. *A History of the Literature of Ancient Israel from the Earliest Times to 135 B.C.* New York: Macmillan, 1922.

BEWER, J. A. *The Literature of the Old Testament in Its Historical Development.* New York: Columbia University Press, 1922; rev. ed., 1933.

CORNILL, G. H. *A Short Introduction to the Canonical Books of the Old Testament*. New York: Putnam, 1907.

DRIVER, S. R. *An Introduction to the Literature of the Old Testament*. Rev. ed. New York: Scribner, 1913.

CREELMAN, H. *Introduction to the Old Testament, Chronologically Arranged*. New York: Macmillan, 1917.

OESTERLEY, W. O. E. *An Introduction to the Books of the Apocrypha*. New York: Macmillan, 1935.

TRANSLATIONS

The Bible: An American Translation. Edited by J. M. POWIS SMITH and EDGAR J. GOODSPEED. Chicago: University of Chicago Press, 1931.

The Holy Bible: A New Translation. By JAMES MOFFATT. New York: Doran, 1926.

The Holy Scriptures according to the Masoretic Text: A New Translation. By MAX L. MARGOLIS and OTHERS. Jewish Publication Society, 1917.

INDEX

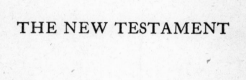

THE NEW TESTAMENT

CONTENTS

iii

CHAPTER I

THE LETTERS TO THE THESSALONIANS

About the middle of the first century, in the Greek city of Corinth, a man sat down and wrote a letter. He had just received some very cheering news from friends of his, away in the north, about whom he had been very anxious, and he wrote to tell them of his relief at this news. As he wrote or dictated, his feelings led him to review his whole acquaintance with them, to tell them about his anxiety and how it had been relieved, and to try to help them in some of their perplexities, and before he closed he had written what we should call a long letter. And this is how our New Testament, and indeed all Christian literature, began. For the writer was Paul, and his friends were the people at Thessalonica whom he had interested in his doctrine that Jesus of Nazareth, who had been put to death in Jerusalem twenty years before, was the divine Messiah, and was to come again to judge the world.

Paul himself had believed this for a long time, and five or six years before he had set out to travel westward through the Roman Empire with this teaching. At first he had worked in Cyprus and Asia Minor, and it was only a few months before that he with two friends had crossed from Asia to Europe and reached the soil of Greece.

Paul was a whole-hearted, loyal friend, and he doubtless made friends everywhere for himself and his teaching; but he never made quite such friends as those who had gathered around him in these first months in Greece. At Philippi, where he stopped first and tried to interest people in his gospel, his friends made him come and live with them; and they thought so much of him that then and for years afterward they sent him money so that he might not have to work at his trade all the time but might have more opportunity to teach and spread his message.[1]

The Thessalonians too had become staunch friends of Paul's. Some of them had risked their lives for him when they had known him only a few weeks, and others were to stand by him all through his life and to go with him long afterward, when he was taken, as a prisoner, from Caesarea to Rome. That was the kind of people in whom Paul had become so interested, and to whom he now wrote his letter. He had been welcomed by them when he first came to Thessalonica, and his very success among them had awakened jealousy and distrust on the part of others. At last Paul had been obliged to leave the city to prevent violence to himself and his friends. He had gone on westward along the Roman road to Beroea and later had turned south to Athens, but all the time he had been anxious about his friends at Thessalonica. What had happened to them? Had the opposition of their neighbors made them forget him and give up what he had taught them, or were they still loyal to him and his gospel? To go back and find out would have been perilous to him and probably to them also. So Paul had decided to send his young friend Timothy to seek them out and learn how matters stood. At the same time Paul's other companion, Silvanus, an older, more experienced man, had been sent on a similar errand to the more distant city of Philippi, and Paul, left all alone, had waited anxiously, first at Athens and then at Corinth, for news to come.

When at last it came, it was good news.[2] The Thessalonians had not forgotten Paul. They still stood by him and his gospel, in spite of all that their neighbors were saying against him. They still held their faith in Jesus as the divine Messiah and were eagerly waiting for his return from heaven, to reward and avenge them; and they were eager to see Paul again. So Paul came to write his letter to them. He wanted to tell them of his relief and delight at their faithfulness and loyalty, which filled his heart with gratitude. He wished also to refute some charges against his own work and character which people whom he had antagonized in Thessalonica had been making against him.[3] Then too Paul wished to tell his friends how much he had hoped to reach them, and how when this had proved impossible he had sent one of his two companions to them to find out all that he wished to know, and to give them encouragement and instruction; how he had waited for his messenger's return, and how he had at last come with his welcome news.

But this was not all. Paul saw his opportunity to help his Thessalonian friends with their problems. Some of them were troubled at the death of friends, who would, they feared, thus miss the joy and glory of meeting the Lord Jesus on his return to the earth. Others were perplexed about the time of Jesus' return, and needed to be told not to trouble about it, but to live in constant readiness for it. Others were falling into idleness and dependence because of their confidence that the time was close at hand. Some needed to be reminded of the Christian insistence on purity and unselfishness of life. To all these people Paul sent messages of comfort, counsel, or encouragement, as their needs required. He was already deep in his new work at Corinth, in some respects the most absorbing and exacting he had ever done.[4] Yet he found time to keep in mind his Thessalonian friends and their problems, and to look out for them amid all his distractions at Corinth. Paul did it all, too, with a personal and affectionate tone which shows how wholly he gave his affection to those with whom he worked.

We can imagine how eagerly the brethren at Thessalonica looked for Paul's letter and read and reread it when it came. They evidently put it away among their treasures, for that is probably how it came to be preserved to us. They certainly pondered over and discussed its contents; for before many weeks had passed Paul had to write them again more definitely about some of these things. Something Paul had said or written to them, or something they had read in the Old Testament, had made some of them think that the Day of the Lord had already come. Some of them had given up work, and were content to live in religious contemplation while their richer or more industrious brethren supported them. In their idleness some of them fell into unworthy ways of life and became a nuisance and a scandal to the church.

Paul was greatly stirred by this. He saw that it threatened the good name and the very existence of the church, and he at once wrote them another letter, our Second Thessalonians. It was a popular Jewish idea that in the last days the forces of evil would find embodiment in an individual of the tribe of Dan, who would make an impious attack upon God and his people but would fail and be destroyed by the Messiah. Paul in his letter appeals to this idea and points out that this great enemy has not yet appeared and so the Day of the Lord cannot have come.[5] There is therefore no excuse for giving up the ordinary industry of life. He reminds them of a precept he has given them before: If anyone will not work, give him nothing to eat. Those who refuse to obey this ultimatum are to be practically dropped from the Christian fellowship.

With these two short letters Paul began Christian literature. Before he ceased to teach the churches he wrote more than one-fourth of what is now included in the New Testament. But in these first letters we see the difficulties that already were besetting the small new groups of Christians, and the patience, skill, and boldness with which their founder looked after their development.

SUGGESTIONS FOR STUDY

1. *References:* [1]Phil. 4:15; [2]I Thess. 3:6–8; [3]I Thess. 2:1–12; [4]Acts 18:1, 5; [5]II Thess. 2:1–3.

2. For an account of the founding of the church at Thessalonica read Acts 17:1–15.

3. Note the occasion of I Thess., 3:6–8, and the progress already made by the gospel, 1:7, 8; 2:1.

4. Picture the receipt of I Thessalonians by the Thessalonian Christians, and read it aloud as they must have done in a meeting of the church, using some modern-speech translation.

5. Note Paul's review of his success among them, 1:2–2:1; his vigorous defense of his methods and motives as a missionary, 2:1–12; his account of his feelings and movements after leaving them, 2:17–3:10; his moral teachings, so necessary for gentile converts, 4:1–10; 5:8–23; his commendation of labor and self-support, 4:10–12; the comfort he gives them about the Thessalonian dead, 4:13–18, and his reminder of the unexpectedness of the return of Jesus, 5:1–6.

6. Observe the prayerful and nobly moral tone of the letter, the intense personal affection Paul shows for his con-

verts, 2:7–12, 17; 3:6–10, and the sanity of his practical advice, 4:11, 12; 5:12–14.

7. What facts about Jesus and what expectations about him does the letter reveal? 1:10; 2:15, 19; 4:14–17; 5:9, 10, 23.

8. Read II Thessalonians, noting its marked resemblance to I Thessalonians in many particulars: I Thess. 2:9 and II Thess. 3:8; I Thess. 3:11–13 and II Thess. 2:16, 17; I Thess. 1:1–7 and II Thess. 1:1–4; the sterner attitude toward the idlers, 3:6–15; the very Jewish argument in 2:1–10 that the Lawless One is not yet openly at work and therefore the Day of the Lord cannot have arrived; and the salutation written by Paul's own hand at the close, 3:17, 18.

CHAPTER II

THE LETTER TO THE GALATIANS

Upon returning to the shores of Syria after his long residence in Corinth, Paul had news that greatly disturbed him. An enemy had appeared in his rear. Among the people who had accepted his teaching about Jesus were many in the towns of central Asia Minor—Iconium, Derbe, Lystra, and Antioch. These places lay in what the Romans called Galatia, though that name included also an additional district lying farther north. They were in the region that has in recent years been traversed by the new railway through Asia Minor. Their people had welcomed Paul as an apostle of Christ and had gladly accepted his message of faith, hope and love.

But there had now come among them Christian teachers of Jewish birth, who looked upon the Christianity Paul presented as spurious and dangerous. Who these men were we have no way of knowing, but their idea of Christianity can easily be made out. They believed Jesus to be the completer of the agreement or covenant God had made with Abraham. In order to benefit by his gospel one must be an heir of Abraham, they held, and thus of God's agreement with him; that is, one must be born a Jew or become one by accepting the rite of circumcision and being adopted into the Jewish people.[1]

8

There was certainly some reasonableness in this view. The men who held it were indignant that the Galatians should call themselves Christians without having first been circumcised and having thus acknowledged their adoption into the Jewish nation; and they considered Paul a wholly unauthorized person and no apostle at all, since he was not one of the twelve whom Jesus had called about him in Galilee twenty years before, nor even a representative of theirs. It was evidently the feeling of these new arrivals that the twelve apostles were the sole genuine authorities on Christianity and what might be taught under its name. This claim also seemed reasonable, and it made the Galatian believers wonder what Paul's relation was to these authorized leaders of the church, and why he had given them so imperfect an idea of the gospel. They admitted the justice of the claims of the new missionaries and set about conforming to their demands in order that they might be as good Christians as they knew how to be.

Where Paul first learned of this change in the beliefs of the Galatians is not certain, but very probably it was at Antioch in Syria, to which he returned from Corinth. He wished to proceed as soon as possible to Galatia to straighten matters out in person. For some reason he could not start at once, and so he wrote or dictated a letter in which he did his best to show the Galatian Christians their mistake. This he sent off immediately, probably intending to follow it in person as soon as he could do so.

The letter Paul wrote is the most vigorous and vehement that we have from his pen. It shows Paul to have been a powerful and original thinker, and is the more remarkable as it was written, not as a book or an essay, but simply as a personal letter, intended to save some of his friends from wrong views of religion. In opposition to the claims of the Jewish-Christian teachers from Palestine, he affirms with his very first words that he is an apostle, divinely commissioned, with an authority quite independent of that of the apostles at Jerusalem. This authority Paul bases on his own religious experience and convictions, in which he feels that the Spirit of God speaks to him; and this rightly seems to him the best, and indeed the only, kind of religious authority that really reaches the inner life.

The demand of the newcomers in Galatia that the Christians there should undertake some of the practices of the Jewish law, such as circumcision and the religious observance of certain days,[2] Paul denounces as unreasonable and dangerous. It is dangerous because if acknowledged it will surely bring in after it the necessity of obeying all the rest of the Jewish law, and will reduce the religious life of the Galatians to the tedious observance of countless religious forms.[3] It is unreasonable because even

in the case of Abraham, long before there was any
Jewish law, faith, that is, an attitude of trust in God
and obedience to his will, was the only thing that
made men pleasing to God.[4] It was when the Galatians came into this attitude of trust and dependence upon God that they felt the presence of his
spirit in their hearts as never before, and in this fact
Paul finds evidence of the genuine worth of the
gospel of faith that he has preached to them. The
Law and the life of religious formalism which it
brings with it can never bring this consciousness,
as Paul knows, for he gave it a long trial before giving it up in despair and turning to the gospel of
faith, hope, and love. In a word, the Law makes
men slaves, the Gospel makes them free. This has
been Paul's experience and it is his teaching.

Galatians is in fact a charter of religious freedom.
Its noble ideal of the religious life, so far from being
outgrown, still beckons us forward, as it did those
obscure townsfolk of the Galatian uplands long ago.
Paul knew its dangers, but he knew its promise too,
and saw that for those who would sincerely accept
it, it opened possibilities of spiritual and moral development which could never be reached by the
lower path. The Christian had received the very
Spirit of God. By that he must regulate his life. If
he did so, he would be in no danger of gross and
vulgar sin, but would find freely springing up in his
life the fruits of the spirit: love, joy, peace, long-

suffering, kindness, goodness, faithfulness, meek-
ness, self-control.

This is the ringing message that Paul sent in hot
haste to the Galatians. He usually dictated his
letters to one of his companions, such as Titus or
Tertius, writing only a line or two himself at the
end. And this he probably did in this case, but emphasized it all, with a touch of humor, by writing
his autograph lines in very large letters.[5] But some
have thought that in his haste he wrote this entire
letter with his own hand. It was carried by some
trusty messenger away through the mountains to
the nearest Galatian church and there read to the
assembled brethren. Then they probably sent it on
to the next town where there was a band of believers,
and so it passed from one church to another until
all had heard it. Some perhaps had the foresight to
copy it before it was sent on its way, and so helped
to preserve to later times Paul's first great letter.

SUGGESTIONS FOR STUDY

1. *References:* [1]Gal. 5:2–8; 6:12; [2] Gal. 4:10; [3]Gal. 5:3;
[4]Gal. 3:6–9, 16, 17; [5]Gal. 6:11.

2. Read the account of the founding of the Galatian
churches in Acts 13:13—14:28.

3. Note that Paul calls himself an apostle in the first
words of Galatians as he has not done in Thessalonians.
Why? Notice the occasion of the letter, 1:6, 7; 3:1.

4. Read the letter through continuously, noting the auto-
biographical chapters, 1, 2, in which Paul shows his practical

independence of the Jerusalem leaders; the variety of arguments, chaps. 3, 4, by which Paul shows the folly of seeking salvation through the observance of law; and the stirring call to Christian freedom and life by the spirit which concludes the letter, chaps. 5, 6.

5. Read the letter through again, noting what you consider the particularly fine passages in it.

6. What does Paul mean by the "marks of Jesus," Gal. 6:17? Can these be the scars of such an experience as that related in Acts 14:19, which befell Paul in Galatia, or that in Acts 16:22, 23, which occurred after Paul's second visit to Galatia and before he wrote this letter? Cf. II. Cor. 11:24, 25. The figure refers to the owner's marks which were branded upon slaves.

CHAPTER III

THE FIRST LETTER TO THE CORINTHIANS

Paul had received a letter. Doubtless he received many, but with all his letter-writing we know definitely of only one letter that came to him. He was settled at Ephesus, working at his trade, and very much absorbed in explaining the gospel to everyone whom he could reach in that city and its neighborhood. Ephesus was a thriving center of life and industry, and people from the other cities on the Aegean were constantly coming and going. Among them were many from Corinth, which lay almost directly across from Ephesus, only a few days' sail away. Some of the Corinthian visitors to Ephesus were Christians, and others were acquainted with Paul's Christian friends at Corinth and brought him word of them.

Their news was not encouraging. The Corinthian believers, though they were probably few and humble in station, had divided into parties.[1] Some of them had begun to look down upon Paul as a man of inferior gifts, as compared with the eloquent Apollos, and of insignificant position in the Christian movement as compared with Cephas, that is, Peter. They had perhaps been visited by Jewish-Christian teachers from Jerusalem, for they were beginning to doubt Paul's right to be called an apostle.² Business disputes among them had led to lawsuits between Christian brethren in the pagan courts.³ Worst of all, immoral conduct in the Corinthian church was reported to Paul, for the Corinthians had not yet fully learned that the Christian faith meant a new life of righteousness and love. With all these abuses the very existence of the little church was being endangered.

Paul was already troubled by these reports when three Greeks who had come over from Corinth sought out his lodgings and put into his hand a letter from the Christians of Corinth.⁴ They had been Christians only a little while and had many things to learn. New situations were constantly coming up which they did not know how to meet. They had their social problems. What were they to do about marriage? Should they marry or remain single? Should a woman whose husband had not been converted continue to live with him? When they were invited out to dinner they might have served to them meat that had first been offered in sacrifice in some pagan temple. Was it right to eat such meat and must they inquire about it before they ate it? Questions were arising about their public worship. What part were women to have in it, and how were they to behave and dress? Even the Lord's Supper was leading to excesses in eating and drinking and bringing out inequalities and misunderstandings.

The Corinthians were much interested in spiritual gifts and their comparative worth. Some rated the ecstatic and unintelligible utterance which they called "speaking with tongues" above prophesying or teaching. Moreover, the persons endowed with these gifts were so eager to be heard that the meetings were becoming confused and disorderly.

On the whole the Corinthians were beset with difficulties on all sides, and they wrote to Paul for advice and instruction regarding their problems. He had already written them a short letter about some immoral practices that had appeared among them or had held over from their heathen days.[5] But that letter had not told them enough. They wanted to learn more about the matter it dealt with, and about a variety of other things.

So Paul came to write what we call First Corinthians. No wonder it is so varied and even miscellaneous. Paul has first to set right the bad practices that are creeping into the church—the factions, the lawsuits, the immoralities—and to defend himself against the criticisms that are being circulated at Corinth. He attacks these abuses with the utmost boldness. They must give up their factions. Christ must not be divided. If Paul preached to them a simple gospel, it is because their immaturity required it. And it was such plain preaching, as they now consider it, that converted them to a life of faith. The gross immoralities which Paul has heard of among them ought to make them humble and ashamed instead of boastful. Their lawsuits against one another disclose their unscrupulousness and self-seeking. Unrighteous men, Paul reminds them, will never enter the Kingdom of God.

From these painful matters Paul turns to the questions the Corinthians had asked in their letter.[6] Married people are not to separate, but the unmarried had better remain as they are. The offering of meat to idols is really meaningless and does the meat no harm, yet we have a duty to the consciences of others, and must not give them offense. When we are guests at a dinner, indeed, we should eat what is offered by our host without asking whether it has been offered to an idol. But in our freedom we are to remember to seek the good of one another.

In church meetings good order and modest behavior are to be the rule for both men and women. The Lord's Supper especially is to be observed in a serious and considerate way. More than any spiritual gifts Paul recommends faith, hope, and love as abiding virtues, much to be preferred to the spectacular and temporary endowments in which the Corinthians are so absorbed.

Some of the Corinthians had found difficulty with Paul's teaching about the resurrection, and probably a question about it had been raised in their letter to him. At all events, Paul comes last of all to the resurrection, and defends his belief in it in an impassioned argument, which rises at the end into a paean of triumph.

So far has Paul brought his Corinthian correspondents—from their petty disputes about their favorite preachers to the serene heights of the lyric on love and the vision of the resurrection. It is instructive to see how he has done it. For he has worked each of their principal difficulties through with them, not to any rule or statute, but to some great Christian principle which meets and solves it. Nowhere does Paul appear as a more patient and skilful teacher than in First Corinthians. And nowhere does the early church with its faults and its problems rise before us so plainly and clearly as here. Someone has said that Paul's letters enable us to take the roof off the meeting-places of the early Christians and look inside. More than any other book of the New Testament it is First Corinthians that does this.

SUGGESTIONS FOR STUDY

1. *References:* [1]I Cor. 1:10–12; [2]I Cor. 9:1, 2; [3]I Cor. 6:1–7; [4]I Cor. 7:1; 16:17; [5]I Cor. 5:9; [6]I Cor. 7:1.

2. Note that Paul had written to the Corinthians before, 5:9. Observe the sources of his information about matters in Corinth, 1:11; 7:1, and the occasion of the letter, 7:1.

3. Read I Corinthians through at one sitting, in some modern-speech translation. Note the immaturity of the Corinthian Christians, as illustrated by the evils Paul tries

to correct—factions, fornication, lawsuits, chaps. 1–6. The Corinthians' letter evidently asked about the further topics of the letter, marriage, meats offered to idols, the Lord's Supper, spiritual gifts, and the resurrection, chaps. 7–15.

4. Observe the extraordinary variety of the letter's contents, in contrast to the unity of Galatians.

5. Read chap. 13, the prose poem on love, and note that Paul commends love as superior to the spiritual endowments which the Corinthians so overprize.

6. Consider the faults and perils with which the letter deals, as typical of the experiences of a young gentile church.

7. Notice how Paul works through problems put before him by the Corinthians to great Christian principles of life, 8:13; 13:13; cf. 6:19.

8. Note the beginnings of dissatisfaction with Paul in Corinth, reflected in 1:12, 13; 2:1–5; 3:1–6, 18; 4:1–5, 8–15. What Paul says of the plainness of his language has been strikingly confirmed by the papyrus discoveries of recent years, which show that he uses the informal Greek of everyday life.

CHAPTER IV

THE SECOND LETTER TO THE CORINTHIANS

First Corinthians was a failure. It has been so useful and popular in every other age of Christian history that it is hard to believe that it did not accomplish the main purpose for which it was written.

The factions in the church at Corinth, so far from sinking their differences and blending harmoniously into a unified church life, shifted just enough to unite all who for any reason objected to Paul, and then faced him and each other more rancorously than ever. His letters, they told one another, might put things strongly, but after all he was, when you actually met him, a man of ineffectual speech and insignificant presence.[1] The old doubt of his right to call himself an apostle still prevailed at Corinth. What right had he to set up his authority against that of Peter and the apostles at Jerusalem, who had been personal followers of Jesus in Galilee? If he were indeed the apostle he claimed to be, he would have expected the Corinthians to give him financial support during his stay among them.[2] His failure to do this suggested that he was none too sure of his ground. While a few remained loyal to Paul, the majority of the Corinthians yielded to these views.

News of this state of things was not long in traveling across the Aegean and reaching Paul, and stirred him profoundly. Perhaps he went so far as to visit Corinth and face his accusers in person. But if he did so, he was not successful in meeting their doubts of him and restoring their confidence, and he must have returned to his work at Ephesus in the deepest discouragement. Yet he was in no mood to give up in defeat or to rest under the slanders of his enemies, and he made one final effort in a letter to regain his lost leadership at Corinth. This letter is what we know as the last four chapters of Second Corinthians.

The chief characteristic of Paul's letter is its boldness. So far from apologizing for himself, he boasts and glories in his authority, his endowments, and his achievements. In indignant resentment at their persistent misconstruing of his motives he fairly overwhelms them with a torrent of burning words. His authority, he declares, is quite equal to any demands they can put upon it; as the recognized apostle to the Gentiles he can without stretching his authority exercise it over them, and disobedience to it will bring vengeance when matters are settled up between them. Conscious that he is quite the equal of those "superfine apostles," as he ironically calls them, whom the Corinthians quote against him, he warns the latter against the teaching of such apostolic emissaries.[3] His policy of self-support in Corinth was designed to save him from any suspicion of self-interest and to make the disinterestedness of his work perfectly unmistakable. The false apostles whom they are now following would find still more fault with him had he let the Corinthian church pay his expenses.

Foolish as boasting is, he will for once outboast his opponents. In purity of Jewish descent he is fully their equal, and in point of services, sufferings, and responsibilities as a missionary of Christ he is easily their superior.[4] More than this, in the matter of those ecstatic spiritual experiences, visions and revelations, which the early church considered the very highest credentials, he can boast, though it is not well to do so, of extraordinary ecstasies that he has experienced.

For all this foolish boasting they are responsible. They have forced him to it by their ingratitude. He has shown himself an apostle over and over again at Corinth, but they have not been satisfied with that. Now he is coming to them again, but not to live at their expense. He prefers to spend and to be spent for them; he and his messengers have asked nothing for themselves. He writes all this not for his own sake but for theirs. They must put aside their feuds and factions if they are to remain in Christ. Paul is coming again to Corinth, and this time he will not spare offenders against the peace of the church, but will exert the authority they have denied.

Paul dispatched this letter to Corinth by the hand of Titus. While waiting for news of its effect he busied himself with concluding his work at Ephesus. Days came and went, and it was time for Titus to return, but there was no news of him. Paul's thought went back again and again to the situation and the letter he had written in such distress. Had it been a mistake? He began to think so, and was sorry he had written it.[5] If it did not win the Corinthians, matters would not be the same as before; they would be much worse. If the breach was not healed by the letter, it would be widened. Paul was still full of these anxious thoughts when the time came to leave Ephesus. He had planned to go next to Troas, and now expected Titus to meet him there, but to his great disappointment Titus did not appear.[6] Conditions were favorable for undertaking missionary work in Troas, but Paul's anxiety would not let him stay, and he crossed the Aegean to Macedonia, still hoping to find Titus and learn the result of his mission to Corinth. There at length they met, and to his immense relief Paul learned of his messenger's success.[7] The Corinthians were convinced. Titus and the letter together had shown them their blunder. They realized that Paul was the apostle he claimed to be, and that his course toward

them had been upright and honorable. In a powerful revulsion of feeling they were now directing their
wrath against those who had led them to distrust
and oppose Paul, and especially against one man
who had been the leader of the opposition to him.
They were eager to see Paul again in Corinth, to
assure him of their renewed confidence and affection, and were even a little piqued that he had not
already come.

Paul's relief and satisfaction found expression
in another letter, the fourth and last of which we
know that he wrote to Corinth. It constitutes the
first nine chapters of Second Corinthians. He wishes
to tell the Corinthians, now that they are ready to
hear it, how much the controversy has cost him, and
how great his relief is at the reconciliation. He acknowledges the extraordinary comfort which Titus'
news has given him, coming as it has after the crush-
ing anxiety of those last days at Ephesus. He is
satisfied with their new attitude, only he does not
wish them to misunderstand his continued absence.
He had intended to visit Corinth on his way to
Macedonia, but their relations were then too painful for a personal meeting and he had put it off.
When he leaves Macedonia, however, it will be to
come to Corinth. He refers in a touching way to
the anguish and sorrow in which he wrote his last
letter to them, and to his purpose in writing it.
His chief opponent whom they are now so loud in

condemning must not be too harshly dealt with. Paul is ready to join them in forgiving him.[8]

Paul describes his anxious search for Titus and the relief he felt when at last he met him and heard his good news. He no longer needs to defend himself to the Corinthians, but he does set forth again in a conciliatory tone, his ideals and methods in his ministry. In every part of this letter Paul shows that warm affection for the Corinthians which made his difference with them so painful to him.

Paul had been engaged for some time in organizing among his churches in Asia Minor and Greece the collection of money to be sent back to the Jerusalem Christians as a conciliatory token that the Greek churches felt indebted to them for the gospel. Such a gift Paul evidently hoped might help to reconcile the Jewish Christians of Jerusalem to the rapidly growing Greek wing of the church. In preparation for this the Macedonians have now set a noble example of liberality, and Paul seeks to stimulate them further by his report that the district to which Corinth belongs has had its money ready for a year past. He wishes the Corinthians to show the Macedonians that he has not been mistaken.[9]

It is natural to suppose that this painful chapter in Paul's correspondence with the Corinthians was not put in circulation at once, probably not at all while the men who were involved in it still lived. The Corinthians could hardly have wished to pub-

lish the evidence of their own even temporary disloyalty to Paul, and visitors from other churches
probably had little desire to take home copies of a
correspondence so hotly personal. But when toward the end of the first century the letters of Paul
came to be collected, the bitterness of the old misunderstanding had been forgotten, and anything
that survived from Paul's hand was thought worth
including in the collection. So these last letters to
Corinth were given forth together, but with the letter of reconciliation first, to take the bitterness off
and commend the writing to the reader by the fine
note of comfort with which it begins. Second Corinthians has never rivaled First Corinthians in usefulness and influence, but no letter of Paul throws
more light upon his character and motives. It is in
these last letters to Corinth that we come nearest to
Paul's autobiography.

SUGGESTIONS FOR STUDY

1. *References:* [1]II Cor. 10:10; [2]II Cor. 11:7–9; [3]II Cor.
11:5, 13; [4]II Cor. 11:21–33; [5]II Cor. 2:4; 7:8; [6]II Cor. 2:12,
13; [7] II Cor. 7:5–7; [8]II Cor. 2:5–8; [9]II Cor. 9:1–5.

2. Read chaps. 10–13, noting the painful stage of the
controversy between Paul and the Corinthians reflected in
them.

3. What is the chief point at issue between them? 11:5,
13; 12:11–13; 13:3.

4. Note what Paul's Corinthian critics are saying about
him, 10:1, 3, 10; 11:6, 7.

5. To whom does Paul refer in 12:2, 3?

6. How does this section, chaps. 10–13, fit the description of the third letter to Corinth given in II Cor. 2:2–4; 7:8, 9?

7. Note in contrast to it the tone of harmony and comfort that pervades chaps. 1–9, for example 1:3–7.

8. Note the occasion of this final letter, II Cor. 2:12, 13; 7:6, 7.

9. Observe the increased prominence of the collection for the saints, mentioned in I Cor. 16:1–4, and now again in II Cor., chaps. 8, 9.

10. Read II Corinthians 1–9 through at one sitting, in some modern-speech translation, considering it as the conclusion of the correspondence.

CHAPTER V

THE LETTER TO THE ROMANS

Paul's work in the eastern world was done. For twenty-five years he had now been preaching the gospel in Asia Minor and Greece. His work had begun in Syria and Cilicia, then extended to Cyprus and Galatia, then to Macedonia and Achaea, and finally to Asia, as the Romans called the westernmost province of Asia Minor. In most of these districts Paul had been a pioneer preacher and had addressed himself mainly to Gentiles, that is, Greeks. From Syria to the Adriatic this pioneer work among Greeks had now gone so far that the gospel might be expected to extend from the places already evangelized and soon to permeate the whole East. Already Paul was planning to transfer his work to Spain, where the gospel had not yet penetrated.

Between Paul in Corinth and his prospective field in the far West lay Rome, the center and metropolis of the Empire. Christianity had already found its way to Rome by obscure yet significant ways. Probably Jews and Greeks who had been converted in the East and had later removed to Rome, in search of better business conditions or the larger opportunities of the capital, had first introduced the gospel there and organized little house congregations. The fervor of the early believers was such that every convert was a missionary who spread the good news wherever he traveled. The fact that Christianity was already established in Rome helps us to understand how Paul could think that Alexandria and Cyrene needed him less than Spain, and to realize how many other Christian missionaries were at work at the same time with Paul.

Paul was eager not only to occupy new ground in Spain, but also to visit the Roman Christians on his way and to have a part in shaping a church for which he rightly anticipated an influential future.

One thing stood in the way of these plans. It was the collection for Jerusalem. For some years Paul had been organizing the beneficence of his western churches, not to sustain wider missionary campaigns but to conciliate the original believers in Jerusalem.[1] The primitive Jewish-Christian community seems rather to have resented the violent eagerness with which the Greeks poured into the churches and, as it were, took the Kingdom of God by force. The Jewish Christians were never altogether satisfied with the way in which Paul and his helpers offered the gospel to the Greeks, and the growing strength of the Greek wing of the church increased their suspicion. It had long since been suggested to Paul that this suspicion might be allayed by interesting his Greek converts in supplying the wants of the needy Jewish Christians of Jerusalem,[2]

and he had already done something in that direction.
A more extensive measure of the same sort was now
in active preparation. The gentile churches of four
provinces, Galatia, Asia, Macedonia, and Achaea,
were uniting in it. For nearly two years the Christians of these regions had been setting apart each
week what they could give to this fund, and Second
Corinthians shows how Paul encouraged them to vie
with one another in this charitable work—a hint of
the importance the enterprise had to his mind. This
collection for Jerusalem has especial interest as the
first united financial effort on the part of any considerable section of the ancient church.

The clearest evidence of the importance Paul
attached to this collection, however, is the fact that
he turned away for a time at least from Rome and
Spain in order to carry the money in person to Jerusalem.[3] This can only mean that he felt that the
whole success of his effort would hinge on the interpretation which its bearer put upon it when he delivered the gift there. In the wrong hands it might
altogether fail of its conciliatory purpose; only if its
spiritual significance was tactfully brought out
could it produce the desired effect of reconciling
the Jewish wing of the Christian church to the
gentile.

Compelled by this undertaking to give up for
the time his plan of moving westward, Paul took at
least the first step toward his new western program.

He wrote a letter to the Roman Christians. The letter would at least inform them of his plans and interest, and so prepare the way for his coming. In it too Paul could embody his gospel, and so safeguard the Roman church from the legalistic and Judaistic forms of Christian teaching that had proved so dangerous in the East. And if this Jerusalem journey resulted in his imprisonment or even his death, as he and his friends feared, this might prove his only opportunity of giving to the Romans and through them to the people of the West the heart of his Christian message.

Righteousness is to the mind of Paul, as he reveals his thought in this letter, the universal need. Jews and Greeks are alike in need of it, for neither law nor wisdom can secure it. But the good news is that God has now through Christ revealed the true way to become righteous and so acceptable to him. This is accomplished through faith, which is not intellectual assent to this or that, but a relation of trustful and obedient dependence upon God, such as Abraham long ago exemplified. This relation is fully revealed through Christ, and the new way of righteousness has been confirmed and illumined by his death. Persons who adopt this attitude of faith are freed by it from sin and from the tyranny of the law. The spirit of God now dwells in them and makes them his sons, never to be separated from his love.

In the failure of the Jews to accept the gospel
more than one early Christian thinker found a serious problem. Was God unfaithful to his promises
in his rejection of Israel? Would the Jews never
turn to the gospel? Paul explains the situation as
due to the Jews' want of faith. They are not ready
to enter into the filial relation that Jesus taught
and represented. But their rejection of the gospel
and God's consequent rejection of them are not in
his opinion final. Some day they will turn to the
righteousness of faith.

This setting forth of Christian righteousness is
the longest sustained treatment of a single subject
in the letters of Paul. From it he passes in conclusion to instruct the Roman Christians upon their
practical duties to God, the church, the state, and
society in general. Few things are more striking in
these earliest Christian documents than their constant emphasis upon upright and ethical living. It is
interesting to find Paul urging his Roman brethren
to be loyal citizens, respecting the authority of the
Roman Empire as divinely appointed, and the friend
and ally of the upright man.[4] The event proved that
in this he idealized the Roman state. Yet, taking
the situation as a whole, his counsel was both wise
and sound, for by virtue of it the church, at grim
cost indeed, disarmed and lived down the Empire's
misunderstanding.

The letter to the Romans is often thought of as

the best single expression of Paul's theology. But it is not less remarkable for its picture of himself. In it he appears as the man of comprehensive mind, not alienated from his own people, though he knows that his life is not safe among them, actively concerned for the harmonizing of Greek and Jewish Christianity, yet even while engaged in a last earnest effort to unite the eastern churches, eager to have a hand in shaping the Roman church and to reach out still farther to evangelize Spain. The apostle is never more the statesman-missionary than in the pages of Romans.

Many years after, when the Christians of Ephesus gathered together a collection of the letters of Paul, a short personal letter written by him to Ephesus from Corinth, probably at about the time he wrote Romans, was appended to Romans, perhaps because, while it was hardly important enough to be preserved as a separate letter, yet, as something from the hand of Paul, the Ephesians wished to keep it with the rest. It was written to introduce Phoebe of the church at Cenchreae, near Corinth, to Paul's old friends at Ephesus, whither she was going on some errand.[5] A Christian traveling about the Roman world on business would find in many cities communities of brethren ready to entertain and help him. The value of this, in an age when the inns were often places of evil character, can be imagined. Most of all, Phoebe's letter of introduction

discloses to us the several little house congregations
of which the whole Christian strength of a great city
like Ephesus was made up in those early days when
the church was still in the house.

1. *References:* [1]Rom. 1:15; 15:22–26; [2]Gal. 2:10; [3]Rom.
15:28; [4]Rom. 13:1–7; [5]Rom. 16:1.

2. Note Paul's circumstances and plans at the time of
writing Romans, as bearing upon its occasion, 1:8–15; 15:18–
33.

3. Note the theme of the letter, 1:16, 17.

4. Observe Paul's argument, 1:18—3:20, that Jews and
Greeks are both in need of the salvation he describes.

5. Read 3:21—5:21, considering it as a description and
explanation of this new righteousness.

6. Read chaps. 7, 8, considering them as reflecting Paul's
personal experience in seeking righteousness through the
Jewish law.

7. Read chaps. 9–11, noting the difficulty Paul finds in
the Jews' rejection of the gospel (9:30, 31; 11:1), and his hope
that they will yet accept it.

8. Consider chap. 16: (1) As part of the letter to the
Romans: how can we explain so wide an acquaintance on
Paul's part with Roman Christians before he had visited
Rome? (2) As an independent letter introducing Phoebe to
some nearer church like that at Ephesus: how can we explain
in this case the letter's present position as part of Romans?

9. Why does Romans stand first among the letters of
Paul, although it is far from being the oldest of them?

CHAPTER VI

THE LETTER TO THE PHILIPPIANS

Paul was a prisoner. His liberty was at an end. On the eve of a new missionary campaign in Spain and the West he had been arrested in Jerusalem and after a long detention sent under guard to Rome for trial. At the height of his efficiency the arm of the Roman Empire halted his career and changed the history of western Christianity before it was begun.

It would be difficult to overestimate the bitterness of Paul's disappointment. The great task of preaching the new gospel in western lands must go undone, or be left to men of far less power and vision, while the one man in all the world fittest for the task wore out his years in a dull and meaningless imprisonment. So it seems to us, and so at least at times it must have seemed to Paul.

Yet in his prison Paul had certain compensations. He could at least talk of the gospel to his guards, and through them reach a wider circle with his message. And he could keep in touch with his old friends and even make new ones by means of an occasional letter to Colossae or Philippi.

The first church Paul had founded in Europe was in the Macedonian city of Philippi, and the

Philippians were among his oldest and truest friends. They did not forget him in his imprisonment. Hardly had his guards brought him to Rome when a man arrived from Philippi with funds for Paul's needs and the evident intention of staying with him to the end, whatever it might be. Nothing could have been more loyal or more practical. Ancient prisoners even more than modern ones needed money if their lot was not to be intolerably hard; and the presence at Rome of one more man to supply Paul's wants and do his errands must have been a great convenience to the apostle.

Unfortunately this man fell sick. Rome was never a healthful city, and we can easily imagine that his first summer there may have been too much for the Philippian Epaphroditus. His sickness of course interrupted his usefulness to Paul; indeed, it proved so serious and even dangerous that it greatly added to Paul's anxieties. When at length Epaphroditus recovered it was decided that he ought to return to Philippi, and to explain his return to the Philippians and make fresh acknowledgment of their generous behavior Paul wrote the letter that has immortalized them.

Paul had of course long since reported to the Philippians the arrival of Epaphroditus and acknowledged the gift he had brought. The news of Epaphroditus' illness too had gone back to Philippi, and worry over that fact, and a certain amount of homesickness besides, had added to the misfortunes of Epaphroditus.[1] As these facts put very kindly and sympathetically by Paul come out in the letter, we cannot escape the feeling that what Paul is writing is in part an apology for the return of Epaphroditus, who, the Philippians might well have thought, should not have left Rome as long as Paul had any need of him.[2]

Paul's letter exhibits from the start his cordial understanding with the Philippians. They are his partners in the great gospel enterprise. From the first day of his acquaintance with them they have been so. Again and again in his missionary travels they have sent him money, being the first church of which we have any knowledge which put money into Christian missions. But the Philippians did it quite as much for Paul their friend as for the missionary cause; for, when his missionary activity was interrupted, they continued and increased their gifts. Amid the divisions and differences—with Barnabas, Mark, Peter, the Jerusalem pillars, the Corinthians, the Galatians and their teachers—which attended the career of Paul, it is refreshing to find one church that never misunderstood him, but supported him loyally with men and money when he was at the height of his missionary preaching and when he was shut up in prison; one church that really appreciated Paul, and did itself the lasting honor of giving him its help.

Paul is able to tell the Philippians that his imprisonment has not checked the progress of the gospel preaching in the West. Not only has he been able to reach with his message many in the Praetorian guard and in that vast establishment of slaves, freedmen, and persons of every station known as the household of Caesar, but the very fact that he is in prison for his faith has given what little preaching he can still do added power, and inspired other Christians to preach more earnestly than ever. On the other hand, preachers of different views of Christianity have been spurred to new exertions now that their great opponent is off the field. So Paul's imprisonment is really furthering the preaching of the gospel, and he comforts himself in his inactivity with this reflection.

The Philippians are of course anxious to know what Paul's prospects are for a speedy trial and acquittal. He can only assure them of his own serenity and resignation. If he is to die and be with Christ, he is more than ready; but if there is still work for him to do for them and others, as he is confident there is, he will be with them again to help and cheer them. Meantime he plans to send Timothy to them to learn how they are, and he hopes shortly to be able to come himself. It would seem that while Paul's situation is still decidedly serious it is not altogether desperate.

With these references to his own prospects and the progress of the gospel in Rome, Paul combines a great deal of practical instruction. The Philippians are to cultivate joy, harmony, unselfishness, and love. In the midst of his letter[3] some chance event or sudden recollection brings to his mind the peril they are in from the ultra-Jewish Christian teachers who have so disturbed his work in Galatia and elsewhere, and he prolongs his letter to warn the Philippians against them.

Or it may be that Philippians as we have it combines two letters, one warning them vehemently against the Judaizers, and acknowledging the coming of Epaphroditus with their gift (3:2—4:23), the other, urging them to be harmonious and unselfish, and sending Epaphroditus back to them after his illness (1:1—3:1).

Paul must have had occasion to write to the Philippians at least four times before Epaphroditus carried this letter back to them. Perhaps those earlier letters were less full and intimate, confining themselves closely to the business with which they dealt. Or perhaps it was the very fact that these were the last letters they ever received from Paul that made the Philippian church preserve and prize them. For out of his narrow prison and his own hard experience Paul had sent them one of his greatest expressions of the principle of the Christian life: "Brethren, whatsoever things are true, honorable,

just, pure . . . . think on these things . . . . and
the God of peace shall be with you."

SUGGESTIONS FOR STUDY

1. *References:* [1]Phil. 2:26; [2]Phil. 2:25, 29, 30; [3]Phil. 3:2.

2. Read the story of the founding of the Philippian
church, Acts 16:11-40.

3. On what occasions did Paul probably write to the
Philippians? Cf. 4:15, 16; II Cor. 11:9; Phil. 2:25; 4:10, 18.

4. Is 3:1 a reference to a former letter?

5. For Paul's experiences since writing to the Romans
cf. Acts 20:4—28:28.

6. What effect had Paul's imprisonment had on the
preaching of the gospel? Cf. 1:12-17.

7. How does Paul view the propagation of other types of
Christian teaching? Cf. 1:18; 3:2-6.

8. Consider whether this letter is less logically organized
than Romans, Galatians, or I Corinthians. How do you explain its informality of structure? Try reading it as two letters, 3:2—4:23 and 1:1—3:1. With 3:2-9 compare the
first part of Galatians after the salutation, Gal. 1:6-14.

9. Notice the type of Christian living it commends, 2:1-
18.

10. Do we know of any other church which helped Paul
with money for his own expenses besides that at Phillipi?
How often did the Philippians do this? Cf. 4:15-18; II Cor.
11:9

11. What does the letter show as to Paul's own attitude
toward his imprisonment and possible execution?

CHAPTER VII

THE LETTERS TO PHILEMON, TO THE COLOSSIANS, AND TO THE EPHESIANS

Of the many letters Paul must have written, only one that is purely personal has come down to us. It was sent by the hand of a runaway slave to his master, to whom Paul was sending him back.

During Paul's imprisonment at Rome he had become acquainted with a young man named Onesimus, who under his influence had become a Christian. In the course of their acquaintance Paul had learned his story. He was a slave and had belonged to a certain Philemon, a resident of Colossae, or the adjacent town of Laodicea, and had run away from his master, probably taking with him in his flight money or valuables belonging to Philemon. He had found his way to Rome and so had been brought by a strange providence within the reach of Paul's influence.

Paul's belief in the speedy return of Jesus made him attach little importance to freedom or servitude. He prevailed upon the slave to return to his master, and sent by him a letter to Philemon, whom he knew, at least by reputation, as a leading Christian of that region. He asks Philemon to receive Onesimus, now his brother in Christ, as he would

receive Paul himself, and if Onesimus is in Philemon's debt for something he may have stolen from
him, Paul undertakes to be personally responsible
for it. Having thus prepared the way for a reconciliation between Onesimus and his master, Paul asks
Philemon to prepare to entertain the writer himself, as he hopes soon to be released, and to revisit
Asia.

While we may wonder at Paul's returning a runaway slave to his master and thus countenancing
human slavery, it is noteworthy that he sends him
back no longer as a slave, but more than a slave,
a beloved brother. It was at the spirit of slavery,
not at the form of the institution, that Paul struck
in this shortest of his letters.

The letter to Philemon was not the only one
that Paul sent to Colossae at this time. There had
appeared in Rome a man named Epaphras, who had
been a Christian worker in Colossae and the neighboring cities of Laodicea and Hierapolis.[1] It was
probably through him that Paul heard that some
of the Colossians had begun to think that a higher
stage of Christian experience could be attained by
worship of certain angelic beings and communion
with them than by mere faith in Christ. They recognized the value of communion with Christ, but
only as an elementary stage in this mystic initiation
which they claimed to enjoy. It was only through
communion with these beings or principles, they

held, that one could rise to an experience of the divine fulness and so achieve the highest religious development. The advocates of this strange view were further distinguished by their scrupulous abstinence from certain articles of food and by their religious observance of certain days—Sabbaths, New Moons, and feasts. Their movement threatened not only to divide the Colossian church, by creating within it a caste or clique which held itself above its brethren, but to reduce Jesus from his true position in Christian experience to one subordinate to that of the imaginary beings of the Colossian speculations.

Paul had never visited Colossae. But his interest in Epaphras and in all Greek or gentile churches led him to undertake to correct the mistake of the Colossians. Still a prisoner at Rome, he could not visit Colossae and instruct the Christians there in person, but he could write a letter and send it to them by one of his helpers, who was also to conduct Onesimus back to his master Philemon.

Paul begins by mentioning the good report of the Colossian church which has reached him, and expressing his deep interest in its members. He proceeds to tell them of the ideal of spiritual development which he has for them, and takes occasion in connection with it to show them the pre-eminent place of Christ in relation to the church. In him is to be found all that divine fulness that some of them have been seeking in fanciful speculations. This is the gospel of which Paul has been a minister, especially to Gentiles like themselves. He wishes them to realize his interest in them and in their neighbors at Laodicea,[2] and his earnest desire that they may find in Christ the satisfaction of all their religious yearnings and aspirations.

As for the theosophic ideas which are being taught among them, Paul warns the Colossians not to be misled into trying to combine these with faith in Christ. In Christ all the divine fulness is to be found. They have no need to seek it elsewhere. The ascetic and formal practices, "Handle not, nor taste, nor touch," which are becoming fashionable at Colossae, are likewise without religious value and foreign to Christianity.

Over against these futile religious ideas and practices, Paul urges the Colossians to seek the things that are above. They are to live true and upright lives, as people chosen of God should do. The peace of Christ must rule in their hearts. Wives, husbands, children, fathers, slaves, and masters all have their special ways of service, but everything is to be done in the name of the Lord Jesus.

Paul says little about the state of his case. Tychicus, who takes the letter to them, is to tell them about that. An interesting group of his friends is gathered about him in Rome, and in closing the letter he adds their salutations to his own. Epaphras, the founder of their church, Mark, the cousin of Barnabas, and Luke, whom Paul here calls the "beloved physician," are among the number. Paul sends an earnest exhortation to Archippus, whom he speaks of as though he were at Laodicea, and asks the Colossians to let the church in the neighboring town of Laodicea read this letter, and to find an opportunity to read a letter he is sending to Laodicea.[3]

What has become of this Laodicean letter? It is very likely what we know as Philemon, which was addressed not only to Philemon but to the church that met at his house, including Archippus, who was evidently the minister of it. But the way in which Archippus is spoken of in Colossians shows that he was not a Colossian but a Laodicean.

Years after, when the publication of the Acts had aroused new interest in Paul, and his letters were being collected, a general letter to all Christians was written by some gifted and devoted follower of Paul, to introduce the collected letters to the churches everywhere, and strike the great note of unity in Christ which the times so demanded. The letter sought to make the churches feel that these several messages to the Romans, Corinthians, or Galatians were in reality for all the churches, and thus put the collected letters, some of which taken by themselves were fire-brands of controversy, into step with the new spirit of unity. The old dividing wall was broken down. There was one Lord, one faith, one baptism. They were all one great spiritual fellowship in their union with Christ. Every spiritual blessing, the writer tells his readers, is theirs in Christ. Through him they are adopted by God as sons. Redemption and forgiveness and the gift of the Holy Spirit they receive through Christ. He would have them realize the greatness and richness of the Christian salvation which God has wrought in Christ, whom he has made supreme. To this thought of the supremacy of Christ, he comes back repeatedly in the letter. He is deeply concerned to have them know in all its vast proportions—breadth and length and height and depth —the love of Christ, through which alone the human spirit can rise into the fulness of God.

Paul appears as one especially commissioned to the Greek world,[4] and the readers are referred to his other letters for a fuller account of his message. It is through Christ that the old separation of Jews from Greeks has been brought to an end, and the same great religious possibilities opened before both. As followers of Christ they must put away the old heathen ways and live pure, true, and Christlike lives. Wives and husbands, children and parents, slaves and masters are shown how they may find in the Christian life the elevation and perfection of these relationships.

Thus what we know as Ephesians was really the first Christian encyclical, and served to introduce to the churches everywhere the first collection of Paul's letters, which were destined to have so much greater influence than when they lay scattered and almost forgotten in the church chests of the generation in which they were written. But this was long after Tychicus and Onesimus journeyed eastward carrying Paul's two letters, one for the Christian brothers at Colossae, and one which Onesimus must with no little trepidation have presented at the door of his old master, Philemon.

SUGGESTIONS FOR STUDY

1. *References:* [1]Col. 1:7, 8; [2]Col. 2:1; [3]Col. 4:16; [4]Eph. 3:1-4.

2. Read the letter to Philemon aloud, and imagine how that Christian gentleman, offended at the conduct of his slave, but full of love and respect for Paul, his friend and teacher, would feel and act toward Onesimus.

3. Note the letter's picture of primitive church life and the light it throws on Paul's character and on his attitude to slavery.

4. Compare the persons mentioned in Philem., vss. 1-3, 10, 23, 24, with those mentioned in Col. 1:1, 2; 4:7-17.

5. What are the ideas and practices criticized in Col., chap. 2?

6. What connection had Paul had with the Colossians, and how did he know of conditions among them? Cf. Col. 2:1; 1:3-8.

7. Note the resemblance of Ephesians to Colossians, comparing, e.g., the injunctions to wives, husbands, children,

fathers, servants, and masters in Col. 3:18—4:1 with Eph. 5:22—6:9.

8. Does Eph. 3:2 sound as though it were written to Paul's old friends at Ephesus? Cf. Acts, chap. 19, and 20:17-38.

9. With the impersonal tone of Ephesians contrast Rom., chap. 16, with its numerous personal references and messages. Consider whether such messages would be likely to occur in a letter sent by Paul to the Ephesians alone.

10. To what letters does Eph. 3:3, 4 refer?

11. How far was this new development in Paul's thought of Christ due to the problems which had arisen among the Christians of Asia and which Paul had to meet?

CHAPTER VIII

THE GOSPEL ACCORDING TO MARK

Peter was dead. The impulsive apostle who had followed Jesus about Galilee had lived to share in the world-wide gentile mission and had met his death in Rome. With him the chief link the Roman church had had with the earthly ministry of Jesus was gone. Western Christianity had lost its one great human document for the life of Jesus.

The familiar stories and reminiscences of Jesus' words and doings would no longer be heard from the lips of the chief apostle. East and west alike had heard them, but in the restless activity of the gentile mission, and especially in the general expectation of Jesus' speedy return, no one had thought to take them down. And so with Peter a priceless treasure of memorabilia of Jesus passed forever from the world.

But there still lived in Rome a younger man who had for some time attended the old apostle, and who, when Peter preached in his native Aramaic to little companies of Roman Christians, had stood at his side to translate his words into the Greek speech of his hearers. His name was Mark. In his youth he had gone with Paul and Barnabas on their first missionary journey to Cyprus, but

had disappointed and even offended Paul by with-
drawing from the party when they had landed in
Pamphylia and proposed to push on into the very
center of Asia Minor.[1] He had afterward gone a
second time to Cyprus with Barnabas, to whom he
was closely related. Through the years that had
passed since then he had probably kept in close
touch with the Christian leaders at Antioch and at
Jerusalem, where his mother's house had been from
the first a center for the Christian community. It
was probably as Peter's companion that he had
made his way at length to Rome, and there until
Peter's martyrdom had served the old apostle as his
interpreter.

Mark saw at once the great loss the churches
would sustain if Peter's recollections of Jesus perished, and at the same time he saw a way to preserve at least the best part of them for the comfort
and instruction of the Roman believers. He had become so familiar with Peter's preaching, through his
practice of translating it, that it was possible for
him to remember and write down much that Peter
had been wont to tell about his walks and talks
with Jesus in Galilee and Jerusalem, more than
thirty years before.

In this way Mark came to write what we call
the Gospel of Mark. But Mark did not call it his
Gospel; indeed it is not certain that he called it a
gospel at all; and if he had thought of naming its

author he would quite certainly have called it Peter's
work rather than his own. But the order and the
Greek dress of the Gospel are the work of Mark,
however much he is indebted to his memory of
Peter's sermons for the facts that he reports.

In the selection of what he should record, Mark
was doubtless often influenced by the conditions
and needs of the Roman Christians for whom he
wrote. But it is Peter's picture of Jesus that he
preserves, not of course just as Peter would have
drawn it, yet with an oriental skill in story-telling
which may be Peter's own. We see Jesus drawn by
John's preaching from his home among the hills of
Galilee, and accepting baptism at John's hands,
and then immediately possessed with the Spirit of
God and filled with a divine sense of his commission
as God's anointed to establish God's Kingdom in
the world. Yet he is silent until John's arrest and
imprisonment, and only when John's work is thus
cut short does he begin preaching in Galilee.[2]
Marvelous cures accompany his preaching, and the
Galileans soon throng about him wherever he goes.
His freedom in dealing not only with Pharisaic
tradition but also with the precepts of the Law
itself soon brings him into conflict with the Pharisees
and their increasing opposition before long threatens
his life. After two or three withdrawals from Galilee
in search of security or leisure to plan his course,
Jesus at length declares to his disciples his purpose

of going up to Jerusalem to the springtime feast of
the Passover. He warns them that the movement
will cost him his life, but declares that God will after
all save him and raise him up. Bewildered and
alarmed they follow him through Peraea up to Jerusalem, which he enters in triumph, now for the first
time declaring himself the Messiah by riding into
the city in the way in which Zechariah had said
the Messiah would enter it.[3] Jesus boldly enters the
temple and drives out of its courts the privileged
dealers in sacrificial victims who had made it their
market-place. The Sadducees, who control the temple and profit by these abuses, on the night of the
Passover have him arrested, and after hasty examinations before Jewish and Roman authorities
hurry him the next morning to execution. Up to the
very hour of his arrest, Jesus does not give up all
hope of succeeding in Jerusalem and winning the
nation to his teaching of the presence of the Kingdom of God on the earth.[4] The book more than
once predicts his resurrection; and in its complete
form it doubtless contained a brief account of his
appearance to the two Marys and Salome after his
burial; but it had by the beginning of the second
century lost its original ending, and while two conclusions have been used in different manuscripts to
complete it, the original one, probably only ten or
twelve lines long, has never been certainly restored.

Informal and unambitious as Mark's gospel narrative is, and lightly as it was esteemed in the ancient church, in comparison with the richer works of Matthew and Luke, no more convincing or dramatic account has been written of the sublime and heroic effort of Jesus to execute the greatest task ever conceived by man—to set up the Kingdom of God on earth.

SUGGESTIONS FOR STUDY

1. *References:* [1]Acts 13:13; 15:37–40; [2]Mark 1:14; [3]Zech. 9:9; [4]Mark 14:34–36.

2. Read the Gospel of Mark through continuously, in some modern translation, noting that it consists for the most part of short units of narrative embodying some crisp saying of Jesus.

3. Judging from Mark alone, how much time would you say its action covered?

4. Observe the expectation of a reappearance of Jesus in Galilee that appears in the Gospel (14:28; 16:7), but is not satisfied in the present conclusion, 16:9–20.

5. Consider how welcome this Gospel must have been to Christians who had before had no written record of Jesus' life or ministry.

6. Is it probable that Peter, in the selection of what he should relate about Jesus in his sermons, was influenced by the needs and problems of his hearers?

7. Is it probable that Mark was guided in part in the choice of what he should include in his Gospel by the situation and conditions of the Roman Christians?

8. How long would it have taken Jesus to utter those sayings of his which Mark preserves?

9. Note the large part played by wonders of healing, feeding, etc., in Mark, and the usually beneficent character of these.

10. What wonders recorded in the Old Testament are most like those of Jesus which Mark reports? Cf. I Kings, chap. 17—II Kings, chap. 2; II Kings, chaps. 2–13.

11. Consider whether the marvelous is peculiar to the New Testament or whether it appears in contemporary Greco-Roman literature—Suetonius, Tacitus, etc.—as well.

12. Do you find much theology in Mark?

13. Does Mark regard Jesus as the Christ? Does Jesus so describe himself in this Gospel? What does he mean by "Son of Man"?

CHAPTER IX

THE GOSPEL ACCORDING TO MATTHEW

The Christian movement had failed in its first campaign. The nation in which it had arisen and to which its founder belonged had disowned it. It was as though the Israelites had refused Moses. This was the more staggering because the gospel had been represented by Jesus' early followers as the crown and completion of Judaism. Jesus was to be the Jewish Messiah, through whom the nation's high hopes of spiritual triumph were to be realized. But the Jews had refused to recognize in him the long-expected deliverer, and had disclaimed his gospel. Who was right? The prophets had anticipated a redeemed and glorified nation, but the nation had refused to be redeemed and glorified by such a Messiah. The divine program had broken down.

Yet the gospel was not failing. Among the Greeks of the Roman Empire it was having large and increasing success. Strangers were taking the places which the prophets had expected would be occupied by their own Jewish countrymen. The church was rapidly becoming a Greek affair. The Gentiles had readily accepted the Messiah and made him their own. To a Christian thinker of Jewish training this only increased the difficulty of the problem. For how could the messiahship of Jesus be harmonized with the nation's rejection of him? The prophets had associated the messianic deliverer with the redeemed nation, but the event of history had disappointed this hope. What did it mean? Were the prophets wrong, or was Jesus not the Messiah? Paul had seen the difficulty, and in writing to the Romans had proposed a solution. It was in effect that the Jews would ultimately turn to the gospel, and so all Israel would be saved. Yet since the writing of Romans the breach between Jews and Christians had widened, and Paul's solution seemed more improbable than ever.

But an event had now happened which put a new aspect on the matter. Jerusalem had fallen. The downfall of the Jewish nation put into the hand of the evangelist the key to the mystery. Jesus was the Messiah of the prophets. He had offered the Kingdom of Heaven to the Jews, finally presenting himself as Messiah before the assembled nation in its capital at its great annual feast. Misled by its religious leaders, the nation had rejected him and driven him to his death. But in this rejection it had condemned itself. God had rejected Israel and the kingdom it had disowned had been given to the nations. In the fall of Jerusalem the evangelist saw the punishment of the Jewish nation for its rejection of the Messiah, and in this fact the proof that the gospel was intended for all nations.

The vehicle for this trenchant and timely philosophy of early Christian history was to be a book. It may be called the first book of Christian literature, for Paul's writings, great as they are, are letters, not books, and Mark for all its value is hardly to be dignified as a book, in the sense of a conscious literary creation. This book was to be a life of the Messiah, which should articulate the gospel with the Jewish scriptures and legitimize the Christian movement. For this purpose a variety of materials lay ready to the evangelist's hand. The narrative we know as Mark was familiar to him. He had also a collection of Jesus' sayings which may have borne the name of the apostle Matthew, and one or two other primitive documents of mingled discourse and incident. The mere possession of these partial and unrelated writings was in itself a challenge to harmonize and even combine them, just as our Four Gospels have ever since their origin invited the harmonist and the biographer.

With a freedom and a skill that are alike surprising, the evangelist has wrought these materials into the first life of Christ. Perhaps it might better be called the first historic apology for universal Christianity. For it is a biography with a purpose. Jesus, though legally descended from Abraham through the royal line of David, is really begotten of the Holy Spirit, a symbol at once of his sinlessness and his sonship. Divinely acknowledged as Messiah at his baptism, and victorious over Satan in the temptation conflict, he declares his message in a series of great sermons, setting forth in each some notable aspect of the Kingdom of Heaven. In the first of these, the Sermon on the Mount, Jesus demands of those who would enter the new Kingdom a righteousness higher than that based by the scribes upon the Jewish law, and he follows this bold demand with a series of prophetic and messianic acts which show his right to make it. The Jewish leaders are unconvinced and quickly become hostile. His nearest disciples at length recognize in him the Messiah, and he welcomes this expression of their faith.[1] Soon afterward they gain a new idea of the spiritual and prophetic character of his messiahship through the transfiguration experience, in which they see him associated with Moses and Elijah, the great prophetic molders of the Jewish religion.

Already foreseeing the fatal end of his work, Jesus yet continues to preach in Galilee, and at length sets out for Jerusalem to put the nation to the supreme test of accepting or refusing his message. They refuse it, and he predicts the nation's doom in consequence. The Kingdom of God shall be taken away from them and given to a nation that brings forth the fruits thereof.[2] The last discourses denounce the wickedness and hypocrisy of the nation's religious leaders, and pronounce the

doom of the city and nation, to be followed shortly
by the triumphant return of the Messiah in judgment. The Jewish leaders, offended at his claims of
authority, cause his arrest and execution. Yet on
the third day he reappears to some women of the
disciples' company, and afterward to the disciples
on a mountain in Galilee, when he charges them to
carry his gospel to all the nations.

Jesus had expressly confined his own work and
that of his disciples, during his life, to the Jews, but
since they had refused the gospel, his last command
to his followers was to offer it henceforth to all mankind, and the curtain falls on the gospel of Matthew
leaving Jesus an abiding presence with his disciples.

The Jewish war of 66–70 A.D., culminating in
the fall of Jerusalem and the destruction of the last
vestige of Jewish national life, must have brought
what Jesus had said of these things powerfully before his followers' minds, and shown them a welcome solution for the problem that perplexed them.
Jesus had not come to destroy Law or prophets;
his work and its fortunes stood in close relation with
them. But as between the Jewish Messiah and the
Jewish nation, the verdict of history had gone for
the Messiah and against the nation, for the nation
had already perished while he was coming to be
worshiped all over the Greek world.

The obviousness of this solution to our minds
is simply an evidence of the evangelist's success in

grappling with the problem; for we owe to him the
solution that seems so simple and complete. Few
any longer stop to think that a triumphant Messiah apart from a triumphant nation is hardly hinted
at in the Old Testament. In this as in other respects the success of the book was early and lasting. As a life of the Messiah it swept aside all the
partial documents its author had used as his sources.
Most of them soon perished—among them the Sayings attributed to Matthew the apostle—probably
because the evangelist had wrought into his book
everything of evident worth that they contained.
Even what we call the Gospel of Mark seems by the
narrowest margin to have escaped destruction
through neglect, and its escape is the more to be
wondered at since practically all that it offered to the
religious life of the early church had been taken up
into this new life of Christ.

For the probably Jewish-Christian circle for
which it was written the new book performed a
threefold task. It solved, by its philosophy of Christian history, their most serious intellectual problem.
It harmonized and unified their diverse materials
relating to Jesus' life and teaching. And it did these
things with an intuitive sense for religious values
that has given it its unique position ever since.
Forty years after it was written it was quoted at
Antioch as "the Gospel," being probably the first
book to bear that name. Twenty years later, when

the Ephesian leaders for some reason put together the Four Gospels, the first place among them was given to it, and its name was extended to the whole group. A new designation had therefore to be found for it, and it was distinguished as "according to Matthew," probably in recognition of that apostolic record on which it was believed to be based. Of its actual author, however, we know only that he was a Jewish Christian of insight and devotion, who preferred to remain unknown, and cared only to exalt the figure of Jesus, the Son of Man and the Son of God.

SUGGESTIONS FOR STUDY

1. *References:* [1]Matt. 16:15–17; [2]Matt. 21:43.

2. In what respects is the scope of Matthew wider than that of Mark?

3. Note the great discourses characteristic of Matt., chaps. 5–7, 10, 13, 18, 23, 24–25.

4. Note that practically all of Mark (all but perhaps 40 verses) is taken over into Matthew. Can you think of any reason for Matthew's omitting Mark 7:3, 4; 8:22–26; 12:32–34?

5. Compare Matt. 16:13–20 with Mark 8:27–30, noting how Jesus' reticence about his messiahship disappears in Matthew.

6. Compare Matt. 21:19 with Mark 11:20. What is the effect of Matthew's way of telling the story?

7. Notice the repeated emphasis on the fulfilment of prophecy, 1:22; 2:15, 17, 23; 4:14; 8:17; 12:17; 13:35; 21:4; 26:56; 27:9. How does this relate to the purposes of the Gospel?

8. Notice the Beatitudes, the Lord's Prayer, and the great parables of Matthew.

9. Consider whether Matthew is richer than Mark (1) theologically, (2) historically, (3) religiously.

10. Read the gospel through at one sitting, in some modern-speech translation.

CHAPTER X

THE GOSPEL ACCORDING TO LUKE

The acts and sayings of Jesus seem from the earliest times to have been taught by Christian missionaries to their converts, and by these in turn to those who afterward became Christians. Paul reminds the Corinthians how he had delivered unto them what he had himself received as to the Last Supper,[1] and the death, burial, and resurrection of Jesus.[2] Paul had been taught these things after his conversion, and he was accustomed to tell them to his converts. In this way the principal facts of what we call the gospel story became known to all Christian believers.

But the story was not always the same. Scores of missionaries were at work about the eastern Mediterranean, but not all of them had been taught the gospel story by Paul or by the men who had taught him. The Christians who fled from Judaea when the persecution in connection with Stephen's work arose, and who carried the gospel into various parts of the eastern world, probably did not tell their converts precisely the same series of acts and sayings of Jesus. After these early missionaries had left Judaea, new stories and sayings about Jesus' work must have come out as the value of such mem-

ories became more evident. Here and there people
took the trouble to write down these stories for
their own instruction and enjoyment or for use in
their missionary work. Fifty years after Jesus' death
there had in these ways arisen a variety of partial
accounts of his birth, his ministry, and his death
and resurrection, which to a thoughtful mind must
have been very perplexing.

It was this perplexity that led Paul's friend
Luke, a Greek physician living somewhere on the
shores of the Aegean Sea, to write his Gospel. With
this confusion of partial narratives and oral tradition intelligent Greek Christians hardly knew what
to believe about the life and teaching of Jesus. One
such at least, a certain Theophilus, a man of position and intelligence, was a friend of Luke's, and
perhaps suggested to him his perplexity and what
ought to be done to relieve it. For him and for the
growing class of intelligent Christian people Luke
undertook to bring together into one comprehensive and orderly record what was most valuable in
the tradition and narratives which had sprung up
in various parts of the world.[3]

Luke traces the ancestry of Jesus not simply to
David and Abraham, but back to Adam the son of
God, thus emphasizing his human nature more than
his Jewish blood, and preparing the way for his later
emphasis on the universal elements in Jesus' ministry. At the same time he declares Jesus to be in a

special and immediate sense the child of the Holy
Spirit. The consciousness that he is God's son at-
tends Jesus even in his youth, when after a visit to
Jerusalem he lingers in the temple, calling it his
Father's house.[4] At the very outset of his ministry
Jesus appears in the synagogue at Nazareth and
declares that Isaiah's prophecy of a Messiah with
good tidings for the poor and wretched is fulfilled
in him.[5] In the spirit of this prophecy Jesus, though
rejected by his townspeople, goes to Capernaum and
by his cures and teaching achieves an immediate
success. Four fishermen of the neighborhood become his followers. He goes about Galilee teaching
the people and healing the sick and demon-possessed.
His disregard of scribal precepts and his claim that
he has power to forgive sins offend the Pharisees,
and they begin to plot against him. He calls twelve
men to him to be his apostles, and in a great sermon
explains to his disciples the moral spirit which
should govern their lives.[6] Accompanied by the
Twelve he continues to travel about Galilee, teaching and healing, and even restoring dead persons
to life. The Twelve, who have now seen something
of his work and spirit, are sent forth through the
country to heal the sick and cast out demons and
to proclaim the coming of the Kingdom of God.

On their return Jesus feeds a multitude with a
few loaves, and afterward asks the disciples who
the people think him to be. They give various an-

swers, but Peter pronounces him the Messiah. Jesus
charges them to keep this to themselves, and tells
them that rejection and death lie before him, but
that the Kingdom of God will soon come. The
transfiguration gives his closest intimates a better
idea of the kind of Messiah he is to be, and he again
foretells his death and resurrection.

At length Jesus sets forth on the momentous
journey to Jerusalem, sending messengers before
him to make ready for his coming in the villages
through which he is to pass.[7] Teaching and healing
as he goes, he is more than once entertained by
Pharisees, and on one occasion is warned by them
of the danger threatening him from Herod; but he
only grows more earnest in his warnings against
them. In the parables of the Lost Sheep, the Lost
Coin, and the Lost Son, he defends his course in
associating with sinners, that is, persons who did
not fully observe the Jewish law. As he approaches
Jerusalem, he reminds the Twelve that death and
resurrection await him there. Reaching the city he
enters it in messianic state amid the acclamations
of the people. He goes into the temple and clears
it of the traders who use its courts for their traffic.
The Jewish leaders protest and demand his authority for this act. His answer does not satisfy them
and they prepare to kill him. But he teaches daily
in the temple, already crowded with those who had
come up for the feast of the Passover, and in the

parable of the Vineyard he sets forth the peril of the nation in rejecting and destroying him. After a series of clashes with Pharisees and Sadducees, he foretells the destruction of Jerusalem, the coming of the Kingdom of God, and the return of the Messiah on the clouds of heaven. He eats the Passover supper with his disciples, and immediately after is arrested in a garden on the Mount of Olives. After a series of examinations before the high priest, the Jewish council, the Roman procurator, and Herod, the tetrarch of Galilee, who is in the city, and although neither Pilate nor Herod find him guilty, he is condemned and crucified. Immediately after the Sabbath, however, he appears, first to two of his disciples, then to the eleven apostles and their company in Jerusalem. He reminds them that all this has been in accord with the Scriptures, declares that repentance and forgiveness are to be preached in his name to all nations, and is taken from them into heaven.

More than any other evangelist Luke claims to have a historical purpose. His aim is to acquaint himself with all the sources, oral and written, for his work, and to set forth in order the results he ascertains. It is this historical aim that leads him to fix the date of Jesus' birth by the Augustan enrolment under Quirinius, to date the appearance of John the Baptist in the fifteenth year of Tiberius, and to tell us how old Jesus was when he began to preach. He is the only writer in the New Testament who sees the need of such particulars and tries to supply them. Indeed we are not to think of the Gospel of Luke as a mere gospel; it is really the first volume of the history of the rise of Greek Christianity, of which Acts is Volume II.

Luke is evidently a Greek writing for Greeks. The fate of the Jewish nation interests him less than the universal elements in Jesus' work. The stories of Jesus seeking hospitality in a Samaritan village, of the good Samaritan, and of the grateful Samaritan leper, suggest Jesus' interest in people outside his own nation and foreshadow the universal mission. Luke's Gospel shows a peculiar social and humanitarian interest; the poor and unfortunate appear in it as the especial objects of Jesus' sympathy and help. A few echoes of medical language in the Gospel to remind us that Luke was, as Paul calls him in Colossians, "the beloved physician."[8]

SUGGESTIONS FOR STUDY

1. *References:* [1]I Cor. 11:23; [2]I Cor. 15:3–7; [3]Luke 1:1–4; [4]Luke 2:49; [5]Luke 4:16–21; [6]Luke 6:20–49; [7]Luke 10:1; [8]Col. 4:14.

2. Read Luke 1:1–4, noting what is implied as to previous narratives about Jesus. Observe that this is not simply a preface to Luke, but to the two-volume work Luke-Acts.

3. Notice Luke's use of the first person in his preface, in contrast to the anonymity of Matthew and Mark.

4. Notice his historical purpose (cf. 1:5; 2:1, 2; 3:1, 2, 23), the sources he has, and how he means to use them.

5. Why did the existence of numerous accounts lead Luke to write another one?

6. Although Luke seems clearly to have used Mark, he omits one account of the feeding of the multitudes and the account of the cursing of the fig tree. Why does he do this?

7. Notice that, in addition to the infancy narrative (chaps. 1, 2), two considerable parts of Luke (6:20—8:3; 9:51—18:14) contain no material found in Mark.

8. Notice the remarkable parables of Luke: the Lost Sheep, the Lost Coin, the Lost Son (chap. 15), the Pharisee and the Publican (18:9-14).

9. The passage from Isaiah which appears in Luke 4:18, 19 has been called the frontispiece of the Gospel of Luke. Why?

CHAPTER XI

THE ACTS OF THE APOSTLES

Within fifty years after the death of Jesus his gospel had spread over Palestine and Asia Minor and had been carried by travelers and missionaries across the Aegean Sea to Greece and over the Mediterranean to Rome. Companies of Christian believers had been formed in the principal cities, and the new faith was spreading rapidly. But few of these new Christians had any clear idea of how the gospel had reached their communities, and by what providential means and through what perils and difficulties the missionary travelers had found their way to Corinth, Ephesus, and Rome. Few had any idea of how the Christian movement had first separated itself from the Jewish faith; how it had ever come to be offered to Greeks, when it had originally belonged exclusively to Jews; where this change in the propagation of the gospel had begun, and who had first undertaken to carry the gospel out of Syria and Palestine into the more western provinces of the Roman Empire.

Some men still lived who had seen this wonderful Greek mission develop and who had learned from others how it had begun. They knew what courage and perseverance and faith it had taken to bring about its spread through the Roman world, and they felt that it would strengthen the faith and stimulate the zeal of the Christian believers around them to hear the story from the beginning. In such a spirit the physician Luke, perhaps in some city on the Aegean Sea like Ephesus, began to write the story of the Greek mission.

He was himself a Greek, and knew little about the beginnings of the movement except what others had told him. For his first volume, as we have seen, he made use of a variety of written sources, which probably did not extend beyond the gospel story. But he was a close friend of Paul, who had done more than any other to carry the gospel among the Greeks of the Roman provinces. He had been with Paul on some of his most dangerous and adventurous journeys and in some of his most extraordinary experiences.[1] With him he had visited Antioch, Caesarea, and Jerusalem, and in these cities he had met people who could tell him much about the strange series of events that had led the earliest Christians to push out first from Jerusalem to Caesarea and Antioch, and then from Antioch to Cyprus and Galatia. Luke had himself witnessed the extension of the movement from Asia Minor to Macedonia and Achaea, and had finally followed its progress to Rome itself. Supplementing his experiences by his inquiries, Luke fitted himself to relate the fascinating story, with its bewildering variety of riots, arrests, trials, councils, voyages, shipwrecks, imprisonments, and escapes. These are set in the most varied scenes: Temples, market-places, deserts, islands, synagogues, the courts of kings and governors, the streets of those splendid flourishing cities of the Greco-Roman world, Anti-och, Ephesus, Corinth, Athens, Rome. And over it all is the writer's conviction of the providential hand of God shaping the decisions and movements of his people to his own great purposes.

The books known to us as the Gospel of Luke and the Acts of the Apostles are really the two vol-umes of Luke's story of the beginning of Chris-tianity and its development in the Greek world.[3] In both of them his purpose is at once religious and historical. He wishes to strengthen the faith of his readers and commend Christianity to them. At the same time he wishes to make their knowledge of Christian history more exact and complete. We should have liked more definiteness in the dating of some events, and here and there we long for a line more about the fate of Paul or of Peter, the work of missionaries in the East and South, or the be-ginning of Christianity in Alexandria or Rome. But we must admit that Luke has told his story to its climax, for with the churches once established in Antioch, Ephesus, Corinth, and Rome, the extension of the gospel to the rest of the Roman world about the Mediterranean was inevitable.

We are now accustomed to view history as a study of popular forces working their way to expression and influence, rather than of battles, reigns, and dynasties. With such a sense of historical values Luke wrote his sketch of the mission to the Gentiles. Kings and wars play little part in it. It is a record of a popular movement, at first obscure, then gradually making itself felt in widening circles and with increasing power. Even when he wrote, it was still little thought of and, indeed, hardly noticed by Greek or Roman historians and literary men. It was left for this Greek physician, the friend and fellow-traveler of Paul, to begin the writing of what we now call church history.

SUGGESTIONS FOR STUDY

1. *References:* [1]Acts 16:11; 27:1, 2; Col. 4:14; Philem. vs. 24; [2]Acts 1:1.

2. Compare the preface of Luke, 1:1–4, with the opening lines of Acts, 1:1, 2.

3. Notice that the conclusion of the Gospel (24:49–53) is reviewed in the following verses of Acts, 1:3–12, so that the narrative of Acts is closely joined to that of Luke.

4. Note that the descent of the Spirit in Acts 2:1–4 is in fulfilment of the promise recorded in Luke 24:49.

5. Notice the many lands from which Peter's hearers at Pentecost came, and to which those of them who were converted would return with the gospel.

6. Notice the constant emphasis of the Holy Spirit, the Spirit of God, and the Spirit of Jesus in Acts.

7. Read Acts 1–7 as an account of the development of the early church in Jerusalem.

8. In chaps. 8–12 note the gradual spread of the movement to proselytes and Gentiles in Samaria, Damascus, Joppa, Caesarea, and especially Antioch (11:20). Locate these places on the map.

9. Note that this instinctive, unorganized missionary movement at length takes definite shape at Antioch, 13:3.

10. Trace Paul's movements through Cyprus, Galatia (chaps. 13, 14), Macedonia, Achaea (chaps. 16–18), and Asia (chap. 19).

11. Observe that after Paul's arrest Luke continues to trace his movements and experiences until he has spent two years at Rome.

12. Consider why Luke should have stopped at this point. Did he write at this time? Or did he purpose to follow Paul's fortunes farther in a third book? Or had he reached his goal in tracing the establishment of churches through the gentile world from Judaea to Rome?

13. Notice those parts of Acts (16:10–18; 20:5–16; 21: 1–18; 27:1—28:16) in which the writer speaks in the first person, the so-called "we sections." Consider whether there is any reason for thinking them to be by another hand than that which wrote the Acts. Where else does Luke speak in the first person?

14. Notice that Acts includes many accounts of wonders performed by apostles and others, not all of which are beneficent in character (5:1–11; 13:11). Cf. Luke 1:20–23.

15. Read the Acts through at a sitting, in some modernspeech translation, noting its variety, vividness, movement, and interest, and the prevailing emphasis upon the Holy Spirit as guiding all this Christian progress.

CHAPTER XII

THE REVELATION OF JOHN

It was a dangerous thing in the first century to be a Christian. Jesus himself had laid down his life for his cause, and the apostles Paul, Peter, James, and John met their deaths as martyrs, that is witnesses, to the new faith.[1] Although Christianity was not yet a "licensed" or "permitted religion," yet to be a Christian was not against the Roman law, and through the first century we can trace the Christians' hope that when at length the Roman government should decide what its attitude toward Christians was to be, the decision would be favorable. Luke points out that Pilate himself was disposed to release Jesus, and expressly says that neither Herod nor Pilate found any fault in him.[2] Luke also brings out the fact that the proconsul Gallio at Corinth would not even entertain a charge against Paul, and that at Caesarea both Agrippa and the procurator Festus declared that Paul might have been released if he had not appealed to the emperor.[3] Paul had encouraged his converts to honor the emperor, and obey the law, and in Second Thessalonians had referred to the emperor as a great restraining power holding the forces of lawlessness in check.[4]

Nero's savage outbreak against the Roman

church must have startled and appalled Christians all over the world, but that attack, though severe, was short, and left the status of Christians before the law undecided as before. Nero's victims suffered under the charge of burning the city, not that of being Christians, and Paul himself, as Luke indicates, was tried and probably executed as an agitator, not as a Christian. It is clear that representative Christians like Luke kept hoping that when a test case arose the Empire would not condemn the Christian movement and put Christians under its ban.

But these hopes were doomed to disappointment. Late in the reign of Domitian, the emperor-worship which had prevailed in some parts of the Empire since the time of Augustus began to threaten the peace of the churches. Earlier emperors had for the most part let it take its course, but Domitian found divine honors so congenial that he came to insist upon them. There was indeed an obvious political value in binding together the heterogeneous populations of the Empire, differing in speech, race, civilization, and religion, by one common religious loyalty to the august imperator, considered as in a certain sense divine. Most oriental peoples found this easy. Worshiping numerous gods, they did not much object to accepting one more.

With the Christians it was very different. Their faith forbade such an acknowledgment, and the scattered churches of Asia, where the matter first became acute, now witnessed the disappointment of their cherished hope of freedom to worship God undisturbed, in their own way. It is hard to realize all that this meant to them. Their early teachers had been mistaken. The Empire was not their friend and safeguard, to be loyally obeyed. It now suddenly appeared in its true colors as their bitter and unrelenting foe. For it inexorably demanded from them a worship of the emperor which Christians must refuse to accord. The church and the Empire were finally and hopelessly at war.

The Christian leaders of Asia must have realized this with stricken hearts, and they must have reviewed the history of the Christian movement from a new point of view. After all, what else could they have expected? Jesus, Paul, and Peter had suffered death for the Kingdom of God, and at the hands of Rome. In Nero's day hundreds of others had perished in Rome at the emperor's bidding. The Empire, as they now saw, had long since recorded its verdict, and it had been against them.

The matter of worshiping the emperor came home to the Christians of Asia in various forms. His name and likeness appeared on many of the coins they used. He had among them his provincial priesthood, charged with the maintenance of his worship throughout Asia. Christians might be called upon, as Pliny tells us they were twenty years later, to worship the image of the emperor. It was customary to attest legal documents—contracts, wills, leases, and the like—with an oath by the fortune of the emperor. Refusal to make this sworn indorsement would at once involve one in suspicion and lead to official inquiries as to the apparent disloyalty of the person concerned to the imperial government. Why not then make the oath? It was after all a purely formal matter with all who used it. Why not simply add to one's business documents, as everyone did, the harmless words, "And I make oath by the Emperor Domitianus Caesar Augustus Germanicus that I have made no false statement"? So slight an accommodation might seem a very excusable way to gain security and peace.

But in even slight concessions to pagan practice the Christian leaders of Asia saw a serious peril. There must be no compromise. The church might perish in the conflict, but the conflict could not be avoided. The church must brace itself for the struggle, and compromising was not the way to begin. On the contrary, the church must absolutely disavow everything pertaining to the wicked system through which the devil himself was now assailing it. For in the Empire the Asian Christians now recognized not a beneficent and protecting power but an instrument of Satan.

Among the first victims of the kindling persecution was a Christian prophet of Ephesus, named John. He seems to have been arrested on the charge of being a Christian and banished to the neighboring island of Patmos, perhaps condemned to hard labor. He could no longer perform for his Asian fellow-Christians the prophet's work of edification, comfort and consolation described by Paul in First Corinthians,[5] though they needed it now as never before. But he might hope to reach them by letters, and, as he wrote these to the seven leading churches of Asia, his message expanded into a book. He uses the cryptic symbolic forms of the old Jewish apocalypses, of Daniel or Enoch, in which empires and movements figure in the guise of beasts and monsters, and the slow development of historical forces is pictured as vivid personal conflict between embodiments of rival powers. Indeed, his message is one that may not be put in plain words, for it contains a bitter attack upon the government under which the prophet and his readers live.

The canon of the writings of the prophets had long been regarded by the Jews as closed, and anyone who wished to put forth a religious message as a work of prophecy had therefore to assume the name of some ancient patriarch or prophet. But the Christians believed the prophetic spirit to have been given anew to them, and a Christian prophet had no need to disguise his identity. John in Patmos writes to the neighboring churches as their brother, who shares with them the agony of the rising persecution.

The task of the exiled prophet was to stiffen his brothers in Asia against the temptations of apostasy and compromise which the persecution would inevitably bring. He would arouse their faith. In the apparent hopelessness of their position, a few scattered bands of humble people arrayed against the giant world-wide strength of the Roman Empire, they needed to have shown to them the great eternal forces that were on their side and insured their final victory. For in this conflict Rome was not to triumph, but to perish.

The prophet's letters to the seven churches convey to them the particular lessons that he knows they need. But one note is common to all the letters "To him that overcometh," to the victor in the impending trial, the prophet promises a divine reward. But this is only the beginning of his message. Caught up in his meditation into the very presence of God, the prophet in the spirit sees him, as Isaiah saw him, enthroned in ineffable splendor.[6] In his hand is a roll crowded with writing and sealed seven times to shut its contents from sight. Only the Lamb of God proves able to unfasten these seals and unlock the mysterious book of destiny, which seems to contain the will of God for the future of the world, and to need to be opened in order to be realized. Dreadful plagues of invasion, war, famine, pestilence, and convulsion attend the breaking of the successive seals, doubtless reflecting familiar contemporary events in which the prophet sees the beginning of the end. On the opening of the seventh seal seven angels with trumpets stand forth and blow, each blast heralding some new disaster for mankind. Despite these warnings men continue in idolatry and wickedness. The seventh trumpet at length sounds and proclaims the triumph of the Kingdom of God, to which the prophet believes all the miseries and catastrophes of his time are leading.

The victory is thus assured, but it has yet to be won. The prophet now sees the dragon Satan engaged by the archangel Michael and the heavenly armies. Defeated in heaven, the dragon next assails the saints upon the earth. In this campaign Satan has two allies, one from the sea—the Roman Empire—the other from the land—the emperor cult of Asia. Again the prophet's vision changes. Seven bowls symbolizing the wrath of God, now at last irrepressible, are poured out upon the earth. An angel shows him the supreme abomination, Rome, sitting on seven hills and drunk with the blood of the saints. Another angel declares to him her doom, over which kings and merchants lament, while a thunderous chorus of praise to the Lord God Omnipotent arises from the redeemed. The prophet's thought hastens on from the fate of persecuting Rome and the im-

prisonment of Satan to the glorification of those
who have suffered martyrdom rather than worship
the emperor. As priests of God they reign with
Christ a thousand years, until the great white
throne appears, and the dead, small and great,
stand before it for the final judgment.

These lurid scenes of plague and convulsion now
give way to the serene beauty of the new heavens
and the new earth, with the new Jerusalem coming
down out of heaven from God who makes all things
new. Amid its glories God's servants, triumphant
after their trial and anguish, serve him and look
upon his face.

The prophet begins with a blessing upon anyone who shall read his prophecy and upon those
who shall hear it read. He closes with a warning
against any tampering with its contents. The book
is clearly intended to be read at Christian meetings.
More than this, by its repeated claim of prophetic
character, it stands apart as the one book in the
New Testament that in its zeal to make its message
heard, claims the inspiration of Scripture. It is thus
in a real sense the nucleus of the New Testament
collection.

The Revelation is not a loyal book. Its writer
hates the Roman government and denounces its
wickedness in persecuting the church in unmeas-
ured terms which every Christian of the day must
have understood. It does not indeed advise rebel-

lion, but it is, from an official Roman point of view, a seditious and incendiary pamphlet. But so symbolic and enigmatical is its language that few outside of Jewish or Christian circles can have understood its meaning, or guessed that by Babylon the prophet meant the Roman Empire. Its value to the frightened and wavering Christians of Asia must have been great, for it promised them an early and complete deliverance, and cheered them to steadfastness and devotion. Their trial indeed proved less severe than they had feared, for twenty years later Ignatius found these same churches strong and earnest, and forty years after the writing of Revelation a Christian convert named Justin found this book still prized by the Ephesian church. Ignatius and Justin both suffered martyrdom in Rome, and joined the army of those who had come out of great tribulation, and had made their robes white in the blood of the Lamb. But in these successive conflicts, and through many more down to the present day, Christians have cheered themselves in persecution with the glowing promises and high-souled courage of the banished prophet of Ephesus, who in the face of hopeless defeat and destruction showed a faith that looked through death, and in stirring and immortal pictures assured his troubled brethren of the certain and glorious triumph of the Kingdom of God.

SUGGESTIONS FOR STUDY

1. *References:* [1]Mark 10:35, 39; Acts 12:2; John 21:18, 19; [2]Luke 23:14–16; [3]Acts 26:31, 32; [4]II Thess. 2:7; [5]I Cor. 14:3; [6]Rev., chap. 4.

2. Read Dan., chaps. 7, 8, as examples of Jewish apocalyptic.

3. Read Rev., chaps. 1–3, noticing the light they throw upon the state of Christianity in Asia.

4. Read chap. 4, the prophet's vision of God, noting its resemblance to Isa., chap. 6, and Ezek., chap. 1.

5. Notice in chaps. 6–11 the seven seals leading up to the seven trumpets, each one symbolizing some invasion, earthquake, slaughter, disaster, or other of the Last Woes.

6. Notice in chaps. 12, 13 the war against the church begun in heaven and continued on earth by the dragon and his allies.

7. Observe in chaps. 15, 16 the seven bowls of wrath preluding the destruction, in chaps. 17, 18, of Rome, the persecutor of the church.

8. Notice that chap. 20 presents the climax of the whole in the judgment scene, while chaps. 21, 22 describe the city of God and the happiness of his people, now delivered from their persecutors.

9. Observe the solemn warning of the prophet against any tampering with his work, 22:18, 19.

10. What are the main religious ideas underlying all this oriental imagery?

11. Read the Revelation through at one sitting in some modern-speech translation.

CHAPTER XIII

THE EPISTLE TO THE HEBREWS

Of all the early centers of Christianity the church at Rome went through the most significant and dramatic experiences. Founded by unknown persons about the middle of the first century, it entertained Paul and Peter, Luke and Mark, witnessed the martyrdom of the chief apostles and piously tended their graves, in a single generation withstood the fires of two persecutions, and served in short as the focus of Christian life in the capital of the world.

All this was not effected without sacrifice and devotion. It is the Christians of Rome who first appear in the pages of the history of the Empire, and it was the extraordinary sufferings they endured that led the historian to mention them.[1] Hardly a dozen years after the Roman church had been established there burst upon it the storm of Nero's persecution, of brief duration but of frightful severity. Many of the Christians of Rome suffered agonizing martyrdom, and all of them faced it with a heroism that wrung sympathy even from the callous populace of that brutal city. In that dreadful August of 64 A.D. the Roman Christians learned what it was to have their dearest friends and leaders torn from them, to attend these friends to prison and to cruel and mocking deaths, to lose their little savings by capricious confiscation, and so to be brought by the events of a single month to the very verge of ruin and despair.

From such a baptism of fire the Roman Christians emerged reduced in property and numbers, but more than ever convinced that they were pilgrims upon the earth and that their citizenship was in heaven. They were sustained in this by the hope in which Paul and Peter had confirmed them, that Jesus would soon return to set up his messianic kingdom, and that then their troubles would be over. Their immediate troubles did soon pass and gave way to a reasonable degree of security and peace, but the hope of Jesus' coming remained unfulfilled.

Years went by. The churches settled down from their first exuberant spiritual enthusiasm into a partial accommodation to a work-a-day world. They had their officers, their meetings, their institutions. They still expected the return of Jesus, but only as people might who had been expecting it all their lives. The expectation could hardly play the part in their religious lives that it had in their fathers'. But evidences were beginning to appear that they were in turn to be put to the test to which Nero had put their predecessors. Domitian was emperor. Conspiracies and losses had embittered and frightened him. He had begun in Rome that reign of terror which so horrified high-minded Romans like Tacitus who had to witness it.

What first led Domitian to threaten the Roman church is not clear. It may have been his insistence upon divine honors for himself, as it was in Asia. It may have been the collection for the benefit of Jupiter Capitolinus, of the temple tax from the Jews, and the incidental confusing of Christians with the latter. Or perhaps the inability of a Christian magistrate to perform the religious duties his office imposed upon him first brought the Christians again under attack. At any rate, toward the very end of Domitian's life, he made a series of attacks upon the Christians of Rome which left a deep impression upon them.

The Roman church had more than made up the losses Nero had inflicted upon it. It had continued to practice that duty of Christian hospitality which its location imposed upon it, and to attend to the needs of Christian prisoners who were brought to Rome as Paul had been. It had not, however, developed any outstanding Christian teachers, nor as yet taken the place of leadership among the churches for which its position at Rome naturally marked it out. It was a practical church, but a church without imagination. The fact that Jesus had been executed like a slave or a criminal was hard for it to understand and to harmonize with the messiahship he claimed. And with the passing of time the expectation of Jesus' return to the earth had declined in eagerness and confidence, leaving the Roman Christians far less ready to withstand the shock of persecution than their fathers had been thirty years before.

But persecution and apostasy were not the only dangers that threatened the Roman church. The very age of the church now exposed it to a peril of apathy and indifference which could never have menaced it in its youth, when enthusiasm was new and hope high. While some might continue to hold in a mild way their expectation of Jesus' coming, others, now that the generation that had known Jesus in Galilee had passed away and Jesus had not returned, felt that the expectation so long disappointed had been vain, and that the Christian movement was played out.

It was to this situation that some Christian teacher, unknown to us but well known at Rome, addressed the letter which from its strongly Jewish tone has come to be called the Epistle to the Hebrews. The writer was not in Italy, though other Christians from Italy were with him when he wrote, and perhaps from what they had told him, or from what he had himself observed in Rome, the perilous situation of the Roman community was clear to him. But the Roman church must not go down. Its noble traditions of devotion and service must not sink into oblivion. Above all the great task for which it was in the writer's mind so clearly marked out must be performed. The church must not only survive but rise to higher forms of service, that should eclipse all that it had yet done. This is the kindling ideal that this great unknown of the first century puts before the wavering line of Roman Christians. Seeing them unequal to their present task, he nerves them for a greater.

The Christian scholar who undertook to meet this situation took as his theme the complete and final character of the revelation made in Christ. As compared with the beings, men or angels, through whom the old Jewish revelation was made, Christ is immeasurably superior. They were at best God's servants; he is God's son. How shall anyone escape who neglects a salvation so supremely authoritative? The Romans must learn the awful lesson of the Israelites in the wilderness. Like them they have had good news and set forth for a better country; let them not like the Israelites, through unbelief and disobedience, fall short of the heavenly rest.

Christ is not only far above the old mediums of revelation; he is far superior to the old priests. This is a difficult matter to explain to the Romans, who for all their long experience as Christians, in view of which they ought to be teaching and leading the churches, are still no better than infants as far as intellectual or spiritual development is concerned.

Only let them remember that persons who have
once had the Christian experience and who then give
it up can never recover it. It is impossible to renew
them again unto repentance. Surely none of the
Christians at Rome will make this irreparable mistake. Their faithful service of helpfulness to their
needy brethren has long commended them to God;
they must not give up now, but hold fast to the end.

To show his readers the extraordinary value of
what they are in danger of throwing away, the
writer proceeds to explain to them the messianic
priesthood of Christ and its superiority to the old
Jewish priesthood. In doing this he uses the Old
Testament in the fanciful Alexandrian manner,
treating it allegorically and typically. This enables
him to find in the Old Testament evidence that
Jesus is the final and eternal high priest, of an order
older than Aaron and even than Abraham. His
ministry is correspondingly superior to that of the
Jewish priests. They had to offer over and over
again, in a tent that was at best only a copy of the
heavenly sanctuary, the same material and ineffectual sacrifices. But Christ as messianic high priest
has offered once for all in the heavenly sanctuary
the supreme sacrifice of himself and taken his seat
at the right hand of God.

With this novel and ingenious interpretation of
Jesus' religious significance the writer couples the
practical lesson of drawing near to God through the

new and living way which Jesus has opened. He
again exhorts the Romans to keep fast hold of their
Christian hope. He who has promised is faithful;
already they can see the Day drawing near. To return to a life of sin after having once experienced
the Christian salvation is to forfeit that salvation
forever and to incur penalties too dreadful to utter.
It is a fearful thing to fall into the hands of the living God. They must remember the heroic devotion
they showed in former days, when in its infancy
their church endured a cruel persecution at Nero's
hands.[2] That same boldness and endurance they
must still show.

Through all the history of God's dealings with
men, that faculty of faith by which men have laid
firm hold on the unseen realities has kept patriarchs,
prophets, and martyrs steadfast to the end. These
veterans of faith are now looking down upon their
successors at Rome to see them run with endurance
the race upon which they have started. Christ himself has set the supreme example of faith. In all the
trials and hardships that they are enduring the
Romans must learn to see God's paternal discipline,
by which the lives and characters of his sons are to
be perfected.

In a final impassioned utterance the writer returns to the thought with which he began. The new
covenant and mediator are far above their old Jewish prototypes, and disloyalty to them is attended

with proportionately greater peril. Our God is a
consuming fire.

Exhortations and warnings conclude the letter.
The Romans must not forget the noble example
of their first martyr-teachers. Considering the issue
of their lives, they must imitate their faith. They
must avoid false teachings and practices, and be
thankful and beneficent. The writer closes his hortatory discourse, as he calls it,[3] with the news of
Timothy's release from prison, promises to visit
them soon, and sends salutations from himself and
the Italian brethren who are with him.

The language of Hebrews shows more elegance
and finish than that of any other book of the New
Testament. Its author was a trained student and
thinker. What he wrote is so eloquent as to be more
like an oration than a letter, and the absence of any
superscription such as letters usually have makes
it seem all the more oratorical. It is worth noting
that the Judaism which the writer has in mind
is always that of the tabernacle in the wilderness,
never that of the temple in Jerusalem. In showing
the superiority of Christ's covenant and revelation,
he first among Christian writers makes free use of
that allegorical interpretation of the Old Testament
which has had such grave consequences in Christian history. Hebrews may be regarded as the supreme effort of early Christianity to state the religious significance of Jesus in Jewish terms—"medi-

ator," "high priest," "Messiah." It is interesting
to observe that the Roman church bravely withstood the attack of Domitian and in the century
that followed made an earnest effort to teach and
lead its sister churches in a way worthy of its opportunities and its history.

SUGGESTIONS FOR STUDY

1. *References:* [1]Tacitus, *Annals* xv. 44; [2]Heb. 10:32–35;
[3]Heb. 13:22.

2. Consider Heb. 10:32–34 as a picture of the experiences of the Roman Christians during Nero's persecution.
Compare with it Tacitus' account, especially these sentences:
"First those were seized who confessed that they were Christians. Next on their information a vast multitude were convicted, not so much on the charge of burning the city, as of
hating the human race. And in their deaths they were also
made the subjects of sport, for they were covered with the
hides of wild beasts and worried to death by dogs or nailed
to crosses or set fire to and when day declined burned to serve
for nocturnal lights. Nero offered his own gardens for the
spectacle."—Tacitus, *Annals* xv. 44 (translation in Harper's
Classical Library).

3. Note the stately, often rhetorical, language of Hebrews, for example, 1:1–4; chap. 11; 12:1, 2.

4. Note that Hebrews calls itself a hortatory discourse,
"the word of exhortation," 13:22. Can it be a Christian
sermon afterward sent to another congregation as a letter?

5. In this case would the personal references and appeals
appropriate to one circle be appropriate also to the other?

6. Notice the successive comparisons of Christ with (1)
the angels, who were in Jewish thought the mediums of rev-

elation, chaps. 1, 2; (2) with Moses, 3:1–6; (3) with Joshua, 4:8–11; (4) with Aaron, 7:11–28.

7. Read 8:1—10:39, observing the argument that Christ performs a priestly service of a higher type than that of the Jewish priests.

8. Read chaps. 11, 12, noting the writer's idea of faith as the faculty of laying hold on the unseen, and his argument that his readers should, like the heroes of faith, find in their trials the discipline of their faith.

9. Notice the frequent paragraphs of practical exhortation: 2:1–4; 3:12–14; 4:1, 2, 11, 14–16; 6:11, 12.

10. What is the writer's view of those who have given up their faith in Christ and apostatized? Cf. 6:4–6; 10:26–31.

11. Who were the martyr-teachers of the Roman church whose example the writer commends to the Romans in 13:7?

12. Notice the rebuke of ascetic practices in the commendation of marriage, 13:4, and the reference to meats, 13:9.

13. Notice the renewed use of somewhat extended letters in the life of the early church. Had Paul's example something to do with this?

14. Read Hebrews through at one sitting, in some modern-speech translation.

CHAPTER XIV

THE FIRST EPISTLE OF PETER

The Empire's condemnation put a peculiar strain upon the churches all over the Roman world. The ignorant masses already regarded the Christians as depraved and vicious and credited them with eating human flesh and with other monstrous practices. But quite aside from this the Empire had adjudged being a Christian a crime punishable by death. The Christian had neither the protection of the state nor the sympathy of his fellows.

In this situation a Christian elder of Rome wrote to his brethren throughout Asia Minor a letter of advice and encouragement. Perhaps the Epistle to the Hebrews had already reached Rome and its ringing challenge to the Romans to be teachers stirred him to write.[1] He styles himself a witness of Christ's sufferings, which may mean that he was himself a Christian confessor, that is, one who had risked his life by acknowledging his faith before the authorities.[2] He sends to the Christians of the chief provinces of Asia Minor a message of hope. They already enjoy a salvation of unutterable worth, and have awaiting them in heaven an imperishable inheritance. All their present trials are to prove and refine their faith. As Christians they are to live lives of holiness and love. By their pure and unobjectionable conduct they must disarm the public suspicion of their practices. They must obey the emperor and his appointed governors. Government is for the restraint of evildoers and for the encouragement of the good. The example of Christ's sufferings should encourage servants when they are mistreated to imitate his patience and self-command. All must cultivate sympathy, humility, and love.

No one can reasonably molest them if they live uprightly, but if they should suffer for their very righteousness they would be only the more blessed. It is better to suffer for welldoing than for evildoing. They must not be afraid, but be ready to give respectful and honest answers to magistrates who examine them, and by their uprightness of life must silence and condemn the popular calumnies. Christ too suffered to bring them to God, and they must live the new Christian life which he opened to them, not their old gross heathen life of sin.

The fiery trial to which they are now exposed must not be thought strange. Through it they may share in Christ's sufferings, and so in his coming glory too. It is a privilege to endure reproach for the name of Christ. To be punished for committing crime carries disgrace along with it, but to endure punishment for being a Christian does honor to God. They can only commit their lives to God, and keep on doing what is right.

Their elders must do their work in a noble and high-minded way, as true shepherds of the flock of God under the chief shepherd Christ. They must all humble themselves under God's mighty hand, and he will in his good time lift them up again. Everywhere their Christian brethren are being compelled to endure this same bitter experience. God is the source of all their help, and after they have suffered a little while he will give them deliverance.

Among the messages which conclude the letter is one from the church at Rome—here as in the Revelation called Babylon—in which the writer is an elder.[3] Who he was it is not possible to say; but in later times the church at Rome came to regard itself as the heir and spokesman of Peter, and if one of the purposes of this letter is to correct the seditious attitude toward the Empire that marked the Revelation, and if the publication of Paul's letters in collected form had recently drawn universal attention to him as an apostolic writer, we can understand how the Roman church might have felt justified in claiming the great name of Peter, its martyr apostle, as the one whose authority really speaks in this letter to the Christian groups which Revelation was most likely to affect. But, whoever wrote it, it gave the imperiled Christians all through Asia Minor a message of hope and courage during the persecution of Domitian, pointed out the difference between suffering for being a criminal and

suffering for being a Christian, and inspired them
to overcome by lives of purity and goodness the
hatred and slanders of the heathen world.

SUGGESTIONS FOR STUDY

1. *References:* [1]Heb. 5:12; [2]I Pet. 5:1; [3]Rev. 17:5, 6, 9.

2. Read First Peter through, and imagine its effect upon
the persecuted Christians of Asia Minor.

3. Notice the districts of Asia Minor in which Christianity was already established, 1:1. Consider whether the
order in which they are mentioned is that in which the bearer
of the letter would naturally visit them.

4. Which of these had Paul evangelized?

5. In view of the hostile attitude of the Empire, how do
you explain the loyal tone of the letter, 2:13–17?

6. How does this compare with the attitude of the writer
of the Revelation, in the same general circumstances?

7. What does the writer imply in speaking of Rome as
Babylon, 5:13?

8. Notice the help for the situation of his readers found
by the writer in the suffering of Christ, 3:18; 4:1.

9. Observe the emphasis upon suffering "as a Christian,"
4:15, 16. Was this a new thing? The victims of Nero's persecution had suffered under the charge of being incendiaries
or haters of the human race.

10. What picture of church life and of Christian morals
does the letter give?

11. Note that four ancient documents relate to Domitian's persecution in Rome and Asia Minor: Revelation, Hebrews, First Clement, and First Peter.

12. On Christianity in Bithynia (1:1) read Pliny's letter
to Trajan (x.97) written about 112 A.D., a few years after
First Peter. Pliny inquires of the emperor "whether the very

profession of Christianity unattended with any criminal act, or only the crimes themselves attaching to the profession are punishable."

13. On the suggestion that "Enoch" has been lost from the text of I Pet. 3:19, compare the following extracts from the Book of Enoch, one of the most influential religious books of the first century, which after long being lost was discovered by Bruce in Abyssinia more than 150 years ago. Chapter 10 tells how Noah was warned of the approaching flood, and the wicked angels who had corrupted the earth were condemned and fettered, and chapters 12, 13 describe Enoch's mission to them. "The Watchers called me and said to me, 'Enoch, thou scribe of righteousness, go, declare to the Watchers of the heaven who have left the high heaven, ... "Ye have wrought great destruction on the earth, and ye shall have no peace nor forgiveness of sin."'"

"And Enoch went and said, 'Azazel, thou shalt have no peace; a severe sentence has gone forth against thee to put thee in bonds' . . . . . Then I went and spoke to them all together, and they were all afraid, and fear and trembling seized them. And they besought me to draw up a petition for them that they might find forgiveness, and to read their petition in the presence of the Lord of heaven. . . . . . Then I wrote out their petition." The petition is refused, and Enoch is shown the prison of the angels, chapter 21. There can be little doubt that this is what is referred to in I Pet. 3:19, 20.

CHAPTER XV
THE EPISTLE OF JAMES

The ancient world was full of preachers. Dressed in a rough cloak, one would take his stand at some street corner and amuse and instruct, with his easy, animated talk, the chance crowd that gathered about him. He would mingle question and answer, apostrophe, dialogue, invective, and anecdote, urging his little congregation to fortitude and self-control, the great ideals of the Stoic teachers. For these street preachers of ancient times were Stoics, and their sermons were called diatribes.

Christian preachers had to compete with these men for the attention of the people they were trying to convert to Christianity, and they naturally adopted some of their methods. In the market-place at Athens Paul did this informal open-air preaching every day, and in doing so came into conflict with some of these Stoic preachers.[1] A later Stoic, Justin, became a Christian, and tells us in his *Dialogue with Trypho* how he continued to practice this way of preaching on the promenade at Ephesus.

We cannot help wishing that one of these street sermons had been preserved to us just as its author gave it, and of course we have in the Book of Acts reports of several sermons of Stephen, Peter, and

Paul. It is true that Luke was not present when most of these were uttered, and probably had to fill out somewhat any outline or report which had come to him; but this only means that the sermon, if not exactly what Paul or Peter said, is what another early Christian preacher, Luke, would have said, and supposes Paul would have said, in those circumstances. But we have in the New Testament at least one ancient sermon preserved for its own sake and not as an incidental part of a historical narrative. It is the book we know as the Epistle of James.

In James the Christian preacher tells his hearers that life's trials, vicissitudes, and temptations will perfect character, if they are met in dependence upon God. But his hearers must not merely profess religion, but really practice purity and humanity. They must be doers that work, not hearers that forget. They must learn to respect the poor, and to feed and clothe the needy. Their faith must show itself in works. They must not be too eager to teach and direct one another. The tongue is the hardest thing in the world to tame. If they wish to show their wisdom, let them do it by a life of good works. They must give up their greed, indulgence, and worldliness, their censoriousness and self-confidence. Their rich oppressors are doomed to punishment; only they must be patient, like Job and the prophets. Above all things, they must refrain from oaths. In trouble and sickness they must pray for one another. The prayer of a righteous man avails much. And they must seek to convert sinners, for God especially blesses such work.

These are the teachings of this ancient sermon. What is the connection between them? Do they constitute a chain of thought? Are they beads on a string, or simply a handful of pearls? As an example of Christian preaching this sermon is not at all doctrinal or intellectual. Little is said even of Christ. The whole emphasis is practical. The preacher's interest is in conduct, in the words and acts of his hearers. He does not care especially about their theological views. For him the only real faith is that which shows itself in good deeds. Honest, upright, and helpful living is what the preacher demands, and he does so with a directness and a frankness never since surpassed. It is this that has given this fifteen-minute sermon its abiding place in Christian literature.

Where this sermon was first preached it is impossible to say. It would have been appropriate almost anywhere. That is the beauty of it. But we may be sure that it was as a sermon and not as a letter that it first appeared. It contains none of those unmistakable epistolary touches that we find for example in Galatians and Second and Third John. It does not end with a farewell or benediction as so many New Testament letters do. Only the salu-

tation contained in the first verse suggests a letter:
"James, a servant of God and of the Lord Jesus
Christ, to the twelve tribes which are of the Dis-
persion, greeting."

But a moment's reflection will show that this
does not prove the Epistle of James to be a letter.
How would one go about delivering it "to the
twelve tribes which are of the Dispersion," that is,
to the Jews scattered about through the Greco-
Roman world from Babylon to Spain? Or, if the
Dispersion is meant in a figurative sense, to all the
Christians outside of Palestine? It is clear at once
that these words are not the salutation of a letter
but a kind of dedication for a published work. That
the Epistle of James was written to be thus published, however, that is, that it is an "epistle" in
the literary sense of the word, is very improbable
in view of its contents, which relate to no single
subject or situation.

It can surely be no cause for surprise or incredu-
lity that we possess among the twenty-seven books
of the New Testament one representative of the
commonest type of Christian literature, the sermon.
It would be a wonder if this were not the case. Like
thousands of other sermons, it was not only preached
but published, with a dedication, boldly figurative,
to Christians everywhere. The unidentified James
whose name is prefixed to it may have been its
author or its publisher, or simply one in whose

name it was put forth. The early church sought to
recognize in him Jesus' brother, who, though not an
apostle, became the head of the church at Jerusalem.[2] But if he was the preacher, the sermon's
reticence about Jesus would be doubly hard to understand.

There is something very modern about this so-
called Epistle of James. Its interest in democracy,
philanthropy, and social justice strikes a responsive
chord in our time. The preacher's simplicity and
directness, his impatience with cant and sham and
his satirical skill in exposing them, his noble advo-
cacy of the rights of labor and his clear perception
of the sterling Christian virtues that were to win the
world, justify the place of honor his sermon has in
the New Testament.

SUGGESTIONS FOR STUDY

1. *References:* [1]Acts 17:17, 18; [2]Gal. 1:19; 2:12.

2. Is the teaching of James as to faith and works incom-
patible with Paul's teaching as to faith, or only different
from it in emphasis?

3. What did Paul mean by "works," and what does the
letter of James mean?

4. Are the rich oppressors of 5:1–6 worldly Christians,
or is the passage an apostrophe in which the preacher condemns the luxury and heartlessness of the pagan world? Cf.
2:6, 7.

5. What evils does the letter principally attack?

6. What are its chief religious teachings?

7. Do the practical teachings of the letter resemble those

of Jesus as we know them from the Gospels, and if so, which ones?

8. Read it through aloud at a single reading, and imagine its effect upon a first-century company of Christians in some house in Rome or Corinth.

9. Do you observe in James any traces of the preacher's acquaintance with First Peter?

10. Compare James with typical prophetic sermons, Amos, chaps. 1, 2; Isa., chap. 1 or chap. 5 or 8:1—10:4 or chaps. 18, 19, the sermon on Egypt.

11. Compare with James a discourse of Epictetus: for example, i, 3, i, 16, or the following: "Have you not God? Do you seek any other while you have him? Or will he tell you any other than these things? If you were a statue of Phidias, either Zeus or Athena, you would remember both yourself and the artist, and if you had any sense you would endeavor to do nothing unworthy of him who formed you or of yourself, nor to appear in an unbecoming manner to spectators. And are you now careless how you appear because you are the workmanship of Zeus? And yet what comparison is there either between the artists or the things they have formed? . . . . Being then the formation of such an artist, will you dishonor him, especially when he has not only formed but intrusted and given to you the guardianship of yourself? Will you not only be forgetful of this but moreover dishonor the trust? If God had committed some orphan to your charge, would you have been thus careless of him? He has delivered yourself to your care, and says, 'I had no one fitter to be trusted than you. Preserve this person for me such as he is by nature; modest, faithful, sublime, unterrified, dispassionate, tranquil.' And will you not preserve him?"—Epictetus, *Discourses* ii. 8 (Carter's translation).

CHAPTER XVI
THE LETTERS OF JOHN

About the beginning of the second century a disagreement arose among the Christians of Asia. It was about the reality of the life and death of Jesus. How could the Messiah, the Son of God, possessed of a divine nature so utterly removed from matter, have lived a life of human limitation and suffered a shameful and agonizing death?

It was a favorite idea in ancient thought that the material universe was intrinsically evil, or at least opposed to goodness, and that God, being wholly good, could not come into any direct contact with it, for such contact, it was thought, would infect God with the evil inherent in all matter. This idea was held by some Christians who at the same time accepted Jesus as the divine Messiah. From this contradiction they escaped in part by claiming that Jesus' divine nature or messiahship descended on him at his baptism and left him just before his death on the cross. They inferred that his sufferings were only seeming and not real, and from this idea they were known as Docetists, that is, "seemists."

The Docetists were probably better educated to begin with than most Christians, and their profession of these semi-philosophical views of Christ's life and death still further separated them from ordinary people. This separation was increased by the claim they made of higher enlightenment, closer mystic fellowship with God, clearer knowledge of truth, and freedom from sin. Expressions like "I have fellowship with God," "I know him," "I have no sin," "I am in the light," were often on their lips. Both their spiritual pretensions and their fantastic view of Christ made them an unwholesome influence in the Asian churches and roused more than one Christian writer to dispute their claims.

There lived at that time in Asia a Christian leader of such influence and reputation that he could in his correspondence style himself simply "the Elder." Wide as his influence must have been, there were some who withstood his authority and refused to further his enterprises. With his approval missionaries had gone out through Asia to extend the gospel among the Greek population. Some Christians had welcomed them hospitably and helped them on their way, but others who were hostile to the Elder had refused to receive them and had threatened any who did so with exclusion from the church.

In this situation the Elder writes two letters. One, known to us as Third John, is to a certain Gaius, to acknowledge his support and encourage him to continue it, and to warn him against the party of Diotrephes. Gaius is probably the most influential of the Elder's friends and supporters in his own community, while Diotrephes is the leader of the party hostile to the Elder. The letter is probably delivered by Demetrius, one of the missionaries in question. At the same time the Elder writes another short letter, our Second John, to the church to which Gaius belongs, urging its members to love one another and to live harmoniously together, and warning them against the deceivers who teach that Christ has not come in the flesh. The advocates of this teaching they are to let severely alone, refusing them even the ordinary salutations and the hospitality usual among Christians. The two letters are brief, for the Elder is coming to them very soon in person; but short as they are they bring us into the very heart of a controversy that was already dividing individual churches and threatening the peace of a whole district.

As missionaries like Demetrius went about the province of Asia, under the Elder's direction, they took with them a longer letter from his pen in which the same pressing matters were more fully presented. We have seen that the short letters are without his name, and the long letter bears not even his title. It hardly required it if it was to be carried by his messengers and read by them as from him in the assembled churches they visited. This longer letter, known to us as First John, deals with the same question as Second John, takes the same view of the matter, and puts it with the same confident authority. But the situation has developed somewhat, for the Docetists, or some of them, have now left the church.[1]

The Elder begins with the most confident emphasis. His own experience guarantees the truth of his message, which he is sending in order that his readers may share the fellowship with God and Christ which he enjoys.[2] The heart of that message is that God was historically manifested in the life of Christ, and that the Christian experience is fully sufficient for anyone's spiritual needs. To claim fellowship with God and live an evil life will not do; the claim is false. The Docetic pretension to sinlessness is mere deceit. The Christian way is to own one's sins and seek forgiveness.

The claim of knowing Christ is meaningless apart from obedience to his commands. Living as he lived is the only evidence of union with him. Those who claim peculiar illumination and yet treat their brethren with exclusiveness and contempt show that they have never risen to a really Christian attitude. The Elder's reason for writing to his friends is that they have laid the foundation of a real Christian experience, and he would warn them against sinking again into a life of worldliness and sin.

The breach with the Docetic thinkers, with their claims of freedom from sin, is complete. It is well that they have left the church, for they have no right to be in it. Those who deny that Jesus is the Christ are not Christians but antichrists. In opposition to their teachings, true Christians should continue to cultivate that spiritual experience upon which they have entered. They must abide in Christ and following the guidance of the Spirit seek, as children of a righteous heavenly father, to be righteous like him. Righteousness and love are the marks of the Christian life. Jesus in laying down his life for us has shown what love may be.

Some who urge the Docetic teaching claim that the Holy Spirit in their hearts has indorsed it. But the Spirit of God authorizes no such teaching. Only spirits that confess that Jesus Christ is come in the flesh are of God. Spirits that deny this are of the world. The Elder declares that he is of God, and that all who really know God will obey his solemn warning against these spirits of antichrist.[3]

Love is the perfect bond in all this great spiritual fellowship. Love is of God and God is love. He has shown it by sending his Son into the world to give us life. We love because he first loved us. If he so loved us, we also ought to love one another. Belief in Jesus as the Christ is the sign of sonship to God and the way to the life of love, since it is the manifestation in Jesus of God's love that kindles love in us. The messiahship of Jesus is evidenced not only by the voice of the Spirit, but by his human life and death. There are three who bear witness, the Spirit, the water, and the blood. The witness is this, that God has given us eternal life and this life is in his Son. To have the life we must see in Jesus the Christ, the indispensable revelation of God.

The Elder writes to confirm his readers in their assurance of eternal life. Sonship to God means the renunciation of sin. The Christian has an inward assurance that he belongs to God, whom Jesus has revealed. Here is the true God and eternal life.

Except for a few touches which mark it very definitely as a letter (2:12–14), this little work might pass for a sermon or homily. It is clearly a circular letter written to save the churches of Asia from the Docetic views which threatened them. The great words of the letter, life, light, love, figure importantly in the Fourth Gospel also, and in its meditative and yet epigrammatic style the letter resembles the Gospel. It has been said that while the Gospel argues that Jesus is the Christ, the letter contends that the Christ is Jesus, that is, the Messiah is identical with the historical Jesus.

Who was this Asian Elder who could so confidently instruct and command the churches of his countryside? Early Christian writers mention an Elder John of Ephesus, who was a follower of Jesus but was not the apostle of that name, and they sometimes refer to him simply as "the Elder," just as the writer of these letters calls himself. There is no need to identify him with the prophet John of the Revelation. But to John the letters have always been ascribed, and we may think of the Elder John as sending them out from Ephesus, one to Gaius, one to the church to which he belonged, and one to that and other churches, in full assurance that the Christian experience and belief in Jesus as the Christ would save them from the mistakes of Docetism.

SUGGESTIONS FOR STUDY

1. *References:* [1]I John 2:19; [2]I John 1:1–4; [3]I John 4:6.

2. Read Third John as an example of a personal Christian letter. Compare it with Paul's letter to Philemon, the only other one of this kind preserved in the New Testament.

3. Read Second John as an example of a letter to a church, analogous with Paul's letters to Thessalonica, Corinth, or Colossae. How does it compare with such letters of Paul?

4. Notice in First John the emphasis on belief in Christ, 2:23; 3:23; 4:15; 5:10–13. How does this compare with the teaching of James? Yet cf. 3:18.

5. Notice the writer's attitude to the world as over against the church, 2:15–17; 3:13; 5:19. Is there anything like this in James?

6. Read First John, noting the spiritual claims made by the Docetists but denied by the writer, 1:6, 8, 10; 2:4, 9; 4:20.

7. Has the reference to antichrists in 2:18 anything to do with what Paul wrote of in Second Thessalonians, or is it merely an application of the well-known name to the new and immediate foes of the church?

8. Does the "going out" of the Elder's opponents from

the church, 2:19, mark the beginning of the rise of heretical bodies professing a modified Christianity not accepted by the church at large? Consider whether the Nicolaitans of Rev. 2:6, 15 may have been such a Christian sect.

9. What are the leading religious ideas of First John?

10. Read 4:7–21, comparing it with Paul's chapter on love, I Cor., chap. 13.

11. The letter begins with basing Christian confidence on Christian experience, 1:1–4. What is its closing emphasis, 5:18–21?

CHAPTER XVII

THE GOSPEL ACCORDING TO JOHN

Christianity and Judaism had parted company.
The Christian movement, at first wholly Jewish,
had after a little tolerated a few Greeks, then admitted them in numbers, and at length found itself
almost wholly Greek. The Jewish wing of the
church withered and disappeared. The Jews closed
up their ranks and disowned the church. Church
and synagogue were at war.

It was plain that the future of the Christian
movement lay among the Greeks, the Gentiles. To
them it must more than ever address itself. Its
message must be made intelligible to them. But the
forms in which it had always been put were Jewish.
Jesus was the Messiah, the national deliverer whose
coming was foretold by Jewish prophets, and who
was destined to come again on the clouds of heaven
in fulfilment of the messianic drama of Jewish
apocalyptic. The church was addressing a Greek
world in a Jewish vocabulary. Was there no universal language it could speak? Was no one able
to translate the gospel into universal terms? The
Gospel of John is the answer to this demand.

Early in the second century a Christian leader
of Ephesus, well acquainted with the early Gospels

and deeply influenced by the letters of Paul, put
forth a new interpretation of the spiritual significance of Jesus in terms of Greek thought. Paul had
laid great emphasis upon faith in Jesus the risen
Christ, glorified at God's right hand, and had attached little importance to knowing the historical
Jesus in Palestine. His Ephesian follower finds in
Paul's glorified Christ the divine "Word" of Stoic
philosophy, and reads this lofty theological conception back into the earthly life of Jesus. The faith
Paul demanded becomes with him primarily an intellectual assent to the messiahship of Jesus thus
understood, that is, to the revelation in the historical
Jesus of that absolute divine will and wisdom toward which Greek philosophy had always been striving.

The form in which this Christian theologian put
his teaching was a gospel narrative. He did not intend it to supersede the familiar narratives of Matthew and Luke, but to correct, interpret, and supplement them. The new narrative differs from the
older ones in many details. In it Jesus' ministry falls
almost wholly in Judaea instead of Galilee, and
seems to cover three years instead of one. The cleansing of the temple is placed at the beginning instead
of at the end of his work. Nothing is said of Jesus'
baptism, temptation, or agony in the garden. His
human qualities disappear, and he moves through
the successive scenes of the Gospel perfect master

of every situation, until at the end he goes of his own accord to his crucifixion and death. He does not teach in parables, and his teaching deals not, as in the earlier Gospels, with the Kingdom of God, but with his own nature and with his inward relation to God. In his debates with the Jews he defends his union with the Father, his pre-existence, and his sinlessness. He welcomes the interest shown by Greeks in his message, prays for the unity of the future church, and interprets the Lord's Supper even before he has established it. His cures and wonders, which in the earlier Gospels seem primarily the expression of his overflowing spirit of sympathy and helpfulness, now become signs or proofs to support his high claims.

The long delay of the return of Jesus to the world had caused that hope which had been so strong at first to decline in confidence and power. The new evangelist at once acknowledges and explains this by showing that the return of Jesus has already taken place in the coming of his spirit into the hearts of Christian believers. He thus transforms the Jewish apocalyptic expectation into a spiritual experience.[1] He foresees that under the guidance of this spirit the Christian consciousness will constantly grow into greater knowledge and power.

Toward the close of his Gospel the writer states his purpose in writing it to be to give his readers faith in Jesus as the Christ, and thus to enable them to have life through his name.[2] This idea of the life to be derived from Jesus is prominent in the whole Gospel. Christ is the source of life of a real and lasting kind, and it can only be obtained through mystic contact with him. This is because Jesus is the full revelation of God in human life. This doctrine, which we call the Incarnation, is fundamental in the Gospel of John: "In the beginning was the Word and the Word was with God and the Word was God. . . . . And the Word became flesh and dwelt among us, and we beheld his glory. . . . . I am come that they may have life and that they may have it abundantly."

While the Gospel of John contains no parables, in a sense it is a parable. It presents an interpretation of Jesus in the form of a narrative of his ministry. The writer feels that the Jewish title of Messiah does not express the full religious significance of Jesus, but by finding for it an expression in Greek philosophical terms he transplants Christian thought and the Christian movement into Greek soil. It was easy for persons of Greek education to understand the claim that Jesus was the divine Logos, or Word, of the Stoic philosophers, and a gospel which began with such a claim would be likely to arrest their attention. The writer still thinks of Jesus as Messiah, and retains his respect for the Jewish scriptures. Indeed, the idea of the revealing Word of Jehovah appears now and again in Jewish literature, and the Jewish philosopher Philo had already identified it with the Logos of Greek thought. This made it all the easier for the writer of the new Gospel to apply it to Jesus, but in this interpretation of Jesus as the divine Word he goes beyond previous Christian thinkers and takes a long and bold step in the development of Christian theology.

The Gospel is the story of Jesus' gradual revelation of himself to his disciples and followers. The opening sentences present its main ideas in words intelligible and attractive to Greek minds. Over against the followers of John the Baptist, who still constituted a sect in the writer's day as they had in Paul's,[3] the evangelist relates John's ready testimony to Jesus as the Son of God and Lamb of God. With a few followers, some of them directed to him by John, Jesus visits Cana and in the first of his "signs" indicates his power to transform human nature.[4] After a brief stay in Capernaum he goes to Jerusalem to the Passover, and there clears the temple of the dealers in sacrificial birds and animals who with their traffic victimized the people and disturbed places meant for prayer. The Jews demand a sign in proof of his right to do this, and he answers with a prophecy of his resurrection. In a conversation with Nicodemus, Jesus explains that a new birth of water and the Spirit, that is, baptism and

spiritual illumination, must precede the new life of
the Kingdom. Jesus comes near the place where
John is baptizing and John gives fresh testimony to
his superiority. To avoid overshadowing John, Jesus
goes into Galilee,[5] and on the way explains the
water of life to a Samaritan woman and reveals himself as the Messiah and the source of eternal life.
In Galilee Jesus is favorably received and performs
the second of the seven signs that punctuate his
earthly ministry. Soon another feast brings him to
Jerusalem. There he heals an impotent man on the
Sabbath and, in the discussions which ensue with
the Jews, expounds his relation to God. Returning
to Galilee, he feeds a great multitude by the Sea of
Galilee and declares himself the bread of life, for
everyone who beholds him and believes in him shall
have eternal life. At the Feast of Tabernacles he is
again in Jerusalem, teaching in the temple, although
danger from the Jewish authorities threatens him.
He declares that he is sent by God and offers his
hearers the water of life, which the evangelist interprets to mean his Spirit, which was to be given
to his followers after his resurrection. He proclaims
himself the light of the world and when the Jews
object claims the witness of God for his message.
He promises truth and freedom to those who abide
in his words, and declares his sinlessness and pre-
existence. He restores a blind man's sight on the
Sabbath, and in the discussions that follow declares

himself the Son of God and the Good Shepherd. Soon after at Bethany Jesus raises Lazarus from the dead and proclaims himself the Resurrection and the Life. The hostility of the Jewish rulers becomes so bitter that he conceals himself for a little while in Ephraim, but as the Passover approaches he goes up to Bethany. Enthusiastic crowds go out from Jerusalem to meet him and escort him in messianic state into the city. Greeks ask to be presented to him, and Jesus answers that he is now to be glorified but that it must be through his death. In his last hours with his disciples he comforts them in preparation for his departure, and promises to send them his spirit to comfort and instruct them. Under the figure of the vine and the branches he teaches them the necessity of abiding in him, the source of life. As he has come from the Father so now he must return to him. Finally, in an intercessory prayer, he asks God's protection for his disciples and the church they are to found, praying above all for its unity.

Leaving the city, he goes with his disciples to a garden on the Mount of Olives. There Judas brings a band to arrest him, but they are at first overawed by his dignity, and only after securing the freedom of his disciples does Jesus go with them.[6] He is examined before the high priests and before Pilate, and on the charge that he claims to be the king of the Jews he is sentenced to be crucified. The evange-

list is careful to show that Jesus retains his sense
of divine commission to the last and dies with the
words, "It is finished," on his lips, and he bears
solemn testimony to the piercing of his side and the
undoubted reality of his death. These details were
important for the correction of the Docetic idea
that the divine spirit abandoned Jesus on the cross.
The writer also indicates that Jesus was crucified
on the day before the Passover, so that his sacrificial death fell on the day on which the Passover
lamb was sacrificed. On this point he corrects the
earlier gospel narratives.

Early on the first day of the following week Jesus
appears to Mary. The same evening he appears to
the disciples, imparts his spirit to them, and com-
missions them to forgive sins. Eight days later he
again appears to them when Thomas is with them
and convinces Thomas of the reality of his resurrection. The Gospel closes with the evangelist's
statement of his purpose in writing it: that his
readers may believe that Jesus is the Christ, the
Son of God, and that, believing, they may have life
in his name.

To the Gospel of John an appendix or epilogue
was afterward added,[7] probably when John was combined with Matthew, Mark and Luke. It reports an
appearance of the risen Jesus by the Sea of Tiberias,
or Galilee, and his conversation on that occasion with
Peter, in which he predicts Peter's death, but seems

to intimate that the beloved disciple may live until his own return. The Gospel never names this disciple, but by describing him several times in this way it makes him more conspicuous than any name could make him. The beloved disciple has perhaps died, for the epilogue explains that Jesus did not exactly say that the beloved disciple would survive until his coming. This epilogue may have been added to the Gospel to correct the popular misunderstanding about Jesus' words to Peter, and to claim the beloved disciple's authority and even authorship for the Gospel. There are indeed some points in the Gospel which seem to involve better information on the part of its writer than the earlier evangelists had. But the whole character of the narrative and its evident preference for the symbolic and theological, as compared with the merely historical, are against the assigning of its composition to a personal follower of Jesus. It is very probable that it was written by that Elder of Ephesus who perhaps after the publication of this Gospel wrote the three letters that bear the name of John.

The Gospel of John was wholly successful in what it undertook. It was not at first generally welcomed by the churches, but in the course of a generation it came to be accepted side by side with the earlier Gospels, and in its influence upon Christian thought it finally altogether surpassed them. Its great ideas of revelation, life, love, truth, and freedom, its doctrine of the spirit as ever guiding the Christian consciousness into larger vision and achievement, and its insistence upon Jesus as the supreme revelation of God and the source of spiritual life, have given it unique and permanent religious worth.

SUGGESTIONS FOR STUDY

1. *References:* [1]John 14:3, 16–18, 23, 26, 28; 15:26; [2]John 20:31; [3]Acts 19:1–7; [4]John 2:11; [5]John 4:1, 2; [6]John 18:8, 9; [7]John, chap. 21.

2. Read John 1:1–18, noting in the passage the leading ideas of the whole Gospel: revelation, incarnation, and Christ the source of life and light.

3. Notice in 2:13–16 that the cleansing of the temple is put early in Jesus' ministry. Where in his work do our other Gospels put it?

4. Count Jesus' visits to Jerusalem in John and the number of Passover feasts mentioned in the course of Jesus' ministry, 2:13; 5:1; 6:4; 7:2, 10; 10:22, 23; 12:1, 12.

5. How long a ministry does this imply? How many passovers and visits to Jerusalem does Mark record?

6. Note the seven signs wrought by Jesus before his crucifixion, 2:11; 4:54; 5:9; 6:11; 6:19; 9:7; 11:43, 44. Cf. 20:30.

7. Why does the evangelist record these signs and how does he interpret them? Cf. 20:31.

8. Are the discourses in John mainly ethical, like the Sermon on the Mount; eschatological, like Mark, chap. 13; theological; or apologetic, that is, in defense of the pre-existence, messiahship, or authority of Jesus?

9. With all its emphasis upon belief (20:31), note the other, mystical, side of the Gospel's teaching, 15:1–19. Do you see any resemblance here to First John?

10. Notice that the writer speaks frequently of "the Jews" as over against Jesus and his followers, though these latter were Jews too in the period of Jesus' ministry. Consider whether this suggests that he wrote at a time when the Christians and the Jews were sharply distinguished.

11. Someone has said that there are a hundred quotations from Matthew, Mark, and Luke in the Gospel of John. Can you find any such?

12. Mark 14:12–17 puts the Last Supper on the day on which the Passover lamb was sacrificed. Are John 13:1; 18:28; 19:14, meant to correct this?

13. Is the writer's conception of Christ more like Paul's or Mark's?

14. Is his idea of Jesus' return to the earth like Paul's?

15. What is the religious value of the Gospel of John?

16. Read the Gospel of John through at a sitting, in some modern-speech translation.

CHAPTER XVIII

THE LETTERS TO TIMOTHY AND TO TITUS

The first Christians were too absorbed in the expectation of Jesus' speedy return to the earth to give much thought to practical detail. They cared nothing about developing a literature, a theology, or an organization. The Lord was at hand.[1] The time was short.[2] Why should people marry or slaves seek to be freed? At any moment the present order might come to an end.

But time wore on and nothing happened. The first leaders passed away, but the churches continued their work. It began to be clear that the end was not to come as speedily as men had thought, and that the churches might have to go on under the existing order for a long time. Christian leaders began to see that the practical side of church life could no longer be neglected. Spiritual enthusiasm and well-meaning devotion were no longer enough. Efficiency must be insured. Church life must be regulated. Church officers must be properly qualified. The several classes of people in the churches must be shown their several spheres and functions and kept to them. Efficiency must come through organization.

Such a state of things, it is true, seems a serious

decline from the high, confident, spiritual enthusiasm of the apostolic age. But after the prophet
must come the priest, to conserve and codify the
other's work. And this was what the letters to Timothy and to Titus sought to do.

Many churches needed to be shown what officers
they ought to have to carry on their work and what
kind of men these ought to be. Marriage, it was now
evident, ought to be encouraged and sanctioned.
The charitable work of the churches must be wisely
directed and protected from abuse. The morals of
the Christian communities needed definite correction. Christian leaders needed to be reminded that
they must set a worthy example of conduct and
character. The homely practical lessons which need
to be taught so often had to be put before the widest
possible circle of churches in compact and telling
form.

In these letters Christians are taught to pray
for kings and rulers and for all men. Perhaps the
empire no longer maintained its hostile attitude to
the church. Yet First Peter, written in the midst of
persecution, bids Christians honor the emperor.[3]
Certainly the Book of Revelation takes a very different attitude toward kings. Prayer is to be offered
by men. Women are not to teach, but to occupy a
subordinate place in the church life. Each church
may have as officers a presiding officer, the bishop

or elder, and his assistants, the deacons. These should be men of good repute and blameless character, who have married but once. A recent convert should not be made a bishop, and only men who have proved their faithfulness in the church life should be appointed deacons.

That practical helpfulness which had characterized the churches from the first finds natural expression in providing for the support of destitute widows in the Christian community. This matter needs to be safeguarded against abuse. It is right that children or grandchildren who are able to do so should provide for their widowed mothers or grandmothers. Only widows past middle life and without any kindred able to provide for them are to become the permanent pensioners of the church.

Novel religious speculations remote from practical life are to be discouraged and avoided. Some teachers have declared that the resurrection has already taken place; an idea perhaps due to a misunderstanding of Paul's teaching that conversion and baptism usher the believer, risen with Christ, into a new and blessed life. Such innovations are to be sternly condemned.

It was the coming in of these new currents of teaching that most perplexed Christian leaders about the end of the first century. How were they to be met and controlled? They sometimes seemed to threaten the life of the churches. To whom, when the first great leaders of Paul's generation were gone, could their less gifted successors appeal in matters of conscience and faith? This is one of the questions these epistles to Christian ministers undertake to answer. It is not easy to realize how far early Christian thought, on a great many matters, was from being definite and specific. The words of Jesus all recognized as authoritative, and also the voice of his Spirit in their own hearts. But one Christian might put forth views widely different from another's and claim for them the authority of the Spirit. Which was right? Who was to decide?

In the midst of this rising confusion of belief and teaching the churches fell back upon the letters of Paul. New teachings that conflicted with his must be false. In addition to Paul's letters and the memory of his teaching there was also what we call the Old Testament. Jesus had disowned various parts of it, and Paul had denied the religious efficacy of the Law, but Christian leaders felt safer in following them in their indorsement of the Jewish scriptures than in their partial rejection of them, and very definitely added the Old Testament to their new authorities. We have evidence of this tendency in the Gospels of Matthew and John, but it is Second Timothy that first puts it decisively and unequivocally. Every scripture inspired of God, it was now felt, was profitable for teaching, reproof, and instruction. The church had adopted the Old Testament.[4]

With the words of Jesus, a few letters of Paul, and the Jewish scriptures at their backs, the Christians could now feel in a measure prepared to test new religious teachings which original spirits in their own community or Christian visitors from distant churches might set forth in the local meetings. The new teaching had to square with the old apostolic teaching. If it conflicted with that, it could not stand. It must be possible also to harmonize it with the Old Testament. That Paul and Jesus did not always conform to the Old Testament did not at once appear nor greatly matter. What was needed was authorities, and with Jesus, Paul, and the literature of the Old Testament the need was satisfied.

That the letters to Timothy and Titus claim Paul as their author may possibly be due to the fact that short genuine letters of his were made the basis of them by some later follower of Paul who composed them. At any rate, the writer felt justified in claiming Paul's authority for what he thought a necessary and timely supplement to the letters Paul had left behind, and doubtless thought he was doing just what Paul would have done had he lived to see the conditions the writer saw. But the value of these letters lay in the practical direction they gave the churches of their time, showing them how to readjust their high hopes of Jesus' return and to

set themselves to the task of establishing and per-
petuating their work. In these little letters we see
the church after the lofty enthusiasm of its first
great experience settling down to the common life
of the common day and grappling with its age-long
task.

SUGGESTIONS FOR STUDY

1. *References:* [1]Phil. 4:5; [2]I Cor. 7:29; [3]I Pet. 2:17;
[2]II Tim. 3:16.

2. Notice that First Timothy is a letter of instruction to
a Christian pastor or minister, 4:6, and that his public functions are reading, exhortation, and teaching, 4:13. What
would he read in church? Cf. II Tim. 3:15, 16.

3. Read I Tim. 3:1–13, noticing the church officers mentioned and the qualifications they ought to have. What is
the chief emphasis in these?

4. Note the writer's somewhat indiscriminate condemnation of the advocates of a different type of Christian
teaching, I Tim. 4:1–3; II Tim. 3:1–9; Titus 1:10–16.
Does he give a clear picture of their teachings?

5. Notice the writer's indorsement of marriage, I Tim.
3:2, 12; 4:1–3; Titus 1:6.

6. Observe the writer's rule as to women teachers, I
Tim. 2:11, 12. Cf. Acts 18:26.

7. What is meant in these letters by "faith"? Is it an
inward attitude of trust and dependence upon God or a de-
posit of truth to be guarded and preserved?

8. In what does the Christian life consist, according to
these letters?

9. Do any of Paul's great characteristic ideas appear in
these letters?

10. Is II Tim. 4:6–8, which we may call Paul's epitaph,
any less appropriate or significant, considered as an early

Christian's estimate of Paul, than when viewed as Paul's own commendation of himself?

11. What would be the immediate practical value of these letters to the scattered pastors and ministers of the early churches?

12. Read the three letters through each at a sitting, in some modern-speech translation.

CHAPTER XIX

THE EPISTLE OF JUDE AND THE SECOND EPISTLE OF PETER

Many ancient thinkers conceived of the supreme God as far removed from the material world and too pure to have anything directly to do with it. The necessary connection between God and the world, they thought, was made through a series of intermediate ideas, influences, or beings, to one of which they ascribed the creation and supervision of the material world. When people with these views became Christians, they brought most of their philosophical ideas with them into the church and combined them as far as they could with their new Christian faith.

In this way there came to be many Christians who held that the God of this world could not be the supreme God whom Jesus called his Father. Their view of Jesus himself seemed to most Christians a denial of him, for they held to the Docetic idea that the divine Spirit left him before his death. They accordingly saw little religious meaning in his death, but they considered themselves so spiritual that they did not feel the need of an atonement. In fact, they felt so secure in their spirituality that they thought it did not much matter what they did in the flesh, and so they permitted themselves without scruple all sorts of indulgence.

Such people could not help being a scandal in the churches, and a Christian teacher named Jude made them the object of a letter of unsparing condemnation. He had been on the point of writing for some Christian friends of his a discourse on their common salvation when word reached him that such persons had appeared among them. He immediately sent his friends a short vehement letter condemning the immoral practices of these people, predicting their destruction, and warning his readers against their influence. He quotes against them with the greatest confidence passages from the Book of Enoch[1] and the Assumption of Moses,[2] late Jewish writings which he seems to regard as scripture. The persons he attacks still belong to Christian churches and attend Christian meetings. He does not tell his readers to exclude them from their fellowship but to have pity on them and to try to save them, only taking care not to become infected with their faults.

Who this Jude was we cannot tell. He looks back upon the age of the apostles, asking his readers to recollect how they have foretold that as time draws on toward the end scoffers will appear. He probably wrote early in the second century. The words "the brother of James" were probably added to his name by some later copier of his letter who took the writer

to be the Judas or Jude mentioned in Mark 6:3 and
Matt. 13:55 as a brother of James and Jesus.

A generation after this vigorous letter was written it was taken over almost word for word into
what we know as Second Peter. In the early part
of the second century various books began to be
written in Christian circles about the apostle Peter,
or even in his name, until one could have collected a
whole New Testament bearing his name. There were
a Gospel of Peter, Acts of Peter, the Teaching of
Peter, the Preaching of Peter, the Epistles of Peter,
and the Revelation of Peter. Most of these laid
claim to being from the pen of Peter himself.

The one that most insistently claims Peter as its
author is our Second Peter. It comes out of a time
when Christians were seriously doubting the second
coming of Jesus. A hundred years perhaps had
passed since Jesus' ministry, and men were saying,
"Where is his promised coming? For from the day
the fathers fell asleep all things continue as they
were from the beginning of creation." The spiritual-
izing of the second coming which the Gospel of John
wrought out did not commend itself to the writer
of Second Peter, if he was acquainted with it. He
prefers to meet the skepticism of his day about the
second coming with a sturdy insistence on the old
doctrine. In support of it he appeals to the Transfiguration, which he seems to know from the Gospel
of Matthew,[3] and to the widespread ancient belief

that the universe is to be destroyed by fire.[4] He repeats the denunciation which Jude hurled at the gnostic libertines of his day, only it is now directed against those who are giving up the expectation of the second coming. Jude has some hope of correcting and saving the persons he condemned, but the writer of Second Peter has no hope about those whom he attacks. He supports his exhortations by an appeal to the letters of Paul.[5] He evidently knows a number of them, for he speaks of "all his letters." He considers them scripture, and says that many misinterpret them, to their own spiritual ruin. This view of the letters of Paul, combined with the use in Second Peter of other New Testament books, proves it to be the latest book in the New Testament. It was not addressed to any one church or district, but was published as a tract or pamphlet, to correct the growing disbelief in the second coming of Jesus; and to enforce his message its writer put it forth, as other men of his time were putting forth theirs, under the great name of Peter.

SUGGESTIONS FOR STUDY

1. *References:* [1]Jude, vss. 14, 15; [2]Jude, vs. 9; [3]II Pet. 1:16–18; [4]II Pet. 3:10; [5]II Pet. 3:15, 16.

2. Note the picture drawn in Jude of the errorists under discussion, vss. 4, 8, 10, 12, 16, 18, 19, and the writer's unsparing denunciation of them.

3. Compare Jude, vss. 4–18, with II Pet. 2:1—3:3, noting the close resemblance.

4. Notice the quotations from late Jewish writings: from the Assumption of Moses in Jude, vs. 9, and from the Book of Enoch in Jude, vss. 14, 15. Does the writer regard these books as scripture?

5. Notice the vagueness of the address of Jude. To whom is it addressed or dedicated?

6. Does Second Peter seem from its salutation, 1:1, to have been sent as a letter or published as a tract or pamphlet?

7. Notice in Second Peter the references to Jesus' prediction of Peter's death, 1:14 (cf. John 21:18, 19); to the Transfiguration, 1:17, 18, most resembling Matt. 17:5; to I Pet. (3:1), and to the letters of Paul, 3:15, 16.

8. What do these last verses imply as to the collection of Paul's letters, the esteem in which they were held, and the sectarian use being made of them in some quarters at the time when Second Peter was written?

9. Observe in II Pet. 3:3, 4 the writer's condemnation of those who have given up the expectation of the return of Jesus.

10. Notice the support the writer finds for his views in the Stoic doctrine that the material universe would ultimately be destroyed by fire, 3:10.

11. Compare the first clause of 3:10 with one in the earliest book in the New Testament, I Thess. 5:2. Is this a quotation—the writer of Second Peter knows some letters of Paul (cf. 3:15)—or a coincidence?

CHAPTER XX

THE MAKING OF THE NEW TESTAMENT

When the latest book of the New Testament had been written, there was still no New Testament. Its books had to be collected and credited with a peculiar authority before the New Testament could be said to exist. What led to this collection and estimate?

For the first Christians the chief authority was Jesus. What he had taught they accepted as true and binding. Believing that his spirit still spoke in their own hearts, they ascribed the same authority to its inward directions.[1] Men who possessed this spirit in an especial measure, the Christian prophets, sometimes wrote down their revelations, and these came naturally to have the authority of scripture, that is, the authority which the Christian believers attached to the writings of the Old Testament. Jesus' teaching was at first handed down in the form of tradition; new converts learned it from those who were already Christians, and in turn taught it by word of mouth to those who became believers later.[2] But when gospels were written these began to take the place of this oral handing down, or tradition, of Jesus' words, and soon the gospel writing, and not simply the sayings of Jesus that it contained, came to be regarded as the authority. Authority thus gradually and naturally passed from the words of Jesus, and the thoughts of believers endowed with his spirit, to books embodying these.

Almost from the beginning, too, Christians had held Jesus' apostles in high esteem. Jesus had committed the continuation of his work to them. Paul, though not one of the Twelve, had by his zeal, devotion, and missionary success, convinced the churches that he too was in a real sense an apostle. His martyrdom gave added weight to the teachings he had left behind in his letters; but it was probably the publication of the Acts with its fine account of Paul that first led to the revival of interest in him and in what he had written to the churches. All the Christian writings that followed Acts show the influence of his collected letters, which in the first years of the second century came to be better and better known among the churches.

In the early years of the second century gifted but erratic Christian teachers began to divide the scattered and unorganized churches into parties or sects. Other Christian teachers, fearful of these schismatic tendencies, opposed these novel views and insisted upon what they considered the true and original Christian belief. In these controversies with heretics, that is, sectarians or schismatics, Christians in general more and more appealed in support of their views to the books and letters which had come down to them from earlier times and which they believed presented Christianity in its true and abiding form. In this way greater emphasis came to be laid upon the letters of Paul, the Gospels, and the Revelation.

The first step toward forming a Christian scripture of which we have any definite knowledge was taken strangely enough by one of these sectarian leaders, a certain Marcion, of Pontus in Asia Minor. He was a well-to-do ship-owner of Sinope. He had become convinced that the God of the Old Testament could not be identified with the loving heavenly Father whom Jesus proclaimed, and so he rejected the Old Testament. Something had of course to be put in its place for purposes of Christian worship and devotion, and Marcion proposed a Christian collection, consisting of the Gospel of Luke and ten letters of Paul. He did not include in this list the letters to Timothy and Titus. He accompanied his list with a work of his own called the Antitheses, in which he sought to show that the God of the Jewish scriptures could not be the God revealed in Jesus. The wide influence of Marcion must have done much to promote the circulation of the letters of Paul, whose interpretation of Christianity he regarded with especial favor. This also doubtless prejudiced many against them.

A few years earlier Christian teachers in Asia put forth the Four Gospels together, perhaps in order to increase the influence of the Gospel of John, which Christians attached to the lifelong use of Matthew or Luke might find easier of acceptance if it were circulated along with the Gospel to which they were accustomed. But it is not until about 185 A.D. that we find anything like our New Testament in use among Christians. By that time a great effort had been made by leading Christians of the non-sectarian type—who regarded their form of teaching as apostolic—to unite the individual churches of East and West into one great body, to resist the encroachments of the sects. The basis of this union was the acceptance of a brief form of the Apostles' Creed, episcopal organization, and a body of Christian scriptures, substantially equivalent to our New Testament. In this way the Catholic, that is, the general or universal, church began.

The New Testament, as it soon came to be called, did not displace the Jewish scriptures in the esteem of the church, as Marcion had meant his collection to do. It stood beside the Old Testament, but a little above it, for the Old Testament had now to be interpreted in the light of the New. The books included in the New Testament were appealed to in debate with schismatics as trustworthy records of apostolic belief and practice. They served an even more important purpose in being read from week to week, in the public meetings of the churches, along with the Old Testament scriptures. The Jewish idea that every part of the Old Testament must have an edifying meaning was definitely accepted by early Christians, and was now applied by them to the New Testament as well. This obliged them, as it had the Jews, to interpret their sacred books allegorically, and so the historical meaning of the New Testament books was neglected and obscured, and finally actually forgotten.

As to what should be included in this library of preferred and authoritative Christian writings, there was agreement among the churches in regard to general outlines, but no little diversity of views as to details. All accepted the Four Gospels so familiar to us, and thirteen letters of Paul, including those to Timothy and Titus. The Acts of the Apostles and three or four epistles, one of Peter, one or two of John, and that of Jude, were also generally accepted. Eastern churches, especially that at Alexandria, holding Hebrews to be the work of Paul, put it into their New Testament, but it was nearly two hundred years before Rome and the western churches admitted this. The West, on the other hand, accepted the Revelation of John as early as the middle of the second century, but the East never fully recognized its right to a place in the New Testament. The lesser epistles of John, Peter, and James were variously treated, some accepting them and others refusing to do so. The Syrian church never accepted them all, but in Alexandria

and in the West they became at length established
as parts of the New Testament, mainly on the
strength of their supposed apostolic authorship.

Other books now almost forgotten found places
in the New Testament in the third and fourth
centuries. One of the oldest Greek manuscripts of
the New Testament includes the so-called letters of
Clement of Rome, one a letter from the Roman
church to that at Corinth, written about the end
of the first century, the other a sermon sent seventy
years later from Rome to Corinth. Another of these
manuscripts contains the Shepherd, a revelation
written by a Roman prophet named Hermas, in
the early part of the second century, to bring the
Roman church and other Christians to genuine and
lasting repentance. The so-called Epistle of Barnabas, a curious work of a slightly earlier time, is
also included in this old manuscript. These oldest
extant copies of the New Testament were made in
the fourth and fifth centuries, probably for church
use, and show what books were considered scripture
in those times in the places where these manuscripts
were written.

The list of New Testament books that we know,
that is, just the twenty-seven we find in our New
Testament today, and no others, first appears in a
letter written by Athanasius of Alexandria at Eas-
ter in 367 A.D. But long after that time there continued to be some disagreement in different places

and among different Christian teachers as to just what books were entitled to be considered the inspired and authoritative Christian writings. This was somewhat less felt than it would be now, because the books of the New Testament were not often all included in a single manuscript. People would have one Greek manuscript containing the Gospels, another containing Paul's letters, a third containing the Acts and the general epistles—James, Peter, John, Jude—and perhaps a fourth, containing the Revelation. It was only when printing was invented that the whole New Testament began to be generally circulated in one volume, in Greek, German, or English.

The value of the New Testament to the Christian church has of course been immeasurably great. To begin with, the formation of the collection insured the preservation and the lasting influence upon Christian character of the best of the earliest works of Christian instruction and devotion. While the purpose of the makers of the New Testament was not historical, they nevertheless did a great service for Christian history. But the idea of establishing a list of Christian writings which should be exclusively authoritative, put fetters upon the free Christian spirit which could not always remain. Indeed, the New Testament itself included in Galatians the strongest possible assertion of that freedom, and so carried within itself the corrective of the construction which Catholic Christianity put upon it. But though Christians in increasing numbers may no longer attach to it the dogmatic values of the past, they will never cease to prize it for its inspiring and purifying power, and for its simple and moving story of the ministry of Jesus. Historically understood, the New Testament will still kindle in us the spirit which animated the men who wrote it, who aspired to be not the lords of our faith but the helpers of our joy.

SUGGESTIONS FOR STUDY

1. *References:* [1]I Cor. 7:40; 14:37; [2]I Cor. 11:2, 23; 15:3.

2. How did Paul, Mark, and Luke regard the sayings of Jesus? Cf. I Cor. 11:24, 25; Acts 20:35.

3. Did Paul believe that he had the authority of the Holy Spirit for some of his teachings? Cf. I Cor. 7:40; 14:37.

4. Did he think himself alone in this? Cf. 2:16; 7:40.

5. What did Paul think of an external written standard for the inner life? Cf. II Cor. 3:6.

6. Did the earliest Christians find their religious authority without, in books or laws, or within, in their spiritual intuitions?

7. Did the writer of the Gospel of Matthew think Mark too perfect to be freely revised?

8. Did Luke regard his sources, including Mark, as inspired or infallible? Cf. Luke 1:1-4.

9. How does the writer of Second Peter regard Paul's letters? Cf. 3:15, 16.

10. Note the classing of prophets and apostles together in Eph. 2:20; 3:5, and in Rev. 18:20.

11. Read Rev. 21:14, noting the high esteem in which a Christian prophet holds the apostles.

12. Note the full acknowledgment of the Jewish scriptures as inspired in II Tim. 3:16, 17.

13. What book of the New Testament claims to be inspired?

BIBLIOGRAPHY

GENERAL

MOFFATT, JAMES. *An Introduction to the Literature of the New Testament.* New York: Scribner, 1911.

The most complete and valuable introduction to the whole literature.

STREETER, B. H. *The Four Gospels: A Study in Origins.* New York: Macmillan, 1925.

BURTON, E. D. *Short Introduction to the Gospels.* 2d ed. Chicago: The University of Chicago Press, 1926. Revised by H. R. Willoughby.

A presentation of the main facts about the purpose and attitude of each Gospel necessary for reading it intelligently.

FOWLER, H. T. *The History and Literature of the New Testament.* New York: Macmillan, 1925.

MCNEILE, A. H. *An Introduction to the Study of the New Testament.* Oxford: Clarendon Press, 1927.

SODEN, H. VON. *The History of Early Christian Literature: The Writings of the New Testament.* New York: Putnam, 1906.

PEAKE, A. S. *A Critical Introduction to the New Testament.* New York: Scribner, 1911.

Good, compact introductions to the several books, with especial reference to modern opinion and discussion, which are clearly summarized and criticized.

BACON, B. W. *Introduction to the New Testament.* New York: Macmillan, 1900.

BACON, B. W. *The Making of the New Testament.* New York: Henry Holt, 1912.

These books cover the literature of the New Testament, the first book by book, the second in a more popular and continuous historical way.

McGiffert, A. C. *The Apostolic Age.* New York: Scribner, 1910.

Chaps. iv–vi deal fully and helpfully with the books of the New Testament in their relation to the history of early Christianity and the development of Christian thought.

Eakin, Frank. *Getting Acquainted with the New Testament.* New York: Macmillan, 1927.

SPECIAL

Bacon, B. W. *Galatians.* (The Bible for Home and School.) New York: Macmillan, 1909.

A short popular commentary with a good introduction and an analysis of the letter.

Massie, John. *Corinthians.* (New) Century Bible. New York: Frowde, 1922.

A good short commentary for popular use.

Lake, Kirsopp. *The Earlier Epistles of St. Paul.* Second Edition. London: Rivingtons, 1914.

Gilbert, G. H. *Acts.* (The Bible for Home and School.) New York: Macmillan, 1908.

An excellent short commentary for the general reader.

Harnack, A. *The Acts of the Apostles.* New York: Putnam, 1909.

The introduction to this volume will serve admirably to put the reader into the atmosphere of the Acts.

Porter, F. C. *Messages of the Apocalyptic Writers.* New York: Scribner, 1905.

A popular treatment of the Revelation showing its historical situation and its relations with kindred Jewish literature.

CASE, SHIRLEY J. *The Revelation of John: A Historical Interpretation.* Chicago: University of Chicago Press, 1919.

GOODSPEED, E. J. *Hebrews.* (The Bible for Home and School.) New York: Macmillan, 1908.

A concise commentary for popular use, with a somewhat full introduction on the occasion, purpose, and date of the letter.

ROBINSON, B. W. *The Gospel of John; a Handbook for Christian Leaders.* New York: Macmillan, 1925.

CARPENTER, J. ESTLIN. *The Johannine Writings.* London: Constable and Co., 1927.

SCOTT, E. F. *The Historical and Religious Value of the Fourth Gospel.* (Modern Religious Problems.) Boston: Houghton Mifflin Co., 1909.

An admirable sketch, for the general reader, of the purpose, ideas, and worth of the Gospel of John.

BURTON, E. D., and GOODSPEED, E. J. *A Harmony of the Synoptic Gospels for Historical and Critical Study.* New York: Scribner, 1917.

TRANSLATIONS

The Twentieth Century New Testament: A Translation into Modern English. New York: Revell, 1900.

MOFFATT, JAMES. *The New Testament: A New Translation.* New York: Doran, 1913.

WEYMOUTH, R. F. *The New Testament in Modern Speech.* Boston: The Pilgrim Press, 1903. Revised Edition, 1924.

GOODSPEED, EDGAR J. *The New Testament: An American Translation.* Chicago: University of Chicago Press, 1923.

INDEX

PRINTED
IN U·S·A·